"The story of the submarine *Wahoo* is significant because it was one of the most successful American boats, sinking 25 enemy ships in seven patrols. . . . The author, who served as *Wahoo's* second in command on her first five patrols, includes the kind of personal details that bring history alive. . . . O'Kane's study is most significant for the lessons it offers."
—*The Cleveland Plain Dealer*

"[*Wahoo*] will bring exciting reading pleasure to the casual reader—and chills to the spines of old submariners."
—Captain Murray B. Frazee Jr., USN (Ret.)
Veteran of eleven World War II submarine patrols

"Once I had commenced reading, I was loath to put it down. *Wahoo* will surely become a classic."
—Martin Sheridan, *Boston Globe* war correspondent
and the only reporter to make a WW II submarine war patrol

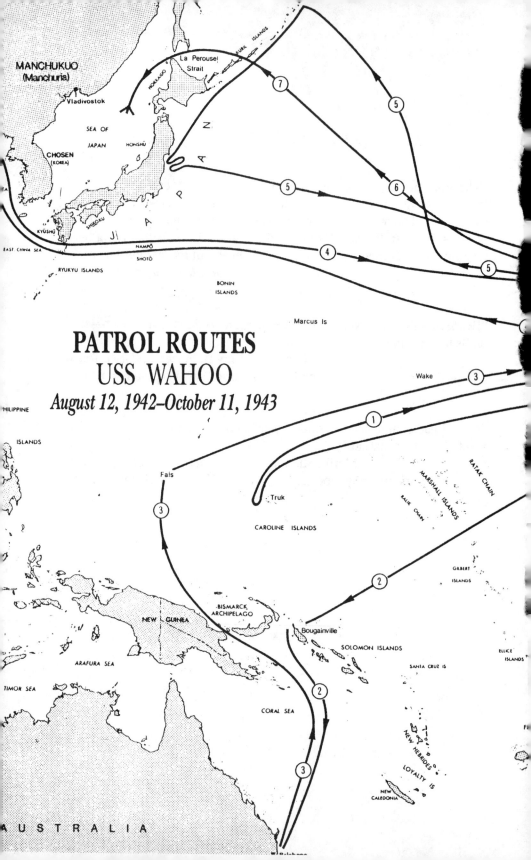

PATROL ROUTES
USS WAHOO
August 12, 1942–October 11, 1943

WAHOO

The Patrols of America's Most Famous World War II Submarine

Rear Admiral Richard H. O'Kane (Ret.)

San Francisco

HAWAIIAN ISLANDS

Kauai
Oahu
Hawaii

PHOENIX
ISLANDS

MARQUESAS IS

TOKELAU IS

TUAMOTU ARCHIPELAGO

SAMOA ISLANDS

SOCIETY ISLANDS
Tahiti

TONGA
ISLANDS

COOK
ISLANDS

★

PRESIDIO

Published by Presidio Press
505 B San Marin Drive, Suite 300
Novato, CA 94945-1340

This paperbound edition published in 1996

Library of Congress-in-Publication Data

O'Kane, Richard H., 1911–1994
  Wahoo: the patrols of America's most famous World War II submarine.
  Includes index.
  ISBN 0-89141-301-4 (cloth)
  ISBN 089141-572-6 (paper)
  1. O'Kane, Richard H., 1911–1994. 2. Wahoo (Submarine) 3. World War, 1939–1945—Naval operations—Submarine. 4. World War, 1939–1945—Naval operations, American 5. World War, 1939–1945—Personal narratives, American. 6. United States. Navy—Biography. 7. Seamen—United States—Biography. I. Title.
  D783.5.W3044 1987   940.54'51   87–6925

Printed in the United States of America

CONTENTS

ACKNOWLEDGMENTS   vii

LETTER FROM AUTHOR   viii

SAILING LISTS   ix, x

PROLOGUE   1

Part One
MARE ISLAND TO PEARL HARBOR   5

Part Two   FIRST PATROL
IN THE CAROLINES   25

Part Three   SECOND PATROL
IN THE SOLOMONS   63

Part Four   THIRD PATROL
BRISBANE TO PALAU AND PEARL   109

Part Five   FOURTH PATROL
THE EAST CHINA AND YELLOW SEAS   173

Part Six   FIFTH PATROL
THE KURILS AND HONSHU   243

Part Seven   SIXTH AND SEVENTH PATROLS
THE SEA OF JAPAN   279

EPILOGUE   331

GLOSSARY   337

INDEX   343

LIST OF ILLUSTRATIONS

CHARTS

Caroline Islands Adjacent Truk	34
Bougainville	77
Vitiaz Strait	132
*Running Gun & Torpedo Battle (Initial Engagement)	146
*Running Gun & Torpedo Battle	152, 155
East China Sea	189
Yellow Sea	198
The Kurils and Honshu	254
Sea of Japan	290
Sea of Japan (showing attack sites)	310

DIAGRAMS

Cutaway Submarine	8
Midship Cross Section	9
Submarine Approach and Attack	37
Twenty-nine cribbage hand	201

PHOTOGRAPHS

Submarine Interiors	following p. 62
Third and Fourth Patrols	following p. 172

*Battle charts by Deville G. Hunter, SM1c (which belie any sensational writing about this action).

Area Charts by Author

ACKNOWLEDGMENTS

I take this opportunity to thank the following individuals, departments, activities, and ships who provided information, documents, and assistance essential to this book:

R. Adm. J. D. Kane and Dr. Dean Allard, directors of the Naval Historical Center for Operation Orders and the later Japanese IJN Report.

The National Archives and Records Service for muster roles.

Mare Island Naval Shipyard for printing microfilm and mutual photographic work.

ComSubPac's staff, who almost prophetically had sent *Wahoo*'s original Battle Charts to me.

Capt. John B. Griggs and author Forest Sterling for their first-hand accounts of *Wahoo*'s sixth patrol.

Rev. Chandler C. Jackson for clarifying letters and phone calls.

All shipmates who filled out the *Wahoo* Watch Quarter and Station Bill on the samples provided.

James E. Lavine for Commander Morton's Night Orders Book.

USS *Dixon* AS 37 for the loan of charts to plot *Wahoo*'s patrols for pantographing to page size.

Photographer Russell Booth for submarine interiors and other exacting work; Tony Mesler for his extensive drafting.

Chief Clint Orr, SubVets WW II Historian, for the timely procurement of the Japanese account of *Wahoo*'s final encounter.

Finally, I am deeply indebted to my wife, Ernestine G. O'Kane, for meticulous editing, suggestions for clarification, and whose support and patience for three years made completion of the book possible.

Forgive me for writing first to the relatives of all who sailed on Wahoo's *final patrol:*

We who had served in *Wahoo* grieved with you when she was pronounced overdue and presumed lost. Your kin were our shipmates, filling billets we had held, with each one of them important to the submarine's success. They all deserve a place in this book, but that being impossible in the narrative, I have prepared exact sailing lists for the accompanying pages, so that no one will be left out. You will find the lists unique, with numerals showing the precise patrols for each crewman.

You may wonder why this account was not written years ago. The answer will become clear in the final pages, and when learning of the brave action of your kin, you will think of him with pride and a misty eye as do I.

I have received concurrence from the Secretary of the Navy that the Presidential Unit Citation goes with the ship's name, not the iron; the type commander to specify the manner of its display. *Wahoo's* PUC passed to her successor, USS *Wahoo* SS 565, who spent her entire commission in keeping the peace. God willing, may the next *Wahoo* fare thus well and fly the PUC pennant with equal pride.

Respectfully,

Sebastopol, California

Richard H. O'Kane

Patrolled in USS *Wahoo* Prior to Seventh Patrol

2	James H. Allen	F3c	6	Donald O. Jonson	TM2c
1–5	Jesse L. Appel	S2c	1–2	Marvin G. Kennedy	LtCdr
1–5	Richard W. Ater	S2c	1–2	John Kochis	MM1c
6	John F. August	S2c	4	Jerome T. Kohl	PhM1c
1–2	Raymond O. J. Baldes	MM1c	1–5	Stephen Kohut	MM1c
5	Charles J. Ballman	MM2c	1–5	Fertig B. Krause, Jr.	SM1c
1–3	Raymond G. Beatty	RM1c	2	Sylvester J. Laftin	TM1c
1–2	Edward L. Bland, Jr.	SOM3c	1	Joseph R. LaMaye	TM3c
1–3	Carl A. Brockhauser	F1c	3–4, 6	James E. Lane	CBM
1–2	Clyde A. Burnum	TM1c	1, 5	James E. Lavine	BM3c
1	Orville F. Chick	F3c	2–6	Richard H. Lemert	MM1c
3	Fred B. Chisholm	MoMM1c	1–3, 5	Andrew K. Lenox	CMM
3	John W. Clary	MoMM1c	1–3	Leslie J. Lindhe	PhM1c
3	Jack E. Clough	TM3c	1	Stanley A. Lokey	BM3c
5–6	Harry Collins	MoMM2c	4	Duncan C. MacMillan	Comdr
5	Kenneth R. Cook	BM3c	4	Clyde C. Mayberry	S1c
1	William E. Coultas	F1c	1	Henry J. Meditz	F3c
5–6	Helmit O. Dietrich	SC1c	1–4	James H. Miller	F2c
1–3	David E. Dooley	S1c	5	John A. Moore	LtCdr
1	Ira Dye	Ltjg	1–4	James Morris	TM3c
3–6	Dennis L. Erickson	EM2c	1–5	Edward F. Muller	MM2c
1	Dale E. Eyman	TM1c	1	Chester M. Myers	TM3c
1	Sidney F. Flateau	CMM	1–5	Richard H. O'Kane	LtCdr
1–4	Oakley R. Frash	MM2c	1	Lester L. Osborn	S2c
5	Donald W. Gilbert	MoMM2c	1–5	Roger W. Paine, Jr.	Lt
2–3	Henry P. Glinski	F2c	1–5	Joe D. Parks	FC3c
1–3	George W. Grider	Lt	3–5	Walter P. Patrick	TM2c
2–4, 6	John B. Griggs	Ltjg	1–5	Ralph R. Pruett	CEM
1–5	James C. Hall	S1c	1–4	Russel H. Rau	CTM
1–2	William J. Hanrahan	MM1c	4–5	Burnell A. Redford	CMM
1–2	Marius S. Hansen	MM1c	3–5	Cecil C. Robertson	F1c
1–4	Daniel J. Hargrave	F2c	1–5	John C. Rowls	SC1c
1–4	Theodore L. Hartman	EM3c	1	Earl C. Schreier	F1c
1	Walter C. E. Heiden	EM3c	1	C. J. Smith	MA2c
5–6	William H. Hodges	EM2c	1	Edward A. Smith	SC3c
4–5	Earl T. Holman	MM1c	2–6	Forest J. Sterling	Y2c
6	Carl C. Hood	FC2c	1–2	Kelly R. Thaxton	MM2c
1–4	Deville G. Hunter	SM1c	1	Maurice J. Valliancourt	S2c
1–5	Chandler C. Jackson	Lt	1–2	Lonnie L. Vogler	S1c
2	Willie James	MA1c	2	Harlan C. Whaley	S2c
5	Clifford T. Janicek	S1c	2–4	William F. Young	S1c
1–3	Edward Jesser	MM1c	3–6	Charles A. Zimmerman	S1c
1–2	Clarence E. Johnson	F1c			

Sailing List of USS *Wahoo* for Seventh War Patrol

2–7	Floyd Anders	F1c		7	Paul H. Lape	F2c
6–7	Joseph S. Andrews	EM1c		7	Clarence A. Lindemann	S1c
7	Robert E. Bailey	SC3c		7	Robert B. Logue	FC1c
2–7	Arthur L. Bair	TM3c		7	Walter L. Lynch	F2c
2–7	Jimmie C. Berg	F1c		5–7	Stuart E. MacAlman	PhM1c
7	Donald R. Brown	Ens		6–7	Thomas J. MacGowen	MoMM1c
6–7	Chester E. Browning	MoMM2c		1–7	Thomas J. McGill	CMoMM
5–7	Clifford L. Bruce	MoMM2c		6–7	Howard E. McGilton	TM3c
1–7	James P. Buckley	RM1c		1–7	Donald J. McSpadden	TM1c
7	William W. Burgan	Lt		6–7	Albert J. Magyar	MM3c
3–7	John S. Campbell	Ens		3–7	Jesus C. Manalesay	St3c
1–5, 7	William J. Carr	CGM		6–7	Paul A. Mandjiak	MM3c
1–7	James E. Carter	RM2c		6–7	Edward E. Massa	S1c
2–7	William E. Davison	MoMM1c		6–7	Ernest C. Maulding	SM3c
1–7	Lynwood N. Deaton	TM1c		6–7	George E. Maulding	TM3c
7	Joseph S. Erdley	EM3c		6–7	Max L. Mills	RT1c
5–7	Eugene F. Fiedler	Ltjg		2–7	George A. Misch	Ltjg
6–7	Oscar Finkelstein	TM3c		2–7	Dudley W. Morton	Comdr
7	Walter O. Galli	TM3c		5–7	Percy Neel	TM2c
6–7	Cecil E. Garmon	MoMM2c		6–7	Roy L. Oneal	EM3c
4–7	George E. Garrett	MoMM2c		1–7	Forest L. O'Brien	EM1c
2–7	Wesley L. Gerlacher	S1c		6–7	Edwin E. Ostrander	F1c
4–7	Richard P. Goss	MoMM2c		1–7	Paul D. Phillips	SC1c
7	Hiram M. Greene	Lt		4–7	Juano L. Rennels	SC2c
6–7	William R. Hand	EM2c		5–7	Henry Renno	S1c
7	Leon M. Hartman	MM3c		3–7	Enoch H. Seal, Jr.	TM2c
2–7	Dean M. Hayes	EM2c		1–7	Alfred Simonetti	SM2c
1–7	Richie N. Henderson	Lt		6–7	Verne L. Skjonsby	LtCdr
7	William H. Holmes	EM1c		1–7	Donald O. Smith	BM1c
6–7	Van A. House	S1c		1–7	George V. Stevens	MoMM2c
6–7	Howard J. Howe	EM2c		6–7	William C. Terrell	QM3c
6–7	Olin Jacobs	MoMM1c		6–7	William Thomas	S1c
5–7	Robert L. Jasa	F1c		1–7	Ralph O. Tyler	TM3c
3–7	Juan O. Jayson	CK3c		1–7	Joe Vidik	EM2c
1–7	Kindred B. Johnson	TM1c		1–7	Ludwig J. Wach	Cox
1–4, 6–7	Dalton C. Keeter	CMoMM		5–7	Wilbur E. Waldron	RM3c
5–7	Wendell W. Kemp	QM1c		1–7	Norman C. Ware	CEM
7	Paul H. Kessock	F1c		1–7	Kenneth C. Whipp	F1c
5–7	Eugene T. Kirk	S1c		7	William T. White	Y2c
5–7	Paul H. Krebs	SM3c		1–7	Roy L. Witting	F1c

PROLOGUE

Her keel had been laid in June of 1941, and about 7 months later at the launching ceremony on February 14, she was christened *Wahoo*. Like all newer United States submarines, she bore the name of a fish, hers being of the Peto family. Her mission had been decreed on the night of Pearl Harbor, "Conduct unrestricted submarine warfare," and after commissioning, *Wahoo* would be the twentieth new submarine to engage the enemy. She would also be my first new ship, culminating seven consecutive years in warships, for threatening wars had kept me and contemporary officers on continuous sea duty.

From the Naval Academy in 1934, I had served a year in the cruiser *Chester* as a junior gun division and then signal officer. From there came over 2½ grand years under mild and wild skippers in the last of our four-pipe destroyers, *Pruitt*. She served as a demanding school in all basic shipboard assignments, and in seamanship unavailable in larger or slower ships. Then during overhaul at Mare Island, north of San Francisco, came the true highlight when my boyhood chum, Ernestine Groves, and I were married on June 1, 1936. *Pruitt*'s change of home port to Hawaii, her conversion to a light minelayer, and subsequent operations twice separated our family, but orders to submarine school squared that away. Together again and with our infant daughter, Marsha, we drove from Mare Island through torrential rains and washouts to Shreveport, Louisiana, and arrived at New London, Connecticut, in the middle of a blizzard. Six months later, I reported to the submarine of my choice, the *Argonaut,* and in the area of our choice, right back in Hawaii.

The USS *Argonaut* SM 166 was our largest submarine, the SM designating her as a minelayer. But she also mounted two 53-caliber, 6-inch deck guns that could hurl 116-pound projectiles over 20 miles,

1

and forward she had four torpedo tubes, carried loaded, with eight more torpedoes in their skids—all of this besides her main armament of seventy-eight mines, launched from great mine tubes aft. Fortunately, I was familiar with all of this, including commissary and communications, my first two assignments. Only underwater sound was new to me, so after the required year, I was able to satisfy the qualification board of two captains, and I wore twin dolphins.

In September of 1939, President Franklin Roosevelt proclaimed a Limited Emergency, and all operations took on a most serious note. Our son James was born the same month. The Pacific Fleet arrived in 1940, and commencing in the fall of 1941, our submarines slipped quietly from Pearl Harbor with their torpedo tube outer doors open for firing, but only if attacked. I had been promoted to lieutenant, my qualification for command had been approved, and again I left my family in Honolulu as *Argonaut* proceeded to patrol south of Midway Atoll.

Orders had specified a submerged patrol, so after arriving in the area, two blasts on the Klaxon sounding diving alarm, AHOOGA, had taken us down during each morning twilight. A skirmish with two destroyers on the night of Pearl Harbor was our only action with the enemy, but ever-increasing humidity, due to lack of air conditioning, caused electrical grounds, and we fought the ensuing small fires instead. The nightly Fox radio schedule had contained briefs of the attack, and one message contained my orders to Mare Island, as executive officer of the submarine *Wahoo* building there. *Argonaut* was scheduled for new engines at the same yard, so now just to get her there.

One after another, the electrical motors of our major machinery had burned until we were compensating the boat by blowing water between tanks and pumping to sea with our one remaining pump. A lesser captain would have taken her home, but our skipper, Steve Barchet, an Annapolis All American, stayed with our mission: to defend Midway. Little did we know that *Argonaut*'s guns, mines, and torpedoes were all that was available to help oppose an expected assault.

On January 22, 1942, with a full section in clean, scrubbed dungarees at quarters, *Argonaut* entered Pearl Harbor to witness devastation far beyond anything we had expected. In charge, I faced the ranks to port or starboard as we passed each damaged, sunken, or capsized ship, some of them vessels in which our older hands had served. But older or younger, the sight became blurred as tears streamed down our cheeks.

We found our families fine and waiting on 1 week's notice for evacuation from the islands. After the unloading of mines, ammunition, and all but two torpedoes, I was able to join Ernestine and the children at the Roy Craws, our gracious landlords, who had brought them to a spare apartment in their Waikiki beachfront home.

On January 29, *Argonaut* sailed for Mare Island Navy Yard, arriving 10 days later, just ahead of our automobile. Thus, I was able to find and rent one of a group of excellent homes across from Hamilton Field, north of San Francisco and 20 miles from Mare Island. One month later, I met the *Lurline,* carrying 5,000 passengers, and brought my family home, where they would have all the facilities of the airfield only a short walk away.

The specified date in my orders arrived, and after a last lunch in *Argonaut,* I left my shipmates and many friends with whom I had served for nearly 4 years and walked along the waterfront towards the submarine in which I would be second in command as her executive officer.

Part One

MARE ISLAND TO PEARL HARBOR

1

From the dock, *Wahoo* appeared ready for sea, but the coming and going of Navy Yard workmen at a hurried pace told that there was much still to be done aboard. That was not yet my business, but the officers and enlisted men who would man her were my concern, so I walked to *Wahoo*'s dockside office across the quay. Looking back, I could see her sleek upper hull, longer than a football field, and thoughts of *Argonaut* faded.

Lt. George W. Grider and Lt. (jg) Roger W. Paine, Jr. greeted me, and over coffee, we brought each other up to date. George, two classes junior to me, had also served in destroyers, and after sub school, in the newer submarine, *Skipjack*. Sandy haired, lean, and with a pleasing southern manner, he would be a fine shipmate. His seniority marked George as our engineering officer, a billet he had already assumed. Roger, 5 years my junior, was similarly lean, but with dark hair and a more serious smile. After attending submarine school, he had served in the *Pompano*, which had a torpedo data computer (TDC). Knowing how to manipulate this machine, which would direct *Wahoo*'s torpedoes, had assured his assignment as torpedo and gunnery officer, and like George, Roger would be an asset to any wardroom.

Chief Torpedoman's Mate (CTM) Russel H. Rau, from New London, had also served in *Pompano,* where he had been chief of the boat, the key enlisted submarine billet, and had two supporters in Roger and George for the same assignment in *Wahoo*. Short, stocky, and muscular with receding hair gave Chief Rau an authoritative, fatherly appearance. If there had been any question, the Watch Quarter and Station Bill he was already preparing would have settled it, for the bill already showed the assignments of many crewmen.

Factually, over half of our complement had already reported to Sub-

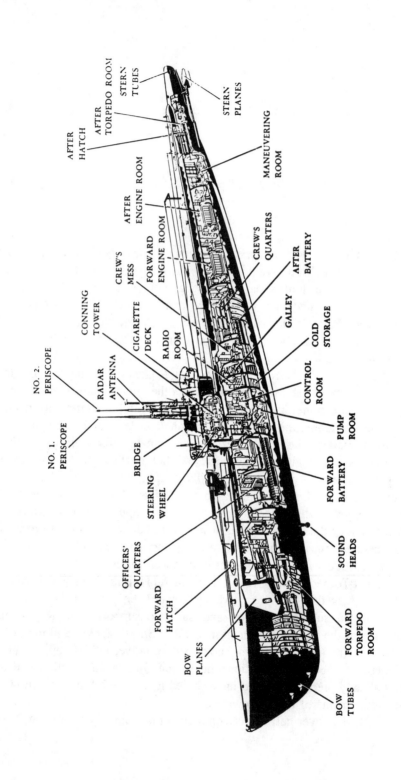

NO. 2. PERISCOPE

NO. 1. PERISCOPE

CONNING TOWER

RADAR ANTENNA

CIGARETTE DECK

RADIO ROOM

CREW'S MESS

FORWARD ENGINE ROOM

AFTER ENGINE ROOM

AFTER TORPEDO ROOM

STERN TUBES

STERN PLANES

AFTER HATCH

MANEUVERING ROOM

CREW'S QUARTERS

AFTER BATTERY

GALLEY

COLD STORAGE

CONTROL ROOM

PUMP ROOM

FORWARD BATTERY

SOUND HEADS

FORWARD TORPEDO ROOM

BOW TUBES

BOW PLANES

FORWARD HATCH

OFFICERS' QUARTERS

STEERING WHEEL

BRIDGE

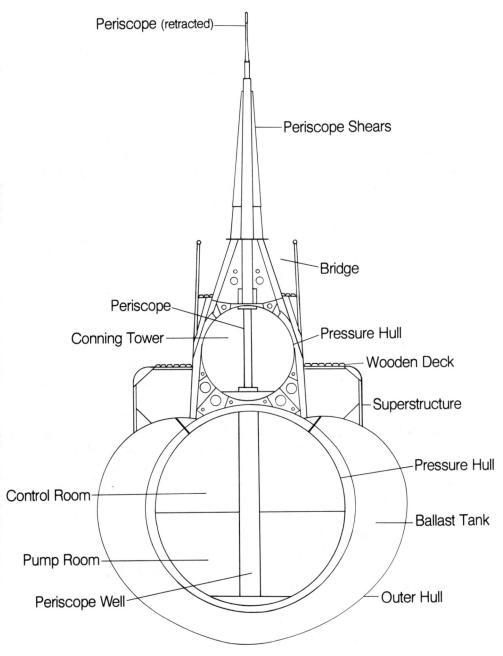

Periscope (retracted)

Periscope Shears

Bridge

Periscope

Conning Tower

Pressure Hull

Wooden Deck

Superstructure

Pressure Hull

Control Room

Ballast Tank

Pump Room

Periscope Well

Outer Hull

MIDSHIP CROSS SECTION

marine Administration (SubAd), Commander Submarine Force Pacific's facility at Mare Island. The men had come from other submarines, submarine school, or other schools pertinent to their rate. A few had come directly from surface ships, or from cities and farms via boot camp. Most important during these final stages of construction were the senior petty officers who had been attending schools at the manufactories of *Wahoo*'s major machinery.

Hand in hand with the billeting at SubAd went the facility's practical schools for lower rates and non-rated men. Training devices, similar to shipboard installations, provided the actual experience men would need to stand supervised watches in their submarine underway. *Wahoo*'s senior petty officers were either instructing or drawing machinery spare parts for temporary stowage adjacent to the office.

Everyone was busy, so I followed suit with my own school, heading for the after torpedo room. There were four tubes, carried loaded, their inner doors secured by heavy bronze bayonet locking rings. Just forward were skids to hold four reloads, and sandwiched with these were twelve pullout bunks. Forward to starboard lay the boatswain's storeroom opposite an enclosed head with outside scuttlebutt (drinking fountain). It was a complete fighting unit, with Torpedoman's Mate, First Class (TM1c) Johnson, who had greeted me, already in charge.

Forward in the small maneuvering room, Chief Electrician's Mate (CEM) Norman Ware introduced himself. This must have been planned and was appreciated. The heart of maneuvering was the encaged control cubicle with operating levers extending aft and rheostats controlling the fields. Here, electricians would direct the electrical output of all diesel generators to the four main motors, two to each propeller shaft through reduction gears, or to the two great batteries when charging. Similarly they would direct the batteries' output to the main motors when submerged. All of this was completely flexible. It was here that all maneuvering bells would be answered, with the electricians calling for more engines as required when surfaced.

Though I would have preferred continuing through the boat, my call on the captain of the Navy Yard took precedence. While there, I learned that Comdr. Duncan C. MacMillan was expected as *Wahoo*'s captain. Back at the office, the reporting of Lt. (jg) Chandler C. Jackson had solved the problem of a communication and commissary officer. A University of Wisconsin and sub school graduate, commissioned in the V7 officer program, he could take these jobs, which included underwater sound, in stride. Tall, lanky, brown haired, and with a bit of a wry smile, he'd fit in well, and I left the Navy Yard with the feeling that we surely must be receiving the best officers and chief petty officers.

A target bearing transmitter (TBT) to send binocular bearings to the conning tower might have brought an attack on the destroyers at Midway. So our senior radioman, James Buckley, RM1c and I set about making one. Lean and dark haired, his southern voice disguised an eagerness of a Yankee, for he soon had a bronze azimuth circle and boat stuffing box from scrap. A Monel shaft with slotted fitting above to receive binocular hinge pins and a pointer below completed the mechanical installation. The optical shop installed a vertical reticle in two pairs of binoculars, and *Wahoo* was now ready for a night surface attack.

Continuing my school below, I met our senior Chief Machinist's Mate (CMM) Andy Lenox as I entered the after engine room. He had just returned from school at Fairbanks Morse, where all of *Wahoo*'s engines had been built. Dark haired, and with about 10 years' more service, he took obvious pleasure in explaining our four nine-cylinder, opposed-piston, supercharged main engine generators. Each was rated at 1,600 horsepower, but could generate volts and amperes the equivalent of 2,000. At the time, we only glanced down to the lower flats at the 500- and 300-kw diesel auxiliaries. On leaving the forward room, we looked over two Kleinschmidt stills, which would supply all of the freshwater needs regardless of the duration of a patrol.

Our TBT and my initial familiarization with the boat had been completed just in time, for Lt. Comdr. Marvin G. Kennedy reported as prospective commanding officer (PCO). He came from staff duty preceded by executive officer of *Narwhal* SS N1, one of our three large submarines, and enjoyed an excellent reputation in torpedo fire control and tactics. Tall, lean, and with a complexion befitting his name, he was quite gentlemanly, but more formal than my previous small-ship captains. He also had his own projects to be completed. First came the installation of tanks to save the air conditioning condensate. Next came an extra set of 8½-by-11-inch card holders in each compartment for close-up pictures of Japanese ships. Chief Rau, now called "Pappy" by his contemporaries, then procured six large cases of ruby-red light bulbs to shorten the time for the eyes of those with topside watches to adapt to the dark. Unlike other boats, all of *Wahoo*'s lights would be red. Since red-marked danger sectors and such on the charts would not be visible, I was allowed a white light in the ship's office, but with a switch that turned it off when the door opened. Finally came a bucket for each stateroom and several for the crew's living spaces, for doing our laundry and taking sponge baths with the condensate, the showers and washing machine being too wasteful. Heretofore, such restrictions were unheard-of in modern boats.

Our major machinery had now been tested at dockside, including the firing of dummy torpedoes. A docking to cut the previously marked flood openings in our ballast tanks had been completed, and the time had come when the responsibility for *Wahoo*'s completion should pass to the PCO. In a ceremony with crew and officers assembled, Lieutenant Commander Kennedy read his orders; Signalman Hunter broke the commission pennant from the main, the jack and national ensign were flown, and on this June 15, 1942, *Wahoo* became a unit of the U.S. Pacific Fleet.

During the following weeks of underway testing, Mare Island inspectors rode with our crew. They attended to their particular machinery together with our responsible officers and petty officers. Those not involved organized their divisions into three watch sections of comparable abilities, and helped the chief of the boat in fitting the names into the Watch Quarter and Station Bill. Measuring about 2 by 3 feet and posted in the crew's mess, this bill would show the watch section, battle station, and duty for each emergency drill for every hand. On getting underway and returning to port, however, experienced men from each section, who took the watch, were known as the special sea detail, a semipermanent and prestigious assignment.

To obtain a satisfactory trim on diving, the diving officer can order pumping from auxiliary (amidships) to sea, or between forward and after trim in any combination including flooding from sea. George had demonstrated during our first dive up the bay when *Wahoo* had fired her first torpedoes, and again on our dive to test depth of 312 feet at sea. Then, however, the Navy Yard had rigged overlapping battens to check the hull's deflection. It was normal, requiring the expected pumping to sea to compensate for the reduced displacement. Commencing with our shakedown to San Diego, the officer of the deck (OOD) would go on down and take the dive.

The final loading was completed and at 1700 on Wednesday, July 15, I reported to the captain, "All hands are aboard and *Wahoo* is ready for sea and shakedown, Sir." He thanked me, and I saw him ashore.

2

Underway from Mare Island at dawn, *Wahoo* followed the Napa to the Sacramento River, and then turned south following the buoys through San Pablo Bay. On course in the channel, Captain Kennedy gave the conn to Chan and went below. Two diesels with 80% load and 90% speed, called 80/90, were driving us on at 14 knots. On Chan's report of San Francisco looming ahead, the captain came topside, changed course into the main ship channel, and on schedule, at 0800, *Wahoo* passed through the Golden Gate. Turning south at the sea buoy, two more engines went on propulsion, and all four worked up to full power for the required 20-hour endurance run. Aboard were Navy Yard representatives from Fairbanks Morse and General Electric to observe and advise, and they were more than welcome.

Quartermaster Hunter and I identified the landmarks and then lights as we piloted *Wahoo* down the coast and then through the Santa Barbara Channel. Below, our hefty senior cook, Rowls, had prepared fine meals, and the odor of lean SC1c (ship's cook, first class) Phillips's baking had roused the oncoming midwatch. George's engineering plant completed its endurance run without fault. The antisubmarine net was opened, and at 1400, our captain brought *Wahoo* alongside the waiting pier at the Destroyer Base in San Diego on schedule.

Waiting were Commander Swinburne, Deputy Commander Submarine Force Pacific Fleet (ComSubPac), whom I had known from early submarine days, and the base commander, Commodore McCandless, an acquaintance since serving in destroyers. While the captain walked to the base with them, we turned back the sections of decking that covered the after and forward torpedo loading hatches. This put the attached skids in place. The slanted hatches were opened, showing the receiving skids below already aligned, and Roger with his torpedomen went about loading the four torpedoes waiting on their conveyor at dockside.

No operation order was needed to tell that *Wahoo* would be underway by dawn for tactical approaches and possible firing during daylight. To avoid lost time, the target ship followed a zigzag plan to confuse the submarine, but so laid down that an aggressive boat, with correct tactics, could close to an acceptable torpedo-firing range. That would set the pattern for nearly 2 weeks, with ship's drills taking up the slack while our destroyer or patrol craft (PC) target and *Wahoo* opened the range for the next run. After firings, specially outfitted PT-type retrievers picked up the torpedoes, whose yellow exercise heads brought them to the surface at the end of their run. Prepared for refiring, they would be reloaded on the second night. So we did get some sleep.

We had learned our battle stations till there would be no mistakes. The captain made excellent approaches, including some by the TBT at night. By the position of the torpedo wakes, or by seeing the fish run under their ships, the escort skippers signaled hits for all but a few of the required firings, and those were difficult with wildly zigging targets.

Only one exercise remained on the schedule—the firing of our deck gun. We did not yet have one, so Captain Kennedy asked me to go to the 11th Naval District Headquarters and schedule an indoctrinal depth charging for Monday morning, the day of our departure, instead.

Upon returning, I found the pier swarming with crewmen, each with a batch of rags, and what appeared to be an allowance of ammunition about the dock. The red magazine flood valve wheel, forward of the flood and vent manifold, had lost its warning red in our red lighting. It must have been inadvertently cracked and then not completely shut during diving. A mess cook had noted one of the hatches in the deck seeming a little squashy. Upon opening it, Paul Phillips, our fine baker, had found the magazine flooded. George had told the captain, who had few words, but seemed a bit in shock.

In the morning, the flooding of the magazine was not mentioned as *Wahoo* departed, rigging for dive en route. Ten miles northwest of Point Loma, Lieutenant (jg) Lassing with his *PC-570* was waiting as had been agreed. *Wahoo* drew ahead on course north and then dived, rigging for depth charge while keeping both scopes exposed. The purpose was to let newer hands know what depth charges are like and so dispel some of the Hollywood myths created by shaking the camera. *PC-570* came roaring past, lest she damage her stern, and laid down a string of four. The instantaneous CRACK then WHACK and swishing rumble through the superstructure, repeated four times, could have convinced the uninitiated that the charges were on top of us, but Hunter on the scope confirmed that they were a hundred yards away. So the final requirement before departing on patrol had been completed, when normally this would have been done off Pearl Harbor.

Our continuing return to Mare Island went well. Loading for patrol kept hands busy, but did not interfere with normal liberty. A final docking fixed an annoying squeal from our port shaft, and after testing at sea, much to the delight of the crew, *Wahoo* moored at Pier 45 in San Francisco. In the morning we would sail for Pearl Harbor and unrestricted submarine warfare against the enemy.

3

A prolonged blast from her whistle warned that *Wahoo* was backing clear from Pier 45. The current caught her stern, commencing a swing that our captain completed precisely with screws and rudder. Two engines were now driving us towards the center of the Golden Gate Bridge, surely man's most beautiful steel structure. As we drew near, the waves from our friends and loved ones, gathered in the observation area, carried their Godspeed, and ours were returned. But then the channel and antisubmarine net required our strict attention. The time was 0930 on this August 12, 1942, as prescribed in our operation order.

Beyond the marked channel, all landmarks were obscured by the seasonal fog, but the two Farallon Islands and the bridge showed clearly on the SJ (surface search) radar as tall dancing pips above the horizontal grassy line. Their bearings and ranges plotted nicely with our dead-reckoning position (DR) on the chart and gave a final departure point by radar, a new experience for me. A lookout report brought me to the bridge; it was our escort, the USS *Kilty,* waiting beyond the end of the swept channel, clear of possible enemy mines. I gave the captain the recommended course and time at the channel's end, and received his, "Make it so." George took the conn and ordered, "Set the regular sea detail," and "Rig ship for dive." The captain left the bridge and I followed, but only as far as the conning tower to get my sextant for a morning sun line.

Normally in submarines, the senior quartermaster or signalman becomes the assistant navigator. So I was surprised to find that SM1c Hunter was to head our quartermaster watch list. The designation was reasonable, for he could now be on watch with our less experienced officers, but I would have preferred making the designation. So I showed Krause, our polite, sandy-haired signalman, second class from New England, how to use the comparing watch, and we took five evenly spaced altitude readings of the sun. The computation gave us an apparently good position line, but the proof would have to await the sun line at high noon. While I went below to consult the captain concerning plans for the rest of the day, Krause consulted our books concerning his new responsibility.

The captain went along with my suggestion for a chlorine gas drill about midafternoon to be followed by a trim dive after our escort had been released. This modest schedule would surely be welcomed by all hands, especially the bachelors, for George, with the duty, and Pappy Rau apparently had experienced a busy night in striking returning hands below. Living only 23 miles north of the bridge, mine had been a quiet night at home, and quite intentionally, I had not inquired about the details, which had obviously been well handled. Other questions were answered by a quick turn through the boat: We were well secured for sea, with no loose gear to cause damage or injury. Some hands were restowing lockers, but most others not on watch were staying out of the way in their bunks. The watch was alert, including the galley, where our expert cook, Phillips, was showing how to turn chicken-fried steaks. Unfortunately, there was no way to snitch one, so I returned to the bridge suddenly quite hungry.

George would have the deck till noon, with Roger and then Chan to follow. Hopefully, we could add three junior officers at Pearl, so in a one-in-three rotation, the extra could serve as operations officer supervising the conning tower watch and as assistant navigator. This had proved desirable in *Argonaut,* so here, with radar also to be interpreted, an operations officer would seem essential. But the sight topside took my mind from such details.

Wahoo was racing through the calm summer seas on course 255 degrees true heading for Point Yoke, the first of five positions that would keep us clear of any shipping while en route to Pearl Harbor. Maintaining a station about 500 yards ahead was *Kilty,* who would accompany us till dark, primarily to identify our submarine as friendly. We would thus avoid diving for planes and could maintain the 16-knot speed of advance required by our operation order. At the moment, three of our four main diesels were driving *Wahoo* at 17 knots so as to allow for temporary reductions during training dives and some of our emergency drills.

Each of the four lookouts was searching his sector as if we were in enemy waters, and that was as it should be. Realism came with an SD (air search) radar contact at 12 miles. It could be in any sector since the SD gives range only and is not directional, but if the plane closed we would dive, for escorted or not, the final responsibility for *Wahoo*'s safety lay with us alone. Probably sighting *Kilty,* the plane withdrew after closing a mile, so by her presence, our escort was accomplishing her mission.

My task, at the moment, was to provide an accurate noon position report. The noon latitude sun line crossed nicely with the midmorning line run ahead at our speed and confirmed our (dead-reckoning) position. *Wahoo* was indeed making good 17 knots. The captain received the formal position slip, a printed form about 3 by 4 inches, that I had signed. After thanking me, he advised that he would be below for the next half hour or so. This was not an order for me to remain on the bridge or in the conning tower, but I gathered that he expected such, so answered that I would be here at hand.

When the noon meal had been served and the mess cooks had squared away the mess room, we held the chlorine gas drill. This deadly gas will be generated if saltwater enters the battery cells. Normally, the rupture of the pressure hull abreast a battery compartment would have to precede such flooding, and in peacetime, this would be limited to a collision. In the coming months, however, depth charges, bombs, and even shelling increased the possibility. So, rehearsing the procedure of identifying, vacating, and isolating the affected battery compartment, with subsequent ventilation, was now more important. It could save many lives. The instructions that had been posted in each compartment, and the detailed procedures contained in the duty chief's folder, proved adequate, and I congratulated Chiefs Rau and Ware on their performances. Chlorine gas was set aside as a drill. Now, the report of chlorine gas would mean the real thing.

Chan relieved Roger, assuming the four-to-eight watch. The *Kilty* was released at 1800, with our "Well-done" and her "Godspeed." Seen broadside, as she raced by, the fine seagoing design of our destroyer escorts was evident: in her I saw the simplicity of *Pruitt* and the essentials from our full-fledged destroyers. I sincerely hoped the enemy did not have comparable escorts. When she was clear, Chan took us down, keeping the lanyard to the hatch in hand to insure that it could not open before our eager Quartermaster Striker Simonetti had spun the wheel setting the dogs. Chan dropped on down to control and leveled us off at the ordered 64 feet, reporting satisfied with the trim. After we had briefly manned battle stations, the captain surfaced our ship in the customary cautious manner and quickly had *Wahoo* at her 17-knot cruising speed. The whole operation had seemed particularly smooth, which is always the way when everyone handles his job properly; this should give our skipper confidence, especially in Chan, who stood an excellent watch and set the pace for his assistants.

The sun line, our escort's departure, the messages, and the dive seemed to make the afternoon go quickly. Then came sunset followed by evening twilight and the first stars. After the noon meal, Krause and I had calculated the approximate bearing and altitude of the stars we might use. Now as the brighter ones became visible, their identification was no task at all. We took a careful series of sextant altitude readings of the six most prominent, with five readings on each one. If the changes in altitude were consistent, we would use the third or middle sight in our calculations; otherwise, we would average them for use with the mid-time. Later, perhaps, when we were more sure of ourselves, we might drop to three readings or even a single one.

We rather raced with the calculations and plotting, which surely wasn't consistent with accuracy, but the captain seemed anxious. The stars were kind, however, and their lines crossed nicely in forming a large dot. The afternoon sun line, run ahead at our speed, just like a ship along a course line, crossed through our point, all plotted to 2000, or twenty-hundred. The completed formal position slip brought a "Thank-you" from the captain, but with just the touch of a frown, for we were a few minutes late. However, Krause and I had used extreme care and knew *Wahoo*'s current position, and to navigators, that is what really counts.

A warmed-over soggy supper, notes for the captain's Night Orders, and the morrow's Plan of the Day finished my day shortly before midnight. In 4½ hours, I'd be called for a round of morning stars and another day.

Though my schedule left little personal time, that of the crew and officers was exhausting. Reveille, breakfast, trice up bunks and clamp down (with a damp swab), emergency drills, and battle stations filled the daytime hours between watches. Only during mealtime was there assurance against interruption. At this pace, we'd be the best-trained ship's company to arrive at the U.S. Submarine Base, Pearl Harbor (if we were still on our feet).

Points Yoke and Zed were now behind us, as we continued to enjoy cruising weather. Lack of sea legs didn't affect the instruction accompanying most watches below decks. Of necessity, many non-rated men had already been designated as strikers and were filling billets of third-class petty officers. Their instructors were our qualified submariners, officers, and petty officers alike. This required no urging, for in the coming weeks their very lives could depend on the effectiveness of teaching. A wavering wake that slowly straightened told of a new hand on the wheel receiving instruction from Hunter or the steersman he had relieved. Keeping the lubber line, representing the ship's bow, on the designated compass-card course requires anticipation and the minimum rudder to correct. It was evident that this new hand had a natural feel of the ship.

Wahoo was now headed for Point Able as she continued following the alphabet. Thus far, any small errors in our navigation would affect only our personal pride, but the coming report to Commander Submarine Force Pacific Fleet, ComSubPac, on crossing the 1,000-mile circle from Pearl must be accurate, for operational control of *Wahoo* would pass to ComSubPac at that time. Of even more importance to us would be an exact position to effect a rendezvous with the ship designated to escort *Wahoo* on approaching Pearl.

My confidence in being able to handle the multiple assignments increased when, for the first time since leaving San Francisco, I was able to turn in before 2300, over 5 hours until morning star-call. Deep in the first minutes of sleep, I became aware of a rocking motion; then of a firm hand on my shoulder, and a far-off voice repeating, "We've got troubles, Lieutenant!"

In minutes, I joined my assistant in the ship's office to find out what was wrong in private. Now the *Air Almanac,* an annual publication, lists the hour angle (the angular distance from Greenwich, England) and the declination (the angular distance from the equator) of the sun, moon, planets, and major stars for each 5 minutes of the day. It is bound with a wire spring, in a semi-loose-leaf manner, so that out-of-date pages can be torn out and discarded. Krause had torn out too many pages and they had already been given the "deep-six" in the weighted sacks of trash and garbage. The detailed data on them was absolutely necessary in calculating the true altitude at the recorded moment of sextant or observed altitude; without it, only latitude lines at high noon are practical.

There was only one solution, lacking the more extensive *Nautical Almanac*. I retrieved my slide rule, and after calculating the rate of change of hour angle and declination in the undisturbed pages, we proceeded to make new tables to replace those that had gone to Davy Jones's locker. It was a monstrous task, but new tables for the missing 3 days were complete, with time for a cup of coffee before going topside. My final word before climbing the ladder was, "Krause, if these work, mum's the word, but if they don't, you're going to stand up with me when I tell the captain!"

Waiting brought apprehension, but morning twilight's first horizon took precedence. Krause had been on the bridge for some minutes spotting the stars we had used on the previous morning. With some doubts, we recorded five sextant altitudes of each one. The rate of change for all seemed reasonably consistent, always an indication of good sights, so we went below to double check the times and then make the calculations.

Every now and then, there seems to be a helping hand, and this time it could truly have been called a guiding star. The star fix was fine, and privately we were off the hook. In 3 days the last of our manufactured tables would follow the others, and we'd be back on the printed pages with no one the wiser.

The required reports on crossing the 1,000- and 500-mile circles from Pearl had been received by ComSubPac; Points Cast, Baker, and Able lay astern; and Steersman Dooley held *Wahoo* on the zigzag legs of her final routing of the voyage. Having kept our temporary navigational troubles strictly private had helped in establishing a mutually respectful rapport, a relationship that I hoped to enjoy with the captain. Our position slips were now delivered on time, or nearly so, and I was thankful for the circumstance that had made Krause my assistant.

It was from Krause that I learned more about our last night in San Francisco. One hand surmised that if he returned to *Wahoo* thoroughly inebriated, sick drunk, the duty officer would have to send him to the hospital. He could then sail on the next submarine instead. But he had underestimated George, an athlete, and Pappy Rau, who had experienced such things before. Though a quarter again the size of either of them, George and Pappy quickly handcuffed and leg-ironed the culprit to the radio direction finder mast aft of the conning tower fairwater. As the chilling San Francisco fog rolled in, they uncuffed one hand at a time, fitting him with a foul-weather jacket. But still immobile, his teeth were chattering and complexion somewhat blue at dawn when he gladly went below.

I was probably the last to learn of this, and hopefully the captain never would. That his submarine could be the first ship in this century to use leg irons, still in the equipage from sailing days, might not sit well. Krause did not mention a name, but from the brief details I surmised that he might have been my assistant navigator.

The evening Fox, a radio schedule from ComSubPac, contained a message with *Wahoo*'s call sign. Chan raced aft to decode it and returned in minutes with the tape in hand. As expected, the message gave the coordinates where we were to meet the USS *Litchfield* at 0400 tomorrow, August 18. A copy of our operation order had been sent to ComSubPac by Clipper Mail; he had our various positions, and the rendezvous plotted nicely 128 miles ahead.

The captain came to the bridge shortly after 0300, unaware, unless he had glanced at the chart, that a midnight star triangle lay astride our track. It was still with some satisfaction, however, that we heard the radar operator announce, "SJ contact, range 14,000 yards, bearing near dead ahead." The time was 0330.

"It really works," whispered Krause.

"The radar?" I queried.

"No, this navigation stuff," he replied.

Till now, Krause's total experience in celestial navigation had produced only positions on a chart. I recalled my first landfall, comparable to this rendezvous; it was the proof of the pudding and I knew just how he felt.

Chan had supplied the correct challenge and reply, while Krause readied the Aldis lamp, a hand-held signal light. *Litchfield*'s silhouette, first as a blur or "blurp" and then tall and sharp, came out of the night. We were ready to challenge or be challenged.

"No, not that," ordered the captain, referring to the Aldis lamp. "Use the blinker gun and go to battle stations!"

These precautions made identification more difficult and downright dangerous when the torpedo tubes were readied and the doors opened. If *Litchfield* had known that six torpedoes were pointed down her throat, she'd have spun on a dime and left us behind. Fortunately, perhaps, she made the correct reply to our challenge and then sent two short messages with her easily read Aldis lamp.

"What did she say?" asked the captain.

Krause stepped across the bridge to deliver them orally, saying, "They're addressed to you, Sir. The first read, 'Welcome to the Islands,' and the second said, 'Congratulations on precise navigation.' " There was no comment, and upon returning Krause uttered a soft, "Jeez."

Piloting, with radar ranges on Molokai and Oahu, and then made more precise with visual bearings at dawn, was a welcome change from stars. *Wahoo* entered the wide Kaiwi Channel between them and set course for Pearl Harbor, an hour's run ahead. Following early breakfast, the welcome orders, "Make all preparations for entering port; station the special sea detail; and rig ship for surface," were announced on the 1MC. *Litchfield* was released with our "Well done," and a section of hands who had not seen Pearl Harbor since the attack were at quarters as we entered the channel. Facing each ship, or her remains, as we passed by would make their blood boil, and I doubted there would be a dry eye. The very sight would exhort them to do their level best in our coming endeavors. The captain conned our submarine through Pearl Harbor, around ten-ten dock, and with a one-bell maneuver to alongside Pier 2 at the U.S. Naval Submarine Base in time for most of a working day.

Part Two

FIRST PATROL
In the Carolines

1

On the pier to greet us at the U.S. Naval Submarine Base were Rear Adm. Robert E. English and Comdr. Frank Watkins, our new submarine force and division commanders. The admiral's submarine service had started before World War I, and his previous billet had been Commander Submarine Squadron Four (ComSubRon 4), which included command of the Submarine Base, the second senior command in Submarine Force Pacific (SubPac). The commander had just returned from a successful patrol in *Flying Fish* and was the only division commander to have made a war patrol in command. Our captain had served with the admiral, so with his support and first-hand advice from the commander, all augured well for *Wahoo*.

Smith, our steward, had carried out Chan's instructions to have just-brewed coffee ready, which was one of the reasons for the admiral and commander's coming on below. A bit of nostalgia—the surroundings played their part, but the coffee was superb. After a cup, I excused myself for there was much to be done. A quick turn aft showed each compartment now sporting at least one white light, so it was no longer blinding when I went topside. Beyond the head of the dock, a medium-sized bus with driver was parked. Pappy Rau assured me that the pending work could be handled by two sections, so one section left to stay with the bus, which would return before curfew at dark, and with the knowledge that tomorrow's section could ride on their return.

Our torpedoes were being winched topside, and by boom onto the waiting conveyor on the dock. Each the weight of an automobile, it was exacting work, but necessary, for they would be replaced by torpedoes precisely prepared at the Base torpedo shop. Roger and Pappy Rau would witness the preliminary and the final adjustments at the shop, and be responsible for the reloading. Though but one of the tasks preparatory to going on patrol, it could determine our readiness date.

The captain had seen the admiral ashore, and after a turn through the boat with the commander, had gone to the Base with him. George left with Machinist's Mate, Second Class Frash, his "Oil King," to record fuel oil soundings at the Base tank farm preparatory to *Wahoo*'s fueling. Chan was off to Base communications to exchange registered publications, and rather by default, I had now assumed the duty. The first evidence of the captain's efforts ashore came at midafternoon when Lt. (jg) Richie N. Henderson reported on board for duty. Tall, lean, sandy haired, and with a slightly wry smile, he immediately gave every promise of being a fine shipmate. From Pennsylvania, and a 1940 USNA graduate, he had survived his battleship at Pearl Harbor. To us, he was a gold mine, submarine school or not, and immediately relieved Chan of commissary.

During the declared Limited Emergency prior to the war, Pearl Harbor boats had been required to submit warm- and cold-weather menus for possible southern or northern patrols, and the estimated provisions. These were approved with some modifications by the force medical officer, though by Navy Regulations this was the responsibility of a ship's captain. The commissary provisioning for patrols during the Emergency satisfied the menus but not the crews. They wanted twice as much bread and baked goods. Skippers took charge for subsequent patrols, but the doctors and staff were slow in revising the recommended commissary stores for new boats. So, like the torpedoes, all of our stores would be unloaded and the ship reprovisioned.

We had surmounted a few problems in *Wahoo,* including that flooded magazine, and believed that such things were behind us. But Richie shook our confidence in his first hour on the job. A battery fresh-water line passed through the commissary storeroom and had an obscurely located shut-off valve. The bonnet of this valve had been leaking, with the water running down the curved contour of *Wahoo*'s pressure hull. We were somewhat abashed to have a surface sailor find what none of us had observed, even on inspections. The cleanup went on into the night, when soggy stores could be dumped, unobserved, in the "Dempster Dumpsters" at the head of the dock.

On our third day in port, the captain hit pay dirt again: Lt. (jg) Ira Dye, an NROTC graduate from the University of Washington, reported for duty. Of medium height, with straight blond hair combed back to an indeterminate part, and displaying an engaging smile, he too would be a pleasant addition to the wardroom. Of more importance, as George saw it, was his engineering degree. So *Wahoo* had an assistant engineer and electrical officer wrapped in one. Like Richie, he would get his submarine school training aboard, but living truly within a ship day and night makes the knowledge come quickly.

Later in the day, still on a need-to-know basis, was the designation of our patrol area. Krause broke out the master chart of the Pacific, which showed the outline and numbers of the detailed charts. At the Base chart pool we drew the charts we would need en route and while patrolling, spreading them out to be sure. Back aboard, we stowed them in the drawers provided below the wardroom's sideboard. Prompted by our earlier experience, both the *Air* and *Nautical Almanacs* were sighted in place and our department was ready for patrol.

Briefings and reading patrol reports and pertinent parts of the Japanese monograph at headquarters had occupied my spare time, but also had provided opportunities to drop by personnel. In proportion, our new hands equaled the captain's efforts, so *Wahoo* would put to sea with a complement of seven officers and sixty-five enlisted men, but still missing and particularly affecting me was a yeoman. Departments were reporting their readiness, and this was well, for the captain announced that we would depart on patrol Monday, August 23, 3 days hence. On Sunday evening, a few minutes after the Base movie, I reported, "All hands are aboard and Departments ready for patrol, Captain," and received his, "Very good."

In the quiet of my stateroom, I considered *Wahoo*'s prospects for the coming patrol, and not without some doubts. How could our captain, who could make good practice torpedo attacks, apparently be so uninformed in modern submarine matters? The probable answer was quite simple: Our new-construction captains had gone to shore duty after qualifying in submarines, the Navy encouraging nonsubmarine duties to broaden their careers. Their executive officers, while starting 5 years later, had served continuously in the boats in most billets and, for many, a war patrol. And so we had the incongruous situation in which some skippers had far less submarine time and experience than their execs. Our peacetime training against warships with air and surface escorts created a bugaboo of periscope sighting. The West Coast Sound School demonstration for PCOs created another bugaboo, for without temperature gradients—always found in the deep Pacific and which reflect echo-ranging sound waves back towards the surface—the S-boat targets could not escape. Attending the new PCO tactical-updating course at New London followed by a PCO patrol in a seasoned submarine was designed for our very situation. Lacking this would demand the sharing of submarine knowledge and expertise, but would this be possible in *Wahoo?*

2

A prolonged blast from our whistle warned that *Wahoo* was backing from her slip. The line handlers on the dock paused in their work, first with their fingers in their ears and then, perhaps following the lead of Commander Watkins, remaining at attention till our ship headed out the channel. It was an emotional moment, deepened by the captain's serious words at quarters and my announcement of our destination. The remaining men who had not seen the devastation were at quarters on the forecastle as the captain conned his ship through the harbor. Below, rigging ship for dive was already in progress, for we had one last submerged operation before proceeding on patrol. Turning west at the sea buoy, *Wahoo* headed for her PC escort; Roger took the conn, and the first section relieved the special sea detail. Our following trim dive served an additional purpose when the PC gave us two indoctrinal depth charges, primarily for our new shipmates. On the surface again, the steersman steadied on 257 degrees, the initial course to our patrol area, and rang up standard speed. The maneuvering room would adjust our propeller turns for 14 knots. A thousand yards ahead, the escort patrolled across our bow and would stay with us till dusk. The time was 1000 (ten-hundred) this August 23, just 1 hour after getting underway, and *Wahoo* was on patrol.

On the conning tower chart, for all to see, was the track we would follow. It had three long legs that passed through points designated in our operation order. More important to us, however, were Taongi Atoll 90 miles to the west of the second leg, Ponape Island to the southeast of the third leg, then Namonuito and Hall Islands. Passing between these two, *Wahoo* would enter her patrol area.

The Nampo Shoto, the Bonins, and the Marianas leading south from Tokyo form an interrupted corridor. Along this route, surface and air patrols could offer considerable protection to Empire shipping to and from the Carolines, a loose line of islands, reefs, and atolls extending from Palau, near the Philippines, eastward over 2,000 miles to the Gilberts. Near the center of this chain lies a small group of volcanic islands with about 1,500-foot peaks and extensive, deep anchorages. Well fortified, they are surrounded by a continuous ring of low islands and reefs. Averaging 30 miles across and with only four navigable passes, this ring made the anchorages immune to gunfire. The atoll, as an enemy naval base, had made possible the control of the Marianas and support of their conquest of the Solomons, about 900 miles southeastward. Sometimes called the Gibraltar of the Pacific, this atoll was labeled Truk on our chart. *Wahoo* would patrol its western approaches and the important Piaanu Pass into the atoll.

Morning- and noon-latitude sun lines crossed conveniently on our track, and I delivered the 1200 position slip to the captain on the bridge. As before, he thanked me, but then said:

Dick, I am going to require two officers on watch when we are on patrol, so if you will stand the four-to-eights, your quartermaster can bring your sextant topside for your morning and evening stars, and since you'll be relieved by a quarter of the hour in accordance with naval custom, that will give you ample time to work up your stars and have the position slip to me by 0800 and 2000. The noon position slip, of course, offers no problem.

This additional duty, leaving *Wahoo* without an effective executive officer during these critical hours, had implications that could undermine *Wahoo*'s potential fighting ability. These thoughts were whirling in my mind, but ours was a ship at war and my answer was, "Aye, aye, Sir."

In addition to radio time checks, Krause would now be responsible for recording the exact difference between the gimbal-mounted ship's chronometer and the comparing watch, essential to the later computation of the Greenwich Civil Time (GCT) of each star sight.

The PC turned back at sunset, sending Godspeed and receiving our "Well-done." The SJ radar now searched ahead; its range greatly exceeding the visibility, and our SD was secured for the night. With the first stars of evening twilight, we took our sights using the same lucky stars that had served us well for the *Litchfield* rendezvous. Then came the wait of nearly 2 hours before we would know if our fix was good, and with the fading horizon, no chance of another round of stars for a precise position.

Promptly at 1945, George and Ira came to the bridge. Chan turned over the watch, while I dropped below to the ship's office, which sported the only white light. Our first lines crossed far from the dead-reckoning position, but a simple correction to the GCT set all aright. Though some minutes late, the captain received the position slip in the usual courteous manner, and I sat down to a warmed-over supper.

Except for zigzagging during daylight, which required 10% more speed to maintain the required advance, *Wahoo* had enjoyed routine surface cruising with a trim dive on the third day, and the always puzzling "sailing into tomorrow" as our boat crossed the international date line. A reported distant plane on the morning watch (the four-to-eight) seemed unlikely with Taongi Atoll still 400 miles away, but on the following day, August 29, we proceeded submerged while passing the atoll. Bona fide patrol planes kept us down while passing Ponape, so the captain, who had spent nearly all surfaced hours on the bridge or in the conning tower, had some real rest in his cabin. I hoped that this would become routine in our patrol area, for in *Argonaut* my captain had found it necessary as well as delegating many responsibilities.

Clear of Ponape, we enjoyed surface running in storms, diving at dawn on September 3 between Hall and Namonuito Islands. From there, *Wahoo* would proceed southwest 40 miles into the assigned area. The wind and seas moderated throughout the morning with the overcast lifting at noon. Though without star fixes, we were confident of our position, especially since the dead-reckoning indicator agreed with our DR position on the chart. We would not see the islands, even using maximum periscope (with shears still submerged) of 17 feet. Passing into our area, and now with 3-foot exposures ordered, any sightings would be of enemy planes or ships.

The very fact that *Wahoo* was now patrolling her assigned area over 3,000 miles from Pearl Harbor added pride and determination to our task. But throughout the day only seabirds came into view during cautious sweeps every half hour, and only fish noises were heard on sound. Just as on our previous submerged days, however, time was not wasted. On surfacing late in evening twilight we headed for a point 15 miles off Piaanu Pass. Krause and I raced in bringing the stars down to a fading horizon and rather surprised ourselves with a good fix. Only

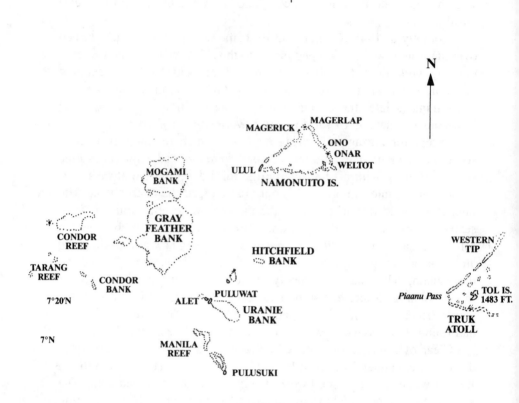

CAROLINE ISLANDS
ADJACENT TRUK
40 MILES

a modest change of course to 185 degrees and slowing to two-thirds speed would put us on station before morning twilight.

We had two officers in each watch section in *Argonaut,* one serving as operations officer in the conning tower or the control room as the situation required. He took the dive when she submerged. In our boat, with radar and sonar to be interpreted in the conning tower, we should have the same, and I was considering such a recommendation to the captain. While at the Submarine Base, however, he had had a metal bunk installed in the conning tower that folded up against the TDC. Presumably, it would be the counterpart of an emergency cabin in surface warships where the captain could rest or sleep near the bridge in pending battle or emergency. Still, in submarines, the captain's cabin was already as close as their emergency cabin. I had the answer when I came off watch: the bunk was made up for the captain this night, and my recommendation would be out of order.

The days of cruising, with routine dives and drills, showed their effect below. Those going on watch or shifting assignments did so with quiet confidence, no longer needing instructions. The battery charge had been in progress since surfacing and would be completed before midnight. Ira had just given permission to dump trash and garbage. In less than a minute the weighted sacks would be passed through the mess-room hatch, and all secured again. Following patrol instructions, the sacks would contain the patrol reports we had been studying, thus insuring that they could not fall to the enemy. Though not covering our area, they contained the lessons of other boats, their successes and failures, and we learned much from them. They had been my only reading since sailing and most certainly superseded many peacetime instructions.

In the bright, clear moonlight, Tol Island, which rises 1,483 feet, could come into view anytime after midnight. As an assistant navigator, unencumbered by watches, Krause was on the bridge early. He called me when the peak was sighted at 2300, and Ira was able to include in his sighting report to the captain that the navigator was on the bridge. The distance (from the height and distance to the horizon tables) was 30 miles, and we slowed to one-third speed while quietly approaching Piaanu Pass.

At this speed, our screws would not appreciably interfere with the supersonic listening sound head (JK), so sound was manned. Buckley, our best soundman, came on watch with us, both as an operator and instructor. Though the chance of hearing the props before seeing a ship was slight in this visibility and with our radar coverage, the ever-present possibility of an enemy submarine outweighed all other considerations, for we could be her target! At 0430, Buckley's report of fast screws sent us down, and I'll never be sure whether the captain or Chan initiated the dive. We searched with the scopes on the reported bearings as they crossed our bow and finally faded in the direction of Piaanu Pass, but saw nothing. However, diving first and asking questions later was correct, so I complimented Chan on his instant reaction. Now with dawn less than an hour away, we continued on submerged.

Krause was busy totalling the daily runs from the chart when the first rays of the rising sun framed Tol with a beautiful corona. I passed the scope to him for a few seconds before pressing the lowering button. "That confirms it," he said, "3,110 miles from Pearl and we're right in our spot." Actually, the confirmation would come on sighting the 70-foot palm trees of the perimeter islands as shown on our chart. Even now, their tops in the sun should be visible from a dozen miles, but my search, interrupted by the arrival of the captain, had shown they were still beyond the horizon.

The captain raised the periscope and went through the search procedure—a quick sweep in low power to be sure all was clear, and then the high-power search. All was quiet until he came on Tol Island, when he fairly burst out, "You'll have us aground!" and changed course to the northwest. Without words, Krause and I gathered that we did not enjoy the captain's full confidence.

By the second day of patrol, we had shelved emergency drills in favor of torpedo fire control. *Wahoo*'s course and speed are fed into the torpedo data computer automatically. The enemy ship's relative position is set from the bearing and range called by the periscope assistant, and the target's course is set from the captain's all-important call of angle on the bow. To port or starboard to 180 degrees, this is the angle formed by the longitudinal axis of a ship and the line of sight intercepting her. Through a series of observations, while the submarine is closing to a firing range, the TDC operator determines the target's speed. If she is zigging, the base course and confirming speed will come from the navigational plot. All the while, the TDC's angle-solver section sets the hitting angle on the torpedoes' gyros.

Fortunately, the TDC, with manual inputs, could generate approach and attack problems. Roger and Richie had composed a goodly number,

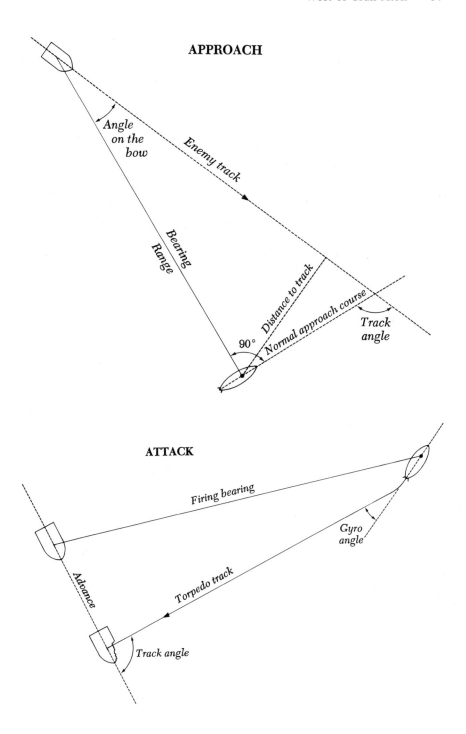

all in a folder and needing only a stopwatch and caller. So our drills, including those directly involved, were realistic, approaching a game. The total party, starting forward and then clockwise, were: Simonetti on the wheel, Chan on plot, Buckley at sound, Roger manning the TDC, Richie at the angle solver to apply torpedo spreads, Krause keeping the log and manning the firing panel, Hunter as periscope assistant, and myself as assistant approach officer, with an ISWAS, a slide rule with azimuth scales, to give desired tracks and distances for the captain, to see that tubes were readied, torpedo running depth set, to compare plot with TDC, and to follow up on any orders from the captain.

The first of the two preceding diagrams shows a submarine during an approach with the elements discussed above. The second shows the attack from stern tubes with small right gyro angles on the torpedoes, the enemy having zigged or changed base course to the right.

3

Under a glassy sea, our search throughout the day was by sound at 90 feet, coming up for 3-foot periscope observations every half hour. A brief study of the chart showed that ships coming from the western Carolines might very well proceed from Gray Feather or Mogami Banks to Namonuito before proceeding on to Truk. If Ulul Island in the Namonuito group had an airfield, as the Japanese monograph surmised, this route would be very likely, and our search would be along their continuing route to Piaanu Pass. I passed this information to Pappy Rau so it would be spread through the watches. The hopes of everyone remained high throughout the day. After surfacing, the SJ more than doubled the distance we had been able to see with 3 feet of periscope, so we were actually searching four times the area this night.

Turning back after the battery charge was completed at 2300, we patrolled back to the vicinity of Truk. This called for stars on the earliest morning horizon. Passing through the conning tower, I noted that we now had two men manning the SJ. Its handwheel, with shafts and gears, to rotate the SJ had become increasingly hard to turn. At night, our auxiliarymen had climbed the shears with grease gun in hand, thoroughly lubricating each bearing on the long, vertical shaft, but it did not help. A misalignment seemed evident, and for the present we would overcome it with manpower. Two on the job could be advantageous, though right at the foot of the captain's bunk, they would have to speak in lowest whispers.

Routinely, Chan and I relieved the watch; the stars came down to a moonlit horizon sharpened by the first sign of twilight, and Chan's two blasts sent *Wahoo* under a calm sea. We searched with both scopes; dawn broke, and in its first light, Krause steadied on an enemy ship. I called battle stations–battle stations over the 1MC; Krause swung down the handle on the general alarm switch, and the electrically generated bell-like notes, called the Bells of St. Mary's, sounded in true earnest for the first time at 0525, Sunday, September 6.

Sitting on the horizon, heading southeasterly, was a modest-sized freighter coming our way. When the captain reached the conning tower, *Wahoo* was steady on an intercepting course that lay at right angles to the bearing of the freighter. This was the action that any skipper would expect. Called the normal approach course (where normal means perpendicular), it would insure reaching an attack position if such was possible.

In record time, Pappy reported battle stations manned, and then the captain slowed for his first observation. His bearing, angle on the bow, and Hunter's range flowed to Roger on the TDC and to Chan on plot. This and subsequent setups showed the approach progressing well, though I found myself mentally urging more speed. But providing the captain with true courses, readying the tubes, and checking plot against TDC kept me busy, so I was surprised when we reached an attack position of 1,450 yards in less than a half hour. Roger reported a good TDC solution; the captain announced, "Standby," and then, "Fire 1," "Fire 2," and "Fire 3" at about 6-second intervals. As previously ordered, Richie, on the TDC's angle solver, applied no deflection to the first torpedo, so it should hit amidships. With the deflection knob, he sent the second torpedo to pass under the stern and the third under the bow. But it was Krause who had the fun of whacking the firing plunger with his palm on each firing command.

A slight shudder forward, the healthy zing of the props, and the momentary pressure on our ears as the poppet valve vented residual air back into the boat showed that each torpedo was on its way. Then came Buckley's report from sound, "All hot, straight and normal." We waited as Hunter called off the 60 seconds till the torpedoes should hit, at least two of them: "Forty-five, Fifty, Fifty-five, Sixty," and so the count continued without explosions. The freighter had turned towards, perhaps just a zig, but with a plane beyond her, glassy seas, and the proximity of airfields, the captain ordered 90 feet. Though no longer counting, Hunter had kept his stopwatch in hand and so timed two unexpected detonations 2 minutes after our firing. Could we have had a range error that great, or had the magnetic exploder mechanism been activated by a field other than that of the ship? Loss of her screw noises would indicate the former, and her possible sinking, but heading northwest, away from the scene and not coming up for an observation, we'd never know.

The initial novelty of living under red lights, with red mashed potatoes, black vegetables, and other unearthly colored foods, had worn off even before reaching Pearl Harbor. There, it had served as a conversation piece, but now, 3 weeks later, I believed it was one of the factors affecting *Wahoo*'s morale. Sinking this first ship would have given a tremendous boost, overshadowing unnecessary restrictions. As it was, the exceptional quiet by those resuming their regular watches reflected disappointment, and these hands, coming from throughout the boat, that of our whole ship's company.

I had read every available patrol report and could remember none in which an enemy ship had been attacked by the second day; in most it would be the second week. Here, we had had an easy setup, far simpler than the destroyer escorts (DE's) at San Diego, but had muffed it. Could it be that individually we were overtrained, so intent on being precise that we had missed the boat, overlooking something obvious?

The hour before returning to periscope depth had provided Krause and me with time to work up our 0800 position; so promptly on George's taking the watch, I dropped below, pausing to talk with Chief Pruett and "Doc" Lindhe who were sharing the watch, before delivering the position slip to the captain on time. Resting in his bunk and reading a Western, he thanked me, looked it over, and slipped it between the pages. On the wardroom table to go with my breakfast was ONI-208J, *Japanese Merchant Ship Recognition Manual*. It had already been flagged to page 270 by the captain, where he had checked the modest-size tanker, *Hoyogo Maru*, as resembling our target; but ours had one stack aft instead of the two, side by side, as shown in the drawing. Chan joined me, and with his long reach, retrieved a pair of dividers from the sideboard. The scale drawing of the ship showed a length of 252 feet. To the same scale, her mast would be about 85 feet, close to the figure the captain had penciled on the page. Perhaps influenced by reports of ships having removed their topmasts to reduce the range at which they might be sighted, the captain had specified using a masthead height of 50 feet in determining the range. Unfortunately this had led to an enemy speed error on both the TDC and plot, unnoted since each had the same 10-knot enemy speed solution. But making the dangerous run for Piaanu Pass, she would surely be running at her maximum speed, which was listed at 13 knots. To be meaningful, the manual's information must be available during an approach. I passed the problem to Lindhe, whose battle station was in the control room.

I was not adequately familiar with our pump room, directly below, so I joined Chief McGill's school. We were standing on safety, a tank as strong as the pressure hull, which could be blown to sea and its flood valve closed for extra buoyancy in an emergency. The deck aft was the top of two auxiliary tanks, while forward it formed the top of negative, giving *Wahoo* 14,000 pounds of ballast for quick diving. To port and starboard were Hardy Tines multistage compressors delivering high-pressure air to 3,500 pounds per square inch on charging the air banks—groups of 11-cubic-foot steel bottles in the ballast tanks amidships.

Aft were the dual piston drain and rotary trim pumps for adjusting the boat's weight and trim (compensating). The compressors for refrigeration and air conditioning were forward. Though the room was pierced by periscope wells and the access ladder, with piping and electric cables running to each machine, the Navy Yard had still provided adequate passageways and even a workbench. Back in the control room, I now had a better appreciation of this normally unseen part of our auxiliarymen's task and even more respect for their chief.

In the wardroom, in addition to the *Press News,* messmates were perusing an innovative entertainment quite likely unique in submarines— an "Al Capp" comic strip complete with Li'l Abner and Daisy Mae. The writers were our radiomen, their shack becoming a private studio after the midwatch, and the artist, you must have guessed, was our versatile battleship lieutenant, Richie. A square a night, with two off for editing, would apparently provide *Wahoo*'s weekly funnies; and if this were just a start, we were in for some wild adventures. This day, their efforts provided the diversion to get us beyond the *Hoyogo Maru;* to treat her as spilt milk and to get on with the patrol.

4

Wahoo's course was 300 degrees true, heading towards the basin formed by Puluwat Island and its reefs on the port hand, Gray Feather and Mogami Banks ahead, and Namonuito Island or Atoll to starboard. That loosely enclosed area measured 100 miles across, and lay the same distance ahead. From anywhere along its arc, a ship could have departed for Truk. So, though we followed the captain's prescribed search procedure, our concentration remained towards that area.

The time between searches was not entirely wasted, for Lindhe had gladly accepted the task of chief identifier and had picked assistants for his identification party. With the manuals spread out on the control room chart desk, the party would receive information about any ship, starting from her masts and then lower structures as they were reported; when settling on the class, Lindhe would bring the marked manual to the top of the ladder. We recorded information and used it as a problem for the party. The drill worked, just as the books had been designed to be used.

Only a reconnaissance floatplane on September 8 rewarded our searches, but it could presage a ship movement through this central area. On sound, our radiomen had a new project: With two positions, side by side, Buckley, Beatty, and Carter were fast training a stable of sound operators, at least as listeners. So, it was Appel who reported distant explosions on September 10. Fast propellers on the following day caused some excitement till they faded away, and then more explosions, seemingly from the northeast, livened up September 13. We hoped that the detonations were torpedoes from our submarine, *Flying Fish,* patrolling to the north, but of course they could be from depth charges too.

Chan was now spending a good portion of his daylight hours, when the captain's conning tower bunk was out of the way, working with Buckley or Carter on our sick SJ. This radar was essentially the same as the surface ship's SG, but with its major components squeezed into deep, rectangular boxes that could be readily lowered through round submarine hatches and would fit snugly against the curved hull of the conning tower. To dispel the heat from the banks of vacuum tubes, small blowers had been installed where they were most efficient. The units could be lifted out of their cases for replacing tubes, but a major cause of their failure was the accumulated heat following one or more of the blowers burning out. Replacing these required a major dismantling of the unit. With few prints and only an ohmmeter to assist, each failure was a monstrous trial and error job, with parts and tools spread out on the conning tower deck. This was the situation when the Bells of Saint Mary's again sounded throughout the ship.

It was 1025, Monday, September 14. Wach, on sound, had heavy screws to the west, and Buckley was handing down a round fiber waste-basket filled with radar parts as the torpedo fire control party was trying to climb the ladder. I could imagine Chan and Buckley's thoughts, wondering if they'd ever get the damn thing together again. Back at periscope depth, the captain made the first observation: a ship on the horizon at about 12,000 yards (6 nautical miles), and presenting an angle on the bow of about 65 port. Plotted on the chart, that showed her heading right for Piaanu Pass, where we should have been.

Lindhe and his party stood by in the control room with ONI-208J and the other publications at hand, but due to an escorting plane, the captain chose the prewar tactic, required on certain exercises when attacking a surface- and air-escorted warship. It was called a sound approach, conducted entirely by sonar information. Here, with an initial broad angle, our best submerged speed would be required to reach an attack position, but that was foiled by the intermittent report of high-speed screws and *Wahoo*'s slowing so that our soundmen could hear the enemy ship. Finally, after a half hour, 32 minutes to be exact, we came up to periscope depth, hoping to fire on accurate periscope bearings. But we were well abaft the enemy's beam at a periscope stadimeter range of 4,000 yards. In this unfavorable position, one that could only grow worse, the captain secured from battle stations, and an estimated 2,500-ton freighter, with no visible surface escort, went on her way.

Ours was a quiet ship, made so by the disappointment of having two ships in eight days go scot-free. Young men, however, don't stay down in the dumps for long, especially when the odor of frying steaks follows the three blasts for surfacing. The change in the menu was Rowls's idea, and with ready permission from the captain, who had directed a course to the north pending our 2000 (twenty-hundred) position report. We had taken our stars on the last distinguishable horizon, and, with a bit of envy, watched the lookouts being relieved after their 2-hour dogwatches. They would be sitting down to hot steaks, while mine and Chan's would be warmed over.

Always punctual, George assumed the watch on time, and I dropped below for the usual mad rush in working up the position. In our exclusive office, still sporting the only white light, the calculations went smoothly. The first line looked good, but a sharp jar, as if *Wahoo* had hit a trawler, sent the second line awry.

5

I burst out of the office into blue smoke and a whining roar like that of a monstrous fire siren getting up to speed. We had fired a torpedo with its warhead into or partway through the tube's outer door, and it was running hot in the tube. The maneuvering telegraphs, two knobs to order speeds, were but a step away, and I killed our headway.

The high-speed trip had shut down the engine when the pitch of the turbine wheels reached about B-flat. But had the impeller that arms the warhead turned dangerously while *Wahoo* was slowing? Since a 400-yard torpedo run was required to fully arm the warhead, the answer was probably no, but it could quite possibly arm if *Wahoo* went ahead.

Roger was reporting the accident to the captain, who seemed to be taking it calmly, or perhaps he was just speechless. But this was a time for action, not explanation, and Pappy Rau already had Boatswain's Mate Smith standing by. On lines, Roger and Smith went over the bow to find the warhead sticking out, but they could not reach the impeller recess on its bottom that arms the warhead. Since the tube was No. 1, the top tube to starboard, and at just about sea level, we could open the inner door without taking too much water, and hopefully pull the torpedo back. A 1½-ton chain fall failed to budge it, so wooden wedges from our shoring gear were driven home so the torpedo couldn't get loose and possibly activate the exploder.

The accident would not have happened if *Wahoo* had had a full-time executive officer; but spending the most important 8 hours of each day, the four-to-eights, as an after lookout or in the conning tower when submerged, I was bypassed by items that should properly have been referred to me. I could visualize Roger's requesting permission to test torpedo firing valves from the captain, who had looked up from his Western and nodded, but had not taken in the full import of the request or the dangers involved. I would have emphatically said, "No! Firing valves are tested during upkeep, with the tubes empty, regardless of what a peacetime manual may require." In a two-month patrol in *Argonaut*, we had not tested these valves, which are operated by the 200-pound air supply, and which instantly release the 400-pound impulse air to eject the torpedoes at over 40 knots. Called differential valves, they are essentially infallible, and during 5 years in submarines, I had not heard of any failures.

Krause had plotted the other star lines, running the position ahead to 2000, and then had made up a position slip. I was tempted to sign and present it, but thought better of the idea and copied it; enough had happened for one night.

From the wardroom to the crew's mess, and probably throughout the boat, there was a new conversation piece. It was a serious one. We had brought *Wahoo* out here to sink the enemy, but so far we'd come closer to destroying ourselves. Even those hands who had not yet officially qualified knew that every hull opening closed with sea pressure, but now we had one that was held against the sea by its bronze bayonet locking ring—No. 1 torpedo tube's inner door. We could still fire torpedoes from the other tubes and evade below the usual temperature gradients, but *Wahoo* was most certainly vulnerable to close depth charges forward.

The battery charge was resumed, and shortly Electrician's Mate O'Brien, with Hartman learning the ropes, passed my stateroom. They dropped down into the battery well, pulling the wooden grill over the hatch opening. After recording the pilot cells' gravity, they would record the percentage of hydrogen shown in the battery ventilation flow meters. It was a continuing part of the charging procedure, and a critical one as the charge approached the finishing rate. Then the charging rate would be reduced following temperature-voltage-gravity (TVG) curves. Exceeding these TVG curves would generate excessive hydrogen with an explosion possible. Chief Ware and these men, in fact all of our electricians carrying out their precise assignments, made sleep possible for those not on watch.

The following days produced no ships, but bit by bit we had become convinced that the exploder had not armed. Though not completely out of mind for some, I am sure, the wayward torpedo had ceased being the conversation piece. In the wardroom, this was prompted by the frown such references brought to the captain's brow. But he was right:

it was high time for *Wahoo* to locate the enemy again. So on Saturday, September 19, having spent 17 days in the southeastern part of our area, the captain elected to patrol to the northwest. There, south of Namonuito Island, the reefs, and other small islands that really form an atoll, *Wahoo* might intercept east-west shipping proceeding to and from Truk's North Pass.

Our submerged run covered half the distance, so we were on station by the time I presented the 2000 position slip. It had been a good decision, for at 2255 the Bells of St. Mary's called us to our battle stations. Under a bright moon and with little wind, Ira had spotted a column of smoke to the northwest. A half-hour surface run closed the range to where a successful submerged approach and attack was almost assured.

6

Two blasts took us down, and shortly the first details of the ship—mast, goal-post, mast, goal-post—flowed down to Lindhe and his party. As she closed, the report of her composite superstructure and short stack completed her classification. Lindhe passed the book to the conning tower and the captain agreed. We had a *Keiyo Maru* class modern freighter that displaced 6,500 tons.

The ship was stopping intermittently, perhaps indicating that she was waiting for an escort before making the dangerous passage to Truk. Dissatisfied with our soundmen, who could not locate any fast escort screws, the captain put George, who had been an instructor at the West Coast Sound School, on sound as our best operator.

And so, with the firing point about 15 minutes away, I took the dive; and incidentally, having been so intent on getting our junior officers qualified in the captain's eyes, this was my first diving experience in *Wahoo*. She was nicely trimmed, and handling her was a breeze compared to *Argonaut*. Not knowing the extent of *Wahoo*'s tendency to rise by the bow on firing, I trimmed her with a 2-degree down angle. Now speed and planes would insure keeping her down.

When all goes smoothly, the assistant approach officer is hardly noticed. This probably led to the facetious title of "yes-man" for the billet. I was now to find out what can happen if the yes-man is suddenly removed. With no one quietly advising the captain of the courses for optimum firing position, a near 90 torpedo track, the distance to the enemy's track, and the other items of readiness for firing, *Wahoo* got too close on nearly parallel and opposite courses. Now on the enemy's starboard quarter, the captain turned away for a stern shot, but too late found that the torpedo run would be too short for the warhead to arm. A second and then, about 4 minutes later, a third torpedo were fired from positions sharper on the freighter's stern, but they were easily avoided since the enemy ship was already turning away from the first torpedo's track. She had it made and could have left us astern, but continued her turn and took *Wahoo*'s fourth torpedo broadside with a tremendous whack and detonation.

What we couldn't hear through the hatch was supplied by the control room's telephone talker, and probably with some embellishment: "She's got a 50-degree port list—getting lower in the sea—sinking by the stern." It was a play-by-play account interrupted by three great explosions and many lesser ones; we rigged for depth charge, and on orders, I started *Wahoo* down to 200 feet. The final report, "She's sunk!" came simultaneously and was followed by the first of a half-dozen depth charges. None of them seemed dangerously close, but they were disturbing, none the less.

At 200 feet, the bathythermograph's stylus traced a short horizontal line on its lampblacked card. Another 30 feet took us below an abrupt gradient that would reflect any enemy echo ranging, and we secured from battle stations.

Having now qualified myself as a diving officer, I turned the dive back to George, who would keep it till surfacing. In an hour we were back at periscope depth, and then surfaced into a still-clear, bright night, but with an indistinct misty horizon. Two comforting diesels had barely pushed us up to cruising speed when an after lookout reported a fuzzy bump on the horizon. I could distinguish nothing, but the captain did, or thought he did, and we commenced an evasion on various courses intermixed with rudder angles and "steady as she goes" all at speeds up to full. Finally, after about another hour, a rainsquall came to our rescue, and we slowed in its seeming sanctuary.

"Where are we?" asked the captain, and upon seeing me plotting our position from the dead-reckoning indicator (DRI), he fairly shouted, "No, not that, I want the position run up!"

Though every order to the steersman had been recorded in the Quartermaster's Notebook, there were few connecting courses, and you can't plot commands. Fortunately, Krause had recorded the DRI position on surfacing, and I had mine in the rainsquall. Starting from close by, I commenced plotting backwards as best I could from the entries, while Krause plotted ahead. I hated doing this, but when our tracks came reasonably close, I drew a couple of quick lines connecting them, and we had a complete plot. It was now time to go on watch, and in a couple of hours we'd have another round of stars for a true 0800 *Wahoo* position.

I was less than proud of our performance, but that did not include the crew. They had all performed admirably, but especially Torpedoman's Mate Johnson, who was in charge of the after torpedo room. Separated by three compartments, four if the maneuvering room is included, he was truly on his own. But just the word from our telephone talker told that he was in charge, and his torpedoes did the job. He should rate high in our ship's company, for every member would now be eligible to wear the submarine combat pin, awarded only if an enemy ship had been sunk. So *Wahoo* finally had a happy crew.

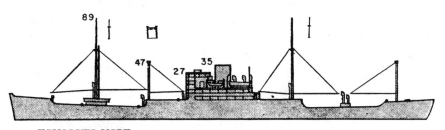

KAMOGAWA MARU
KEIYO MARU, SINKO MARU, TAMAGAWA MARU, YAMAGIRI
MARU, YAMAZUKI MARU, YODOGAWA MARU, ZENYO MARU

Tonnages:
  Gross: 6,438–80
	D. W.: 9,301-413	Constructed:
		  1935–39
			Japan

Length:
  W. L. (B. P.): 439′
	O. A.: 456′	Propulsion:
		  Machinery:
		  Screws: 1
			Diesel
			N. H. P.: 1165
			B. H. P.: 4,700

Beam: 58′			
Drafts: Loaded: 26′	Light: 9′ 6″	R. P. M.: 110 R. P. M.: 133	@ Knots: 14 @ Knots: 17

Speed:
  Normal cruising:14–15
	Max.: 17–19	Fuel: Oil	Capacity: 2,500
			  tons including
			  deep tanks

Radius: 47,000 miles at 14 knots

Potential naval value: AP, AK, AV.

Remarks: Heavy lift gear for 60-ton lift in No. 2 hatch. Can mount six 5″ or 6″ guns.

7

The executive officer, above all, should know what is going on in a ship, and preferably ahead of his commanding officer. Such was still not the case in *Wahoo,* for 2 days after the sinking, when I presented the 0800 position slip to the captain, he ordered me to write up the details for the general court-martial. I answered, "Aye, Aye, Sir," and headed aft to find Pappy Rau. Inquiring from the chiefs up had served well, and this was no exception. Pappy filled me in: One of our lookouts had gone to sleep on watch, a general court-martial offense that in time of war could carry the punishment of death. Further, the offender had also come to *Wahoo* from *Argonaut.* Be that as it may, it just couldn't happen; something was fishy about it. Doc Lindhe came through the control room—there was my investigator. In about 30 minutes, he returned with Deaton and McSpadden, torpedoman's mates who had also come from my old submarine. They told that the accused was known to drop asleep quite suddenly at times, and on one occasion, while working in the superstructure, to fall asleep with an air-driven chipping hammer still banging away in his hands.

The offender simply suffered from narcolepsy, but was such a good shipmate and ball player that the crew had covered for him and stood his watches when *Argonaut* was underway while he mess-cooked. For the remainder of the patrol, we'd have an extra mess cook. Then, of course, he would have to be disqualified for duty in submarines, but we'd see if there was a spot for him on the Base.

The captain knew, of course, that we could only recommend a general court-martial, and for some reason did not seem pleased or amused with my report.

Chan's dive was slow the following morning, due to a sluggish bow buoyancy vent. Chief McGill and his auxiliarymen had been greasing the fittings nightly, so the trouble probably lay in a bent shaft. Bow buoyancy serves well in giving an extra lift when surfacing in a heavy sea, or in an emergency in correcting an excessive down angle. We could live without these features, but not should it stick closed and prevent diving. After surfacing, and when it was quite dark, McGill took care of the situation by removing the adjacent manhole cover and bringing it below. It would now vent and flood by itself, and in heavy seas would act like the blowholes found along some rocky coasts.

Except for a patrol heading west at night, we had sighted nothing. There had to be shipping, and it could be just beyond the horizon of our 3-foot periscope exposures. The seas were glassy, so between exposures we were running at 90 feet. George quietly checked; the captain had dozed off, so on coming up for the next look, George had his understudy, Ira, come up on a gradual arc through 54 feet, then easing back to 64, our customary keel depth. If the captain noticed the maneuver, Ira's training was a logical answer. I had the scope already raised; George and Ira went through their maneuver smoothly, but only the speck of an apparent fisherman on the new horizon showed in my scope. We would try again after a ship would have had time to come over the horizon. But by then the captain was awake.

Now, patrolling in an area the size of Rhode Island, common sense told that we could take a sweep-around, and if clear, use all the scope, 17 feet to the shears, and even surface to cover the horizon and then dive. We were being held back by the peacetime training against warships that had surface and plane escorts. The planes were from the utility squadron, SNJs, and did this screening on a regular basis. The pilots could observe both the target group and the diving submarine at the start of the run, and through experience knew the firing position within a mile or so, and the firing time within a couple of minutes. When the sea was without whitecaps, they would dip a wing and point out the submarine to us—the junior officers from other boats who were observers. So having periscopes sighted by planes became a bugaboo for some, while in truth, the scopes would never be sighted in the open seas. How many ships had passed within the reasonable search area of our periscopes with impunity?

On the second forenoon watch, all necessary conditions held again. Quietly, Ira started *Wahoo* up with a small bubble; the planesmen were doing their part, and Hunter followed my hands with the scope. A sweep-around, and then another when the depth gauge read 55 feet.

"Bearing–Mark!" Hunter read 278, and we had a medium-sized mast-funnel-mast freighter with superstructure amidships. She was partially hull-down, beyond our new horizon, but her angle on the bow of no more than 45 degrees starboard meant that we could reach her. I nodded to Simonetti, who had the brass handle of the round, green box in hand; he swung it to the right and the Bells of St. Mary's sounded throughout our submarine.

Wahoo had steadied on the normal approach course at 7 knots by the time the captain reached the conning tower. He ordered one-third speed and waited until the Bendix log read 3 knots before making his first observation. Of course he saw nothing with 3 feet of scope. I suggested a higher search, but he chose to wait for the enemy to close. A second 3-foot search brought his comment, "If you saw a ship before and she's not in view now, then she's going away," and then, "Secure from battle stations," as he went down the ladder. I believe that we had covered all of the angles, except the obvious one—you can lead a horse to water, but you cannot make him drink.

We would have to think of another ploy or perhaps a gambit that would put *Wahoo* in front of an enemy ship. But we may have already done just that, for the captain changed our course to north, towards the track of the ship that went free beyond our 3-foot periscope's horizon. If we continued in that direction, we would approach our area boundary, but also the shortest unprotected route to Truk's North Passage.

Hunter sighted three planes shortly after diving on Wednesday, September 30. They were in formation, a few miles to the south of us, and were headed west. Any plane could signal activity, a formation of three almost assured it, and our just-plotted position, 45 miles northwest of Truk, couldn't have been better.

With whitecaps for protection, we manned both scopes for the first time, but with *Wahoo*'s standard 3 feet. At 0545, the Bells of Saint Mary's held reveille; we had the tops and sharp bow of a warship coming over the horizon. She bore 322 degrees true, and the captain's angle on the bow put her on course 170 degrees, as if she were heading for Piaanu Pass, but according to other patrol reports, deep-draft ships used the North or South Passes. We moved towards an attack position, only to have the warship zig away about 45 degrees, and then our 7 knots were meaningless unless she zigged back. In another 3 minutes, she zigged again another 30 degrees away, giving us a good view of her starboard quarter as her 20 knots took her over the hill.

Lindhe and company had quickly identified the warship, which looked like our heavy cruisers forward, but aft of the stack had a flat deck and cranes. She was a seaplane tender of the *Chiyoda* class, and as consolation, the party was allowed to watch her go.

The captain did not hold "postmortems"; having a ship get by was painful enough. Amongst the watch officers, however, each ship, and the attack if it followed, became a natural conversation piece. And so, in discussing the *Chiyoda,* we came to some realistic conclusions. These were not intended as criticizing our captain—any layman armed with all of the postwar facts can make the general look foolish—but for our own education. After all, both George and I would be coming up for command in a year or so, and though each of us had been designated as qualified for command, that was during peacetime. Now, in war, we had further obligations to learn as much as we could from the successes and the mistakes of others. This was not all pure dedication; our very lives could depend upon it.

With the *Chiyoda* the lessons were simple: More periscope would have led to earlier detection. Best submerged speed on the normal approach course would have reached an attack position, and if the enemy had continued towards Piaanu Pass, then *Wahoo,* on the other side of the track, could fire stern tubes. That was the same lesson repeated so often: Base your tactics on enemy capabilities, not on his intentions.

Two planes to the north, flying east in the afternoon, and another one at breakfast time gave the hope that more ships would follow, but only distant smoke to the southwest came in view, our plot showing that it lay above a fast ship on an easterly course some 18 miles away. The day was not a total loss, however, for Krause, on the bridge early, retrieved two flying fish that had fallen on deck. Only New Englanders who eat alewives would tackle the bone-infested flying fish, so Krause and I each enjoyed one with breakfast on this Thursday, October 1.

8

The northern limits of our area sliced across the logical shipping lane between Namonuito and Truk's North Pass. Trying to patrol it would likely take *Wahoo* over the line into the area of *Flying Fish,* commanded by Lt. Comdr. Glynn R. Donoho, a taut, successful submarine skipper. To avoid this, our captain decided to patrol just to the west of our area boundary, between Ulul Island, of the Namonuito Atoll, and Mogami Bank. In fact, it was a western extension of the Truk-Namonuito route and should have been included in *Wahoo*'s area, since it also formed a north-south passage. The only disadvantage would be air patrols from Ulul.

Moving to an untried area was like trying a new riffle on a trout stream. Just the word, which had passed quickly through the boat, raised our spirits. A quick turn showed hands busy, with an unusual number working on their course books. They had been figuring too, for, not counting today, October 1, *Wahoo* had just 6 more days to patrol. A new rate to go with the submarine combat pin would set them apart indeed.

We searched along the track followed by the *Chiyoda,* with Richie spotting Ulul Island after lunch on October 3. Bearing 035 degrees and 9 miles distant according to our height versus distance tables, this was only the second landfall since leaving Pearl Harbor. Two fishing boats later in the day were followed on the evening of October 4 by a combination of two horizontal white lights with a red flare-up between them. It could be a beacon for incoming aircraft or ships, so *Wahoo* lay to, waiting.

The Fox schedule received at 0400 on October 5 contained a message with *Wahoo*'s call sign, and Chan went below to decode it. We were assigned the sector south of Truk Atoll in addition to our present area.

ComSubPac or his staff could not, of course, know our present location, but might have guessed that any boat would be near the northern boundary when the patrol had only 2 days to go. There must have been some reason, and amplifying instructions could be following, so the captain felt obliged to leave the sight of the beacon and head southeast.

We had moved only 15 miles when dawn sent us down. There would now follow the period of blindness until there was sufficient light for our scopes, fortunately short here closer to the equator. It passed quickly and we commenced our routine periscope searches. At 0654, I sighted a large ship, still slightly hull-down and presenting a 40-degree starboard angle on the bow (presenting a little more than half a ship's length). That put her at 12,000 yards and on course north. Her deck was flat; we had an aircraft carrier in our grasp, and the Bells of St. Mary's bonged as they never had before.

Simonetti, with the quartermaster watch, took the wheel, bringing *Wahoo* to 310 degrees, the normal approach course, and rang up standard speed—my first actions on sighting. *Wahoo* was steady and on her way by the time battle stations were manned. The captain approved of the action with a nod; it would reach any desired firing range, but he could not quite bring himself to the point of trusting me. *Wahoo* was passing 8 knots, going to 9, when he ordered, "All ahead one-third." I expected that this was just to slow our screws for a moment so that Buckley and Carter would be able to get a bearing on the carrier, and then we'd go ahead again at standard or full. But we continued to coast down slowly to 3 knots for a periscope observation. The sound bearings on the carrier confirmed Roger's 12 knots on the TDC; we'd still be all right if we went ahead immediately at standard or full, but any further observations would have to be shortened by backing to kill our headway. As Simonetti called 3 knots, Buckley reported the escorting destroyers' screws. Hunter raised the scope, and after a sweep-around, the captain steadied on the carrier, calling the angle starboard 50. It checked with the TDC.

During a careful approach, the carrier was positively identified as the *Ryujo,* which had probably been damaged in early actions of the Battle for Guadalcanal. But on each observation the enemy had drawn further ahead, and a zig towards would now be necessary. The *Ryujo* did not oblige—her base course had shown this was not likely—and she went over the hill leaving *Wahoo* back on her starboard quarter. Dejected, the captain went to his cabin, leaving *Wahoo* at battle stations.

If you are capable of half again the speed of an enemy, even more if required, he is not in the clear. I drew up a simple plan, to approximate scale, on a pad of lined paper. It showed *Wahoo*'s track in overtaking and passing up the *Ryujo* while remaining hull-down on her port hand. We would be able to keep track of her by observations with one of our periscopes, which she would not be able to see.

In his cabin, I found the captain depressed, but he immediately nodded approval, saying, "Yes, we have to do that." An hour passed before we surfaced, and as usual, I found myself guarding the after sector. All engines were on the line, however, so we should spot the *Ryujo* in about 2 hours dead ahead. With contact regained, I would plot our courses on a maneuvering board, a special plotting sheet designed for relative movement situations.

We had surfaced under an overcast that was now developing into passing squalls. About an hour had passed when the sun, momentarily, broke through. It was not where I had expected to see it. Abandoning my lookout station, I went forward and checked the gyro repeater. *Wahoo* was on a course parallel to the *Ryujo*'s last observed zigzag leg. It lay 30 degrees to the right of the enemy's base course that Chan had laid down on the chart. Our 18 knots would have gained little in the general direction of the carrier, and we would be a little further away, approximately broad on her starboard quarter. I reported this to the captain, recommending a course change 60 degrees to the left. In all the patrol reports I had read, no boat had surfaced during daylight as close as we were to an airfield to pass up any ship, so I should not have been surprised when the captain replied, "It won't make any difference, we can't stay up here any longer." Two blasts took us down.

9

Chan had encoded a contact report on the *Ryujo,* containing the standard information of what, where, how many, and what doing. The transmitter was warmed up and tuned to the second harmonic of SubPac's frequency. Only plugging the output lead into the antenna trunk remained before transmitting. The captain made a final sweep-around, and three blasts sent *Wahoo* to the surface. The bridge was manned, but the turbos were not started. After allowing a minute for the saltwater to drain from the antenna insulators, Buckley keyed the five-letter groups through the transmitter, paused for a possible receipt, and then repeated the procedure for 5 minutes. NPM, the high-power naval radio station at Pearl, did not answer, and we submerged again at 1315, presumably to try again after dark.

Our course was southwest, essentially the reverse of *Ryujo's* track. In the whole patrol, this was the route most likely to produce a ship, for the *Chiyoda* had undoubtedly passed this way too. But now we had only one night and daylight tomorrow to find the enemy. We had another bright moon coming up, and the submerged attack under moonlight had produced our only success of the patrol. Especially with an assistant approach officer, we could do it again, but this one night would be asking too much.

In *Argonaut,* I had been the fourth officer. However, the exec had been completely involved in navigation and the engineer with his diesels and electrical fires, while I enjoyed a complete rapport with the captain. Since it was possible there, it should be here; I would make one more attempt. After taking my round of stars, in the privacy of the cigarette deck, I reviewed the coming tactical advantages with the captain, and recommended that with the contact report, we request a week's extension of the patrol so we could sink another ship.

The captain was quick with his answer, indicating, I believe, that he had reviewed our situation similarly, but it was not the reply that I expected.

"No, Dick," he said. "We're going to take *Wahoo* back to get someone in command who can sink ships; we're never going to win the war this way."

It must have been a very difficult statement for a captain to make, and I respected his honesty.

Another attempt to raise NPM on the night of October 6 also failed, and at noon on Wednesday, October 7, *Wahoo* left the patrol area. Our return route to Pearl was easy to plot; it lay 30 miles to the west of our previous track, which was still faintly visible on the chart. We would proceed at two-engine speed. The 80% speed and 90% load (80/90) should make good 14 knots, but dawn dives, other submerged time, and prevailing head seas could reduce that.

Radioman Carter, hearing a clear signal from NPM, on his own initiative keyed the *Ryujo* contact report and obtained the receipt. Just 1 week en route, it may still have been of use, and he was commended.

In addition to the watch, the captain usually remained on the bridge during daylight. When Krause and I were getting a noon sun line, that made three extras; three more to clear in an unexpected dive. I was in the process of delivering the position slip to the captain as usual when a Mitsubishi two-engine bomber came out of the overcast at about 2 miles. Urged by the heels of lookouts on our shoulders, we made it below, and for some reason no bombs fell.

On the following day, October 13, I prepared the message that was required on crossing the 1,000-mile circle from Pearl Harbor. The captain added the words, "a portside mooring is requested," and after Ira finished the encoding, Radioman Beatty sent the message to ComSubPac.

Winds and increasing seas made a third engine necessary in order to maintain the required speed of advance, but the extra fuel was no problem, for *Wahoo* would return with enough diesel oil to take her on to the States. The rendezvous with our PC escort was specified in ComSubPac's reply to our report. Like shorebirds prior to a landfall, our PBY patrol planes were viewed on October 15 and 16; then at 0630 on Saturday, October 17, we found our escort dead ahead, just where she was supposed to be.

Rigged for surface, and with a section in hand-scrubbed dungarees on deck, *Wahoo* put up a good front as she entered Pearl Harbor. The captain conned his ship past the drydocks and damaged warships to starboard and port, and then around the end of ten-ten dock—the final turn to the Submarine Base. There, he ordered, "All stop," and then backed to kill our headway.

We had lost eight submarines since Pearl Harbor—four S-boats and four fleet type—and by the size of *Wahoo*'s reception, all hands were relieved and happy to see us return. There was a catch, however, for band, dignitaries, and well-wishers filled Pier 1, which required a starboard side mooring.

"Didn't you include my words in the arrival message?" barked the captain.

In anticipation, Krause had already manned the signal searchlight, and on the captain's "Well, send it again," started the shutter clicking. I could read the message he was sending by watching his hand, and obviously he couldn't resist improving and embellishing my words. It read simply:

HAVE POSSIBLY ARMED TORPEDO
PROTRUDING TO STARBOARD
STILL RECOMMEND PORT SIDE MOORING

The signalman, or his recorder, grabbed the message and ran round and round down the great steel staircase that circled the 100-foot-tall escape training tank and took a beeline to the admirals on the dock. There followed a great exodus with only the band reforming after reaching the relative safety of the escape training tank. *Wahoo* was quickly assigned a berth at a vacant pier, where the captain promptly put her alongside, port side to. There, the Base line handlers and braver seniors greeted us as the band struck up "Aloha-Oe" from its sanctuary beyond the tower.

U.S.S. Wahoo (SS-238) departing Mare Island.

After torpedo room.

Maneuvering room: operating levers, field rheostats, meters, and tachometers.

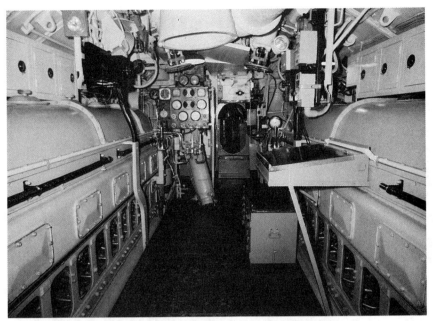

After engine room. Door leads to forward engine room.

After battery living space.

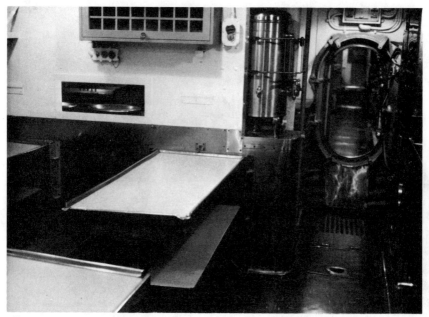

Crew's mess.

Galley.

Radio room, forward of galley.

Control room: diving controls.

Control room: High pressure air manifold.

Flood and vent manifold.

Conning tower, looking forward, with steerman's wheel in center. Torpedo tube ready-light panels to port, with firing plunger below. Sound gear is aft to starboard.

Conning tower, looking aft to port. TDC visible beyond the radar.

Wardroom, aft of torpedo room, viewed from forward doorway.

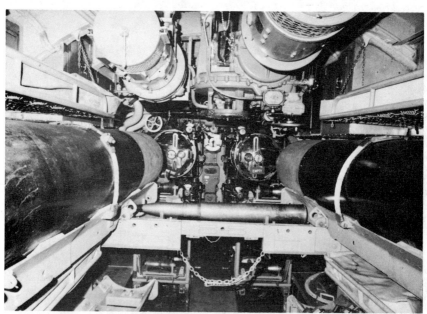

Forward torpedo room. Four-inch shell on display in center.

Part Three

SECOND PATROL
In the Solomons

Always the first business had been the crew's payday, traditionally held in the wardroom, where its two entryways made a convenient passage. This also moved the visitors along: Comdr. Frank Watkins, our division commander, to walk through the ship with our captain, and the others topside through the escape trunk in the torpedo room. I saw them ashore for the captain.

The crew's records had remained at the Submarine Base, so all pay chits had been prepared in advance and arranged alphabetically. Our officers witnessed the men's signatures, and the line moved rapidly. With moneys and necessary gear in hand, all except the senior petty officers were off to the waiting busses and to the Royal Hawaiian Hotel, the submariners' rest camp.

The department heads and leading petty officers held a quick arrival conference with the submarine tender USS *Sperry*'s repair officer. Three of our departments had at least one major work request: George with two cracked cylinder liners in one engine to be replaced, Roger with his torpedo tube, and Chan with his SJ radar units. Only Richie, our battleship sailor, needed no help, but he and the other three would stand a day's duty in rotation. The duty officer would oversee jobs and call the responsible officer back from the Royal when necessary.

The captain had prepared the narrative of the patrol report and the paragraph concerning health and habitability. I had done the tabulation sheets on enemy ship and air contacts, and the required paragraphs about weather, navigational aids, currents, and tidal information. The others had written concise reports concerning their materiel failures, while Roger, in addition to a required sheet on torpedoes, had prepared the formal casualty report concerning the accident to our torpedo tube. The whole patrol report had 18 precise pages, and with comments by immediate reporting seniors, it would enjoy widest confidential distribution, ranging from individual submarines to the chief of naval operations. All in order, the report was delivered to the division commander's (Div-Com) office by our typist, Lindhe, who might get us a yeoman.

After the leading petty officers turned over individual assignments to their counterparts in the relief crew, we would have been on our way too, but a final word from the captain left us stranded. A new directive permitted answering correspondence in ink and returning it when copies were not required in the ship's files. I interpreted this rather liberally, and by the end of an hour we had whittled the 2-months' accumulation down to a pile that George, with the first duty, could handle.

Unlike most skippers, the captain chose to stay with friends in Honolulu instead of joining us at the Royal. That was too bad, for over a few beers the ice might have cracked a bit and led to a better understanding. I had respected his confidence concerning another assignment, but shortly after reaching the Royal, I overheard a conjecture concerning *Wahoo*'s next skipper. But there were more important things at the moment, the first being a long, hot, fresh-water shower with lots of soap and rinses. Chan followed, not because of seniority—we'd knock off rates and ranks at the hotel—I just beat him to it.

Next came mail from home, delivered as soon as the mail orderly had *Wahoo*'s room numbers. With feet propped up, we just plain relaxed—reading our mail, enjoying a $75 room, and watching the occasional patrol planes departing and returning from their respective sectors. All was well at home, across from Hamilton Field, probably the best place possible in wartime. Chan's letters were mainly from Iona, the pretty Wave he had met at Mare Island.

We both had light complexions, further bleached by 2 months with negligible sunlight, so waited until an hour before sunset for our first swim. Having lived only three short blocks from Waikiki Beach, I showed Chan the second reef where it's deep enough to enjoy the therapy of the surf, but still touch bottom between the rollers. Shipmates had found it too, but soon swam ashore for dinner. An hour later, a bit exhausted but completely relaxed, we headed for the Royal, too, where dinner was served continuously over a 2-hour period.

Wahoo's officers would gladly have spent all of the hours of every day at the Royal, but other than their duty days and a change from

Sperry to the Sub Base 5 days into the refit, each one had departmental responsibilities. Mine were overall and would involve presenting a ship ready for patrol to our new commanding officer. Thus, I had been back aboard on the second day when the torpedo was removed from the tube. It had apparently worked loose during a month of pounding into the sea, and slid back onto the skids before the chain fall was taut. The outer door and gear quadrant was another matter. This was a Sub Base job from the start. Finally cast loose, the mangled mess was swung onto a waiting truck by a portable crane. A replacement from Mare Island would surely be required.

Another such trip was a pleasure, however, for Ens. John B. Griggs III and George Misch reported on board for duty. John, or Jack, as he preferred, had been in the class of '43 at the Naval Academy that had graduated a year early. He would take over commissary, freeing Richie to become gunnery officer. George, an NROTC graduate, from the University of California, would replace Ira Dye, who had orders as a division engineer. George was tall and hefty, wearing a smile, and he would get along anywhere. Jack, slight by comparison, was a Navy-junior, so knew the ways of the Navy thoroughly. Both were submarine school graduates and would be a big asset to *Wahoo.*

Back at the Royal, we learned from an older copy of *Time* that the *Ryujo* had been reported sunk by our carrier aircraft on August 24 in the Battle of the Eastern Solomons. There was no mistaking *Ryujo,* since she had four masts alongside her flight deck that could be lowered during flight operations. We had seen them in their raised position. It had been a long haul getting her as far as Truk, and by now she had undoubtedly reached Tokyo. To us, this should serve as an example of the enemy's tenacity. Also of interest, especially to me, was the brief report of the very successful Makin Atoll attack by Colonel Carlson's Marine Raiders. My old *Argonaut* and the *Nautilus* had transported them and lent their tremendous firepower, that of a light cruiser.

The Royal was supposed to get us away from the war, but almost invariably the conversations turned to patrols. Mostly by listening, we learned of others' missed opportunities, and that *Wahoo*'s was about average for a first patrol. Encouraged, we salted away techniques that should be a true asset for any new skipper. The crew had been doing better in relaxing and unwinding. Curfew came at dark, when the island was blacked out and cars moved only with dim, blue lights. It would seem that if a young man could keep his date engaged until close to curfew, he had a very good chance of staying all night. Actually, the shore patrol was very lenient with submariners, normally just depositing them at the Royal's gate after dark, but this was surely given little publicity.

A change of pace came on the second Sunday, when we called on Mr. and Mrs. Roy Craw, who lived beyond the Kapiolani Park, quite close to Diamond Head. They had been our landlords for 3 years before Pearl Harbor, and back then it had been customary to pay the rent in person and stay for a meal. So I had been invited to Sunday dinner, but using their tightly rationed meat points would not have been fair, and I suggested Sunday afternoon, adding that I hoped there would be a piece of cake for my friend and me. That was not brazen, but a compliment, for her cake was famous.

Mr. Craw had been a seafarer, but was now retired from the Tidewater Oil Company. Mrs. Craw was an Hawaiian, a cousin of Olympic swimming champion Kanakanui. When we arrived, she had a large bowl of cake batter on her lap, mixing it with her hand and trying the texture between her thumb and fingers. "How else can you tell when it's properly mixed?" she had replied to my query some years ago, and when I had tried the cake, there were no further questions.

Roy Craw liked scorpions made with okolehau—cane whisky—and mint, much like a julep, but bottled in gallon jugs, which were stacked in his basement like wine bottles in a rack. It was his supply for the duration, and on seeing it, I just hoped the war would not last that long.

When my family had moved to our landlord's spare Waikiki apartment, Mrs. Craw had insisted on their dining with them. It was a gracious gesture, with the added advantage of not having to lay in supplies. Ernestine accepted only after they had agreed to receive compensation, and one of my reasons for calling was to ask Mrs. Craw to cash or deposit three checks. After two rounds of scorpions and butter cake, which seemed to please both of them, I made the request concerning the checks.

"Oh, I wouldn't cash those; I tore them up long ago," she replied, and with a generous smile, inquired further about my family.

We left before sunset with a warm feeling, far beyond that imparted by the scorpions, and spoke of the future and whether or not such hospitality could survive such a vicious war.

Our mail came daily, and was delivered as soon as a batch had accumulated. On the table was a brown, slightly squashy package from home. A peek confirmed my guess—2 months or thereabout of Sunday comics. If we broke them out here, they would be lost, while on board there would be funnies for a whole patrol.

2

A part of each day now required shipboard presence of our officers and leading petty officers: George to try out his refurbished engine; Roger and Richie to approve the torpedo tube's outer door and our long-awaited, 4-inch deck gun; and Chan to draw new, confidential publications. Pappy had to rework the Watch Quarter and Station Bill for fourteen new hands, and other leading petty officers were similarly involved. My own tasks revolved about two things: to clear up any correspondence so our new skipper would not come aboard to a basketful of paperwork (his job would be to sink ships), and to check the necessary charts that Krause was drawing for our next patrol. The first of these tasks was greatly simplified by Yeoman Forest Sterling, who had reported early enough to get things in hand, with the incentive of being able to join his new shipmates for the last week at the Royal. Back on board, I signed and he mailed.

The day before our 3-day readiness period, the troops returned. I was in the crew's mess, checking the final charts as Krause laid them out on the after mess table, when word came back from the control room: "Guess who's come on board as our new skipper?" No one ventured a name, and then we were filled in, "It's Lieutenant Commander Kennedy!"

Properly, I should have gone forward to greet him. Improperly, I bounded up the mess room ladder and made a beeline for headquarters. Comdr. Elton W. Grenfell, popularly called Joe by his contemporaries, had commanded *Gudgeon*, sinking an enemy submarine shortly after Pearl Harbor, and was now chief of staff. He hadn't read *Wahoo*'s patrol report, which was truthful, as the captain saw it, taking the blame for failing to close the *Ryujo*, and stating that this was his usual manner of making approaches, and if faced with comparable situations he would act similarly. Indirectly, he did put some blame on his officers by stating: "Had I but required a more rigorous and alert watch, we might have picked her up sooner." He was apparently not even aware of curtailing action already taken that might have brought success. Of course, Commander Grenfell was unaware of this, and of the captain's oral statement concerning getting a new skipper for *Wahoo* who could sink ships. The patrol report was asking just that; it was there for seniors to read and I gave a brief, including the captain's routine.

"Commander," I stated, "*Wahoo* and our captain need your help."

"Dick," he replied. "The Admiral just had his arm around your captain's shoulder, saying, 'Now you sank one ship, and I want you to go out there and show what *Wahoo* can really do.' They've served together and are friends, you know."

"All the more so," I replied. "Five years our senior, he cannot bring himself to delegate, and I doubt that he can last another patrol without someone closer to his seniority to lean on for advice."

"We have Lt. Comdr. Dudley W. Morton, who commanded *R-5* on patrol, has attended the PCO School, and has command of the *Dolphin* undergoing extended upkeep and repairs. He can be relieved of this temporary assignment to make his PCO run in *Wahoo*. With his support, she should enjoy a less trying patrol."

If it worked, this should be far and away the best solution, since my assignment as executive officer would not be affected, and we agreed to keep this matter private.

Late in the afternoon of November 7, I reported all aboard and *Wahoo* ready for patrol. Captain Kennedy thanked me, saying that he would be spending the night with friends ashore.

At supper, I told the officers that we might be receiving a PCO this evening or early in the morning, and suggested that we keep our conversations clear of the problems on our first patrol. An hour or so later, almost as if it had been staged, Lt. Comdr. Dudley W. Morton came aboard with his gear, and orders in hand for his PCO patrol in *Wahoo*. Misch tossed the gear onto the vacant upper bunk in the captain's cabin and then joined our get-acquainted session in the wardroom. Tall, broad shouldered and with facial features to match, Dudley greeted each of us with a friendly smile and a hand twice the size of ours, except

Misch's. His genial personality seemed contagious, perhaps emphasized by the vacuum it had filled. In varied conversations, we learned that, though born in Kentucky, he had been raised in Miami, Florida, playing high school football before Annapolis. Hope had replaced apprehensions concerning our coming patrol before I hit my bunk.

3

Two diesels commenced rumbling impatiently, always a signal to the seniors aboard to finish their coffee. The captain went directly to the bridge, while I saw Admiral English and the others ashore. The brow was snaked to the pier, the two remaining lines let go, and our prolonged blast announced that a submarine was backing from her slip. Admiral English, at attention, set the pace when he saluted our colors, now broken at the main. Except for a scheduled dive, they'd fly till sunset.

Off Fort Weaver, 5 miles to the west of the channel, the *P 28* was waiting. Pappy's voice announcing, "Ship rigged for dive," came over the bridge and conning tower speakers, and Roger's two blasts took us down. As prearranged, the *P 28* steamed by about 100 yards from our raised scope, indoctrinating our new hands with eight shaking depth charges. After surfacing, *Wahoo* countered with ten rounds from her new deck gun and a pan of 20mm rounds from the dual-purpose AA gun. Still on schedule, we set course 238 true for our patrol area to the north of Bougainville Island in the Solomons 3,000 miles away. The time was 1000, Sunday, November 8, 1942, and *Wahoo* was on her second patrol.

For 2 months, *Argonaut* had patrolled off Midway when attack on the island was believed imminent, only to miss the Battle of Midway while getting new engines. At Truk, *Wahoo* had come closer with the opportunity to sink *Ryujo*. Now we would have another opportunity, since the battles for Guadalcanal were raging to the southeast of Bougainville, and Japanese forces would pass to the north or south of this mountainous island. About 100 miles long, it was joined, beyond a narrow passage, by the smaller island, Buka, to the northwest. Within Bougainville Strait, to the southeast, lay Fauro and Shortland Islands, followed beyond the strait by major long islands and passages extending about

400 miles. All of this as far as Guadalcanal, 300 miles distant, was controlled by Japanese land and sea forces. But on the large island of Guadalcanal and the small island, Tulagi, 20 miles to its north, our Marines were still ensconced. In great sea battles, we had lost more ships than the Japanese, but the enemy had failed to reach our transports and support ships. Had our orders to patrol to the south of Truk come earlier, we might have sunk supporting ships, leaving that bastion for the Solomons; at least I was convinced that no major ships used Piaanu Pass. The struggle was not over, and in our new area, *Wahoo* would get a second chance. It would be a better one, for she would be astride Japanese shipping from the west, and at a likely terminus for support ships from Truk as well.

Reviewing these facts, while looking over the detailed chart of the Solomons, helped me put the past aside, and for the first time, to feel enthusiastic about this patrol. A glance at the clock above the chart table showed just enough time for a turn through the boat before our first sun line. The majority of our crew were now old salts and had done a commendable job in securing for sea, and this included at least one crate of oranges in most compartments, a trick we had used in *Argonaut* where we had chill room for them too. For sure, there'd be no scurvy in *Wahoo,* and what better way to enjoy fruit than when the mood strikes.

Our noon latitude sun line, crossing our track on the chart, showed *Wahoo* making good the prescribed 12 knots. On presenting the position slip, I told the captain about the oranges, including the additional advantage of freeing space in our very small chill room. He nodded, thanked me for the position report, and then advised that now, with sufficient officers, it would not be necessary for me to stand the four-to-eights. We were making progress, but I gathered that we would still have an officer lookout on the cigarette deck.

Battle stations after lunch, with George Misch on the standby Mark-8 angle solver and Jack gaining first experience on the dive with George Grider, was followed by a complete round of emergency drills. Surrounded by men who were qualified in submarines, or nearly so, our new hands performed admirably, and by the time we reached Bougainville, they'd need no coaching. An afternoon sun sight was worked out immediately and plotted. Surely the captain could see the advantage; if it hadn't checked, we could have done it over again.

At sunset, *P 28* turned back, sending the customary, but no less heartfelt "Godspeed." The captain thanked her with a "Well-done" and ordered our zigzag to commence. It was a modest plan, with legs of 5- to 15-minute duration to either side of our base course, still 238. Chief Pruett added turns to our screws to make up for the 5% loss along the base course, but this would be necessary only until dark, when *Wahoo* would steer a steady course again.

Our evening star sights were worked out in the ship's office, with its white light as usual, but there was a change—the crew's mess and the wardroom now sported white lights, like other boats. Somehow, white mashed potatoes and green beans just taste better! This innovation for *Wahoo* had been made possible by the issue to all boats of sufficient pairs of dark red goggles. They were designed as a mask with sponge rubber border and a single, dark ruby-red celluloid insert. An elastic head strap held them firmly against the face so other light could not enter. Members of the oncoming watch who would be going topside donned the masks a half hour ahead of time, and would have their eyes night-adapted as quickly as before.

Wahoo had another innovation that would eliminate the requirement for one of the hands on all-night watch sections. An ordinary General Electric washing machine motor was now rotating our SJ. When any pip showed on the grassy horizontal line, the operator merely pushed a lever that opened a clutch, and then, using the same old handwheel, he could examine the bearing of the pip. Apparently, many other boats had experienced troubles similar to ours, so we now had an installation designed and built by submariners at the Base. Surely they must have raided every junkyard around Honolulu to get the motors, for now, nearly a year into the war, they would not have been obtainable commercially.

Our patrol planes from Pearl had given our lookouts some practice during the first 2 days, but since then the skies and horizon had remained clear. Planes from any sector were now a near impossibility, so our lookouts concentrated on the seas for an ever-possible enemy periscope. Far from a casual view, it was a demanding task, and our new hands welcomed the watch rotation after 2 hours. They would now take a trick at the wheel or another station not requiring such strain on the eyes.

We skipped November 12 as we crossed the 180th meridian, and suddenly it was Friday the thirteenth, which turned out to be a fine day. I had not pinpointed it before, but it was the presence of Dudley at mealtime that had lifted our faces out of our plates.. He was best described as a big, overgrown Kentucky boy who had never been told that adults weren't supposed to smile. His large, square jaw and prominent mouth resembled that of Mushmouth, a character in the "Moon Mullens" comic strip. The upperclassmen at the Naval Academy had dubbed him Mushmouth, but that was quickly shortened to Mush, a nickname used by seniors and contemporaries; but only Dudley, never Mush, was heard in *Wahoo*.

On crossing the latitude line of 7°50′ north after midnight, *Wahoo* automatically passed to the command of Commander South Pacific, Adm. William F. Halsey. There were no dispatches, but should such become necessary, they would come from Commander Task Force 42, the submarine command located at Brisbane, Australia. Towards noon on November 14, we came within aerial search of Mili Atoll and submerged for the rest of the day. Again on the fifteenth we dived for the day, but the lost miles were put to good use in sharpening our planesmen and new officers prior to reaching the patrol area. Only seabirds came in view, so on the sixteenth *Wahoo* continued on the surface, with Mili, Jaluit, and Makin Atolls about 120 miles distant. The seabird warning was correct, and a plane at 6 miles on the SD sent us down for another day.

Small, passing squalls increased in number and intensity each day. This was to be expected in November at our latitudes, as was the storm that greeted *Wahoo* as she entered Patrol Area Dog, whose boundaries had been contained in Commander Task Force 42's encoded dispatch. Behind us lay 2,987 sea miles; all of our gear had worked flawlessly, even our formerly troublesome bow-buoyancy vent, so the success of this mission rested with us personally. Adding emphasis was news on the Fox schedule concerning the continuing Japanese raids against Guadalcanal. Their supplies would pass through our area.

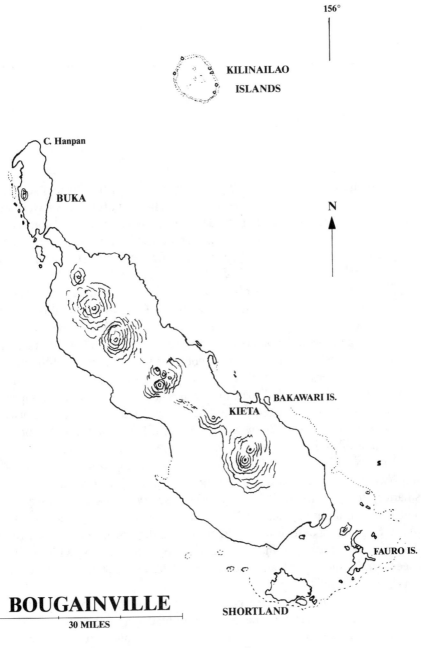

156°

KILINAILAO
ISLANDS

C. Hanpan

BUKA

N

BAKAWARI IS.

KIETA

FAURO IS.

BOUGAINVILLE

30 MILES

SHORTLAND

TREASURY IS.

4

Our submarines had been developed to operate with the fleet as scouts, but lost that role to aircraft. The only operations with the fleet were as a part of opposing forces or to provide target services to our antisubmarine forces. In these, we withdrew at night and turned on our running lights. This was deemed necessary because a surfaced submarine is hard to see at night, and any collision would probably result in the loss of the boat. In spite of these minor roles, we were still called fleet submarines.

Our actual role, in accordance with the Geneva Convention, was to sink enemy warships. It was presumed that they would be escorted by surface and air antisubmarine forces just as were our own warships, so great emphasis was placed on slender periscopes that are difficult to see. The top portion of our search scope, above the taper, was thus about the size of a baseball bat; that of the attack scope would compare with a softball bat. An enemy's sighting either one of these, when used judiciously during an attack, was extremely unlikely, and virtually impossible when the submarine is just patrolling in an open sea area.

But you can't have it both ways: our small-tipped scope was good into twilight, and the larger into brighter nights. The British had been smarter, not fully trusting the post–WW I Geneva Convention's warfare and arms limitations, and had two scopes, one for day and one for night. Ours was a defect that could not be rectified overnight, but barring that, the fleet boat was the best submarine in the world, with surface speed, endurance, payload, and accommodations that no others could approach.

During the Limited Emergency, training in night torpedo attacks using the azimuth ring of the bridge-mounted gyro repeater had commenced, and we had used our TBT at San Diego. But to date, determining a satisfactory submerged firing bearing, after surface tracking, had not been solved. I had participated in the transition from TBT to sound bearing on the night of Pearl Harbor; it could work, but on that attempt it led to confusion.

So this was now our problem as we continued slowly through our area towards the great island. Heavy seas and near gale winds impeded our progress at night, while passing rainsqualls kept our lookouts in foul-weather gear. Submerged during daylight, we could see little through the scopes, while the intermittent heavy rain completely blanked out JK sound when passing overhead. On the third day, with moderating weather, the peaks of Bougainville came in sight, and so did another periscope—somewhat modifying my beliefs on periscope sighting. Chan knew what he had seen, however, and correctly took *Wahoo* deep while putting our stern to the bearing of the other scope. The other submarine might have been tracking us, but for sure, we had not been tracking her. And there was the possibility that we had been spotted and the submarine had been vectored to our track and was waiting for us to surface. The time of 1711 was well into evening twilight, so indicated just that. We waited until it was completely dark, according to Krause's figures, before surfacing.

At dawn, both Bougainville and Buka Islands were in sight. The latter extends to the north and is separated from the big island by Bougainville Strait, a navigable passage. The captain picked an area that could cover shipping rounding Buka or using the strait, and we headed for it. Though passage across this area offered the shortest protected route from the Empire to the Solomons, a week of intensive search disclosed no ships, not even a fisherman.

No week of patrol is a complete loss, for Chief McGill had again chalked the outline of *Wahoo*'s variable tanks, including safety and negative, on the pump room deck. The auxiliaryman with the watch held school daily, whenever new hands were designated by the duty chief. If we had carried paint, I would have suggested that this marking be permanent, for on every patrol, we could expect the task of qualifying new hands. For our part, Dudley and I stood parts of Jack's and Misch's conning tower watches so they could obtain experience with the dive. Otherwise, with *Wahoo*'s present system, they'd never learn.

Since I couldn't discuss our first patrol with Morton and avoid criticism of my captain, I did not bring up the subject and changed the conversation when Dudley did. He quickly understood my position and went elsewhere for the answers he needed to know. You might find him in the engine room with a bucket, scrubbing his clothes, or elsewhere in most any informal attire, even skivvies. So he was not only receiving answers, but becoming personally acquainted with our crew. This night, after a final check topside, I came quietly down to the control room to hear Dudley ask, "What's wrong with your Kleinschmidt stills, Chief?" Chief Lenox came right back, "There's nothing wrong, except they use juice and that means fuel, so they're reserved for drinkin', cookin', and the batt'ries." Morton paused a moment and then continued, "Well, the captain's asleep and I'm going to steal a shower; please send your messenger forward on the double if he gets up." Turning, and with a half wave and smile, knowing all the time that I was there, Dudley ducked through the control room's forward door just as the Bells of St. Mary's bonged for the first time in earnest on this patrol.

The conning tower clock read 2230, and the track on the chart showed *Wahoo*'s position 15 miles east of the northern tip of Buka. In the lightning flashes of the passing squalls, our lookouts had spotted a column of smoke. George had taken true (compass) bearings, and *Wahoo* was already swinging to that direction, 150 degrees, when the captain reached the bridge. Out into the stormy night, I could see indistinguishable shapes (blurps) when chain lightning illuminated the sector on our port bow. I believed we had a convoy. At 2240, 10 minutes after the lookouts' report, another violent lightning display revealed the source of the smoke, a large ship with considerable freeboard presenting a sharp starboard angle. Ahead, on her port bow, was a destroyer-type escort. The range to these ships was perfect, about 6,000 yards; we could track them while here on the surface and then move in submerged for the attack, but two blasts took us down. It was the same mistake my captain had made just south of Midway nearly a year ago.

Periscope observations during lightning flashes seldom seemed to be on the same ship twice in a row and made meaningful tracking on plot and the TDC nearly impossible. Sound tracking did little better, for different screws faded in and out, so we could not coach Buckley or Carter onto the correct bearing. Finally, at 2256, Hunter, with hands on the barrel of the scope and watching the azimuth scale, aligned it with the first consistent sound bearings. Lightning cooperated, and the captain had a destroyer presenting a 90-degree starboard angle. The torpedo gyro angles already showed 50 degrees, so without the reasonably accurate range required for a large-angle shot, the captain withheld fire and swung *Wahoo* to reduce the angle. Our swing was not fast enough, and a few minutes later all enemy sounds ceased.

5

Wahoo resumed her nighttime patrol, with the captain again in his emergency bunk. Having a whole convoy get by had pumped too much adrenalin into my system. Sleep was impossible, and I moved across the passageway to the wardroom. Rather quickly, Dudley joined me and we proceeded to take it out on the cribbage board. Shortly, having finished his watch, George joined us for a triple hand, but cribbage was not foremost on any of our minds. We pushed the board aside and got down to the details of the potential attack we had just muffed. Again, I did not feel we were being disloyal to the captain; he would have been more than welcome. The three of us agreed that *Wahoo* could have stayed on the surface without fear of detection, while gaining a position ahead of the convoy. From there she could have dived at dawn for an accurate periscope attack. This would, of course, require abandoning the prewar concept of a submarine as a submerged vessel of opportunity. Some boats had done this, but as far as I know, it had come about with a change in command.

We had the officers' opinion of the convoy's composition, but not that of the lookouts. They had seen more than we had, and I set Pappy to work with interviews. As expected, their sightings differed. The variations were wide enough, however, to convince me that *Wahoo* had indeed had a convoy within her grasp. And there was one more note of interest: it was Seaman Hall who made the first sighting for their pool.

The following week produced only a propeller-sounding fish noise and then at night strong screws that speeded up for a few minutes before fading from sound. It didn't take much imagination to picture an enemy submarine pulling away and then diving, but our SJ was hot and had revealed nothing with a sweep in that sector.

Not imaginary, however, was a message with our call sign on the first evening Fox after surfacing. Within, it carried the Ultra designation, signifying that the message contained intelligence of the enemy and had highest operational priority. This was a first for *Wahoo* and only the second I had seen. Chan put the special wheels, with their hundreds of contacts, into the coding machine, and the tape came out as he typed the five-letter groups. Enclosed by the padding (words to increase the length and security) the message read:

EIGHTEEN THOUSAND TON LOADED TANKER PROCEEDING TRUK TO SHORTLANDS SCHEDULED ARRIVE MIDMORNING DECEMBER EIGHT OVERALL SPEED PLOTS AT EIGHTEEN KNOTS

There it was: no submarine could have a greater challenge, for sinking this tanker could arrest the Tokyo Express, the almost weekly raids down the New Georgia Sound, called the Slot, that continued to threaten our forces supporting the Marines on Guadalcanal. Krause and I, checking each other, stepped back the hourly positions from the Shortlands and laid down the intercepting track that the captain had desired. It was just past midnight, and in 2 hours *Wahoo* would be on station, waiting.

Though the content of the message was, and would remain, secret, an air of excitement swept through our ship. Frankly, there is no such thing as a secret in the confines of a submarine, further shown by the serious manner of the watch. The battery charge was now complete, and a second engine went on propulsion. I would have preferred three engines on the line as a safety measure, but two would get us there.

Wahoo closed the track laid down on our chart, slowed, and commenced searching into the black night with sound, radar, and lookouts equipped with 7 × 50 binoculars. The SJ with its power train had been performing well in hand train as well as power, so Seaman Gerlacher, with Hunter supervising, was searching to the north with wheel in hand. There had been little time, but obviously enough for first-contact pools. I had been expecting SJ to win, but "Weak echo ranging on a broad front to the north!" came over the bridge speaker. Due to its varying intensity as the enemy escort trained his echo-ranging sound head, such distant bearings are not sharp, but as an early warning are extremely valuable. This spurred radar in efforts to pinpoint the enemy. We were still peering into the night when Hunter reported SJ range 18,000 yards bearing 062. The range matched the speed and the tonnage. We came to the normal approach course, diving when the range had closed to 10,000 yards. An expected course change towards, showing that the tanker was indeed going to enter the Bougainville Strait, put *Wahoo* in fine position. The range was 5,000 yards; at two-thirds speed we would close to 2,500 for firing.

"Echo ranging on our starboard quarter!" came from sound.

"Reciprocal! Reciprocal!" called Dudley, but this advice that the soundman had read the wrong bearing didn't register in time. The captain ordered, "Flood negative and take her deep," apparently with the thought that an escort was closing our quarter to attack.

Recovery in time to pursue the attack was impossible. It would take many minutes to regain periscope depth, and while blowing negative our sound would be blanked out.

To avoid a confrontation, Dudley went on below, while the rest of us listened to the tanker's great screws pounding through our hull and then growing fainter as she proceeded on her way. I took the conn, and the captain, more shaken than by the *Ryujo,* went down the ladder to the control room and to his cabin.

Unlike *Ryujo,* there had been no possibility of overtaking the tanker, so we secured from battle stations as the regular section took the watch. All was clear, and *Wahoo* surfaced on a calm though unfriendly sea. As the captain had instructed, I set course for the top of Buka, that plotted as 310 on the conning tower chart and would keep us well off the jagged coast. Routinely, we took our stars on morning twilight, and then Chan took us down for the day.

Working out the same morning stars used for several days speeded the work, and our correct position was plotted on the conning tower chart in minutes. Without other demands for awhile, I took the conn, sending Jack to control to take the dive with Chan, and then made the next periscope search. The sky and the horizon were clear, so I opened the copy of *Navy Regulations* that I had first brought to the conning tower following the *Ryujo* incident, inquiring into my obligations as executive officer and navigator: concerning assumption of command, it would have to have been in time to sink the ship, but since both of my offices required advice and action to keep our ship off the rocks, or be equally culpable with the captain, should not the same hold for an attack? So I had vowed to speak out in the future. This day, I had laid the book open atop the SJ radar, and between periscope searches, I examined the Quartermaster's Notebook and the regulations, assuring myself that no opportunity had been missed as far as the tanker was concerned.

The tube of our attack periscope was faulty with numerous sharp-edged pits. These tore the flax packing, so droplets of saltwater ran down the tube and frequently over the optics. For some reason, the captain broke his established routine; he was supposed to be asleep, but suddenly appeared through the conning tower's lower hatch. Mistaking the book atop the SJ radar for the *Construction and Repair Manual,* he commented, "Well, I see you've finally broken out the manual to find out how to properly pack that periscope," and stepping over to the SJ, picked up the regulations, which were still open to the flagged pages, and commenced reading.

It was one of life's touchy moments: no words were exchanged, but now each knew exactly where he stood with the other.

6

It was now Wednesday, December 8, still the seventh in Hawaii. All had not gone too well in the Pacific during the first year of the war. Midway had been a victory, stopping the Japanese advance and inflicting heavy major ship losses, though many of the Japanese warships had been able to withdraw to fight again. We looked upon the Battle of the Coral Sea as a victory because the enemy had again been thwarted, and we already knew of the battles for Guadalcanal, with our marines dug in but still threatened. To a belated report that the Japanese carrier *Ryujo* had been sunk by our carrier air, we had taken exception. She would probably be nearing another readiness-for-sea from Tokyo.

To any soldier or sailor, a war is where he fights, but commanding a close second place in our interest was the antisubmarine battle of the Atlantic, and then the African campaign. Casablanca, on the African coast, had been secured, and success in the assault on Algiers, in the Mediterranean, had come in on the Fox. A landing on the continent would still be far away, but the knowledge that at least we were moving towards Europe was surely spurring our efforts in the Pacific.

George had taken the dive and his namesake, George Misch, the conn. Bearings of the taller mountains showed that we were probably approaching the Kieta Peninsula at 1100. If the mountain shown as having a volcano would smoke, we'd be sure, but here in the open sea our DR position, run ahead from the morning twilight star fix, should satisfy any skipper. Dudley took the conn, so Misch could keep pace with Jack in acquiring diving experience. Now alone, except for Krause who had temporarily taken the wheel and the soundman wearing earphones, Dudley commented, "Of all boats, why did I draw *Wahoo* for my PCO run!" I couldn't disguise a slight smile; guessing the truth, he poked a finger against my chest, broke into his friendly grin, and mouthed, "Why you SOB!"

During the night we passed Cape L'Averdy and moved into the gulf formed by the broad northern end of Bougainville and Buka, and which opened to the northeast. Patrolling there would cover the areas of our first weeks, but being deeper in the gulf, *Wahoo* might intercept east-west shipping using Buka Passage. I had put off taking a turn through the boat, frankly because I was still embarrassed by the tanker incident, but this was a new area, with new prospects, and it was time to look ahead. I found all to my liking, especially the resilience of our crew, which continued to amaze me. Apparently, as a group, they could talk things out and get on with the future. I kicked myself for being broody, but with whom could I have discussed *Wahoo*'s predicament and have maintained the military loyalty that my position required?

Nothing, other than the occasional seabirds, came in sight during the first day, and after surfacing we moved north. The captain had selected the 30-mile-wide passage between Cape Hanpan, on Buka's northern tip, and the Kilinailau Islands lying to the northeast for the next day's patrol. What could we expect to find out there? Diving immediately after morning stars, the day progressed as might have been expected: reveille, my position slip, breakfast, trice up bunks and then clamp down, a fire control drill, another position slip, and the noon meal filled half of our day. Nothing moved.

To improve our chances of a sighting, we had been trying another experiment that was quite simple. When the OOD was about to lower his scope, still knowing that all was clear, the quartermaster with the watch would raise the other scope and continue the search. When Dudley or I was in the conning tower, one of us would take over. This would at least insure the earliest possible sighting.

7

Roger had the dive and Richie the conn on a likewise uneventful after-noon. Another hour would bring Chan and Misch to relieve the watch. That meant four more periscope searches to go in *Wahoo*'s standard procedure, but each search was now lengthened, so nearly half the time one scope was up. Why not a continuous search so we'd always know what was going on above us, and would not have to search for planes during the first few minutes? But again, that would be a too radical departure from our worn-out peacetime doctrine; best that we stick with our ploy and try to make it last.

I had just come to the conning tower to see Sterling on sound. I was interested, for in my experience, motivation was the key ingredient in a good soundman. Sterling didn't have to stand that watch, so motiva-tion must have been a factor. Richie was just completing an observation, and as his scope came down, Hunter was just grasping the handles of the search periscope; it was like passing the baton, but from there on it was careful scrutiny of the whole horizon. I watched with approval, and then turned to go on below when Hunter calmly announced, "Heavy smoke on the horizon," and then stepping back, he called the relative bearing from the azimuth ring below the packing gland, 315. He had blasted my strategic theory in favor of the captain's guess, which bothered me not at all. We quickly converted the relative bearing to true, 293, just 23 degrees to the north of due west. Having just appeared, the ship or convoy would be coming our way, and since there were no other major ports, heading for the Shortland area. I drew the enemy's base course lightly on the chart; asked Duty Chief Ware to call the captain; and after giving him a minute to get ahead of the stampede, nodded to Hunter, who had his hand poised on the handle of the general alarm's switch box. The Bells of St. Mary's sounded in earnest for the third time on this patrol.

Another observation showed the smoke drawing slightly to the right. The captain confirmed this, and then sighted two topmasts. Conning *Wahoo* to the north took our submarine to a position almost ahead of the enemy. Within minutes the tops of two more ships came over the horizon, and then the thin stick of the escort. Chan and Roger were having trouble with too many reports on the various ships as their hulls came into view, as during the lightning flashes. I asked the captain to please give angles and ranges on just one ship; he did, and then provided us with the overall composition of the convoy between his periscope observations: we had three ships in column, escorted by a large antisubmarine vessel. The ships were zigging in unison while the escort patrolled across the van. Our talkers were now experts, who could likely get jobs as barkers after the war. So the details went to each compartment, undoubtedly including the reports and actions of the fire control party as well as those of the captain.

Barring a change of base course, which certainly was not expected, *Wahoo* was already nearing an attack position on the convoy's starboard flank. The angles, now opening, permitted further identification. We had three freighters, all loaded, and with the largest, our prospective target, in the middle. All of this was good, but not their escort. Lindhe had passed the warship identification section up through the hatch, and the captain put his finger on the flagged picture. She was an *Asashio* class destroyer, patrolling a good mile to each side of the convoy and about a mile ahead of the leading ship.

The captain's problem was to time our movement in to the firing point to coincide with the destroyer's passage to the convoy's opposite side. Her echo ranging seemed menacing, and the captain considered torpedoing the destroyer first. The range on that pass to our side was too short for our torpedoes to arm, so the captain switched back to the large, second freighter in the column and came right to lengthen the torpedo run. I provided the course for a 120 track that would make the torpedoes come in from 30 abaft her starboard beam. Both Chan's plot and Roger's TDC had speed at 11 knots. Two torpedoes were still set to run at 6 feet below the surface as for the destroyer, the other two at 16 feet; the outer doors were open, and the captain steadied *Wahoo* on the final course.

Hunter raised the attack scope for the final bearing. (It didn't leak; Chief McGill's new packing was holding.)

The captain swung the scope, bringing the wire to the middle of the freighter, and announced, "Final bearing and shoot!"

Glory be. Nothing could stop us.

Richie, on the spread knob, directed four torpedoes to hit along the freighter's length, and Krause, on the firing panel, sent each one on its way.

Four times we felt *Wahoo* shudder, followed by a healthy zing of the torpedo props, and then the slight pressure of the residual impulse air being vented into the boat. Finally came Buckley's report, "All hot, straight and normal."

Hunter was counting the seconds till our torpedoes should hit on their 700-yard run—46—and had picked up the count at 30: "Twenty, ten, five, three, whack!" The first detonation, louder than the depth charges off Pearl, was followed by two more. The destroyer was on the far side of the convoy, allowing our skipper ample time to describe the scene of the freighter listing, and to let me take a squint before his orders, "George take her deep. Rig for depth charge and silent running."

The *Asashio* destroyer would probably have the remnants of four torpedo wakes emanating from one point, our position on firing, as a target for her first salvo of depth charges. She would at least know that we had fired from on the freighter's starboard hand, probably near abeam. She seemed to know both, for the first pattern detonated fairly close to our stern as *Wahoo* passed 120 feet. They were close enough to raise our great main induction valve, over 40 inches in diameter, for a healthy slug of sea into the piping. The antenna trunk flooded; some lights broke; a small circulating waterline in the pump room carried away; and some odd nuts, bolts, and paint chips flew around. Altogether, it was enough to raise the pulse a bit.

Twenty separate attacks followed during the next hour and a half, but the only hair-raiser was of our own making. When George blew negative to level off at 250 feet, the vent's rubber gasket blew out; the flood valve that closes with sea pressure hadn't yet seated, and the pump room bilges filled before the vent's stop valve was closed. *Wahoo's* depth was now 350 feet, but who knows, maybe this had taken us to safety below the enemy's deepest depth charges! Negative was designed to give an initial down angle and negative buoyancy on diving. Its use to gain depth is fraught with troubles, since the sea flooded in has to be expelled with excessively noisy, high-pressure air.

The bilges and negative were pumped to sea; George had us back to 250 feet, and at 1726 up to periscope depth. The ship was still afloat, so we crept towards her to see about ten boats standing by. Her well decks were under water, but not until dark did she sink on this Thursday, December 10, 1942.

Our surfacing demonstrated one more argument against flooding negative to gain extra depth quickly. After a normal all-day dive, an increase in internal air pressure of about an inch is not unusual. This comes from the normal use of compressed air, which is vented into the boat, including that from venting negative. On surfacing, this is bled off by cracking the hatch, still held by the dogs, and then opening the hatch after the boat's pressure has equalized with the atmosphere. This night, with all of our blowing, we had nearly 3 inches to vent, and the noise, at least internally, was that of a monstrous foghorn announcing our presence as the seconds dragged by. To open the hatch prematurely would blow those close below topside. Under normal circumstances, a submarine would have brought the pressure down with her air compressors in a half hour; too slow for us.

But *Wahoo* was on the surface heading east, with a happy crew below. New hands would now rate wearing the prestigious submarine combat pin, and others would affix a bronze star to theirs. The captain had ordered a shot of depth-charge medicine (LeJon brandy) for everyone, which was welcomed more by the way of celebration than for soothing jangled nerves. The camaraderie carried even into the wardroom, where our blowing fiasco was not even mentioned by the captain. We did discuss the approach and attack, and certainly found it more rewarding to review the details that had led to a successful day, so we could salt away the positive for a change.

The captain had been exhausted at the completion of the attack, as if he had just finished a grueling race. He still seemed fatigued and went to his cabin for a Western before going to the conning tower. I went to the bridge, hoping that he would spend this night below so as to get some real rest. The sea was calm; trash and garbage had been given the deep-six. Though the night was bright, the phosphorescence of the disturbed sea shone along our waterline. I tried to analyze the day. Had the captain made this excellent attack because we had only 9 more days in our area, and it was now or never? Certainly for him it had required a great effort; his face was flushed after each observation. Or had our silent confrontation had its effect? Perhaps he had said to himself, "I'll show that whipper snapper!" Whatever it was, *Wahoo* needed more of it.

The answer might come sooner than expected, since before midnight we received two encoded messages. The first concerned the convoy that we had already attacked (they didn't know that), and the second extended our patrol to the east and gave the routing of a large freighter heading for the extra area. We had, at the outside, 24 hours to get in position, but 12 of them would be submerged, so we had best be on our way. The captain got up and looked at the chart; we could get there at our present one-engine speed, and he elected to continue as we were to give the crew a rest after the forty-odd depth charges.

No drills were in the Plan of the Day for December 11; it would be a rope-yarn Sunday for hands to catch up on laundry and such, or to continue with one of the paperbacks always supplied by the Red Cross. When I presented the position slip, I found the captain reading ONI-208J instead of a Western. He had underlined the *Syoei Maru* of 5,684 tons as closest to the class of ship he had sunk. In the 1942 edition of the same manual, which Lindhe and the crew were using, the same type of ship appeared as an 8,748 tonner, probably dead-weight tonnage.

Feeling that I could now take a turn through the boat with my head a bit higher, I found different conversations in most compartments, but

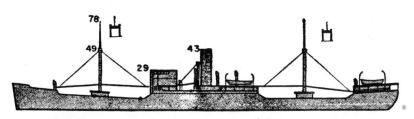

MEIYO MARU
SYOAN MARU, SYOEI MARU

Tonnages:		Constructed:	
Gross:	5,624– D. W.: 8,539–8,610	1937–40	Japan
	5,645	Propulsion:	
Length:		Machinery:	Reciprocating
W. L. (B. P.): 407'	O. A.:	Screws: 1	N. H. P.: 306–379
Beam: 55'		R. P. M.:	@ Knots:
Drafts:		Fuel: Coal	Capacity: 650–950
Loaded: 25'	Light: 10'		tons
Speed:		Radius: 6,300 miles at 12 knots.	
Normal cruising: 12 Max.: 15		Potential naval value: AP. AK.	
		Remarks:	

all were about the same two subjects—the sinking and the depth charging. In the mess room, undoubtedly for the second time but now for my benefit, Deaton and McSpadden (now TM2c's) patted the pressure hull. That told it all. We spoke of *Argonaut* and whether her riveted hull could have taken that drubbing without leaking oil. On through the ship, no one brought up the question, though I am sure it had been in their conversations: Had *Wahoo* finally turned the corner? In a few hours we might know. One other item was lacking; no mention was made of any tactical mistakes. That was the key to sending any ship to Davy Jones's locker, and this time *Wahoo,* including the fire control party and the captain, had made none.

8

The captain had requested a call at 0200, 2 hours after his submarine would pass into her extended area. I had placed mine with the duty chief for an hour earlier. It was a longer safety interval than normal, but when your captain has instant access, on the scene, he leaves his second little option. But in this I had no complaint, for on the last patrol with its 8 hours of watch, I would have been stumbling around trying to wake up. As it was, I'd finished my coffee and was rather enjoying a bright, calm night and the ever-scrubbed fresh air of these tropics. I would have preferred being deeper into our area. We weren't just meeting a train; it was more like going to the station without a timetable—you get there early.

Krause had brought my sextant to the bridge. We took a round of stars, just in case we didn't have a chance later, but we wouldn't work them out now. It was well, for within a half hour, sound reported either echo ranging or a fathometer ahead. The time was 0130, Sunday, December 12, and shortly we had a large freighter in sight. Her broad port angle gave her heading as northerly. She was now showing on radar too; we called the members of the fire control party involved in tracking, but did not go to battle stations.

The initial SJ range was 10,000 yards, 5 nautical miles, and her large angle offered nothing that we couldn't overcome during the 4 hours till dawn. The freighter was zigging frantically, obviously having been informed that there was an enemy submarine in the area. Her angle on the bow seemed never the same, but this was not all bad, for it slowed her progress along the base course to the northward. Tracking finally had a mean solution of 020, but we were doing nothing to pass her up. At the moment, her great stern showed ahead, but she would zig left. We were actually still on her quarter, while we should have been off her port bow by now. I could not let this simple tactical situation deteriorate to the impossible when three more engines would put all aright. I do not talk with a raised voice unless it is necessary. This was one of those occasions and I said rather strongly, "Captain, we have to go after her!"

The captain's reaction rather surprised me, but I guess it should not have. In the presence of George Misch and within full earshot of the forward lookouts and Krause, he replied in an angry, disdainful tone, "Don't be stupid; you can't attack a ship from here!"

He must have known what I had in mind; I had sketched it out for the *Ryujo*. We simply were not on the same wavelength, and tactically, in different wars. For a long moment, I considered pressing the point, but realized that in this agitated situation, he would undoubtedly send me to my stateroom. That would do neither me nor *Wahoo* any good, but at least the troops would have a conversation piece for the next day or so.

9

When last seen, the freighter had a large starboard angle, and the captain surmised that she might be following a circuitous route to the Shortlands, within Bougainville Strait. I provided the course from our plot, which was modified to 190 after we had worked out the stars. That would take us there also, and presumably would cross the freighter's track. Three engines moved *Wahoo* smartly along the route, but with a brilliant dawn there were no masts to eastward, and we pulled the plug for the day.

Our submerged daylight run on December 13, and then two engines throughout the night, brought *Wahoo* to a position 20 miles north of the irregular 100-fathom line across the strait. From there, we would continue to close the small islands that dot the wide entrance, while the two narrow passages lay still another 12 miles beyond. It was an intriguing area, shaped like a funnel split lengthwise, and it was now easy to see that we should have been here early in the patrol.

But we still had 4 days before running the length of the island in making our departure. Breakfast time brought our first contact, with stocky masts of a large ship coming over the horizon. They appeared not much out of line, indicating a sharp port angle. We should be able to reach her handily, and the Bells of St. Mary's bonged again.

Wahoo was off to intercept, and I do believe the captain was trying to make amends for his lack of action and outburst on December 12. Her upper works came over the horizon, and as her angle opened, the captain identified her as a large transport, not the freighter that we had guessed. She had not zigged; there was no escort, and we now had misgivings, but continued the approach, closing the range with a 10-minute run at standard speed. *Wahoo* was now in a beautiful position for a broadside attack. All was in readiness except for opening the forward tubes' outer doors, but on the next observation, now with better light, the captain saw that her side was painted white, with the unmistakable horizontal green band and red cross amidships. Lindhe had the privilege of taking a look and agreed with the captain that this hospital ship was similar to the *Manila Maru* shown in ONI-208J. From without, she appeared to be complying with international law in all respects, and may well have had casualties from Guadalcanal aboard. We watched her go, a bit disappointed, but thankful for a realistic drill.

On securing from battle stations, we came to course 210 to put Oema Atoll and Oema Island on our port bow. Ships coming from the strait could leave them on either side. We could not cover both broad passages, and the captain had chosen the one nearer Bougainville. The rest of the morning was uneventful, except in the freezer room, where Phillips had volunteers sorting the meats and fresh-frozen fruits. He would serve only the best during the remaining days, and turn in the rest, some of which seemed to have acquired an odd taste.

The noon meal passed, and I returned to the ship's office to work on the information that would be my part of the patrol report. A commotion beyond the door caused me to step into control to see what was going on, just as the Bells of St. Mary's bonged throughout our ship. Sterling, on sound, had picked up propeller noises. Jack, with the OOD watch, had swung his scope to the same bearing, and there was a big surfaced submarine heading our way. Calling George to the conning tower, they had already swung *Wahoo* for a 90 track. The range was close, an estimated 1,200 yards.

The captain reached the conning tower wearing a towel Suma style, and still soapy from the shower (a no-no). On his first sweep-around with the scope, the towel came loose and fell down the periscope well. Until the mess attendant arrived with pants and shirt, the captain, quite unperturbed, made the periscope observations while naked as a jaybird. They were among his best, giving Roger an almost immediate TDC solution. Now clothed, he further identified the submarine as an I-boat, Japan's largest attack submarine.

Chan and Roger agreed; her speed was 12 knots and course 015. From the ISWAS, I reported that we were 800 yards from her track. The tubes were ready, outer doors open, and the torpedoes set to run at 10 feet.

Hunter brought the scope up till the handles cleared the well; the captain flipped them down, and then Hunter brought the scope on up to the height of the captain's hands. It would be a water-lapping look. It took no more than 3 seconds, and we heard, "Final bearing and shoot!" Hunter called the bearing; Roger replied, "Set"; Richie directed three torpedoes: the first amidships, the second under her bow, and the third under her stern, while Krause had the privilege of sending each on its way. The shudder, zing, and momentary pressures were all normal.

Then came the report from Buckley that we all awaited: "All hot, straight and normal!" She was a dead duck, for one or two of the three torpedoes would hit, and any sort of hit will sink a submarine.

The torpedo run for the 800 yards would take 38 seconds. The captain raised his scope 10 seconds ahead of the expected hit, and the WHACK! of the detonation blanked out the first words of his description. The first torpedo hit about 20 feet forward of the conning tower, throwing a column of spume high in the air. She commenced sinking instantly with her bridge still manned and then the bridge watch jumped into the sea as she went to Davy Jones's locker.

A look, and I thought of taking a prisoner, but decided to leave well enough alone. It was well, for the captain ordered 200 feet. At this moment, *Wahoo* was shaken by a great muffled WHOMP with an intensity far greater than the detonation of the warhead, but lacking its WHACK. In the Quartermaster's Notebook, it was recorded at 2½ minutes after the torpedo hit, and had to be the collapse of the submarine's hull. Now we knew what it sounded like, if that was any comfort.

After George had leveled *Wahoo* at 200 feet, undoubtedly glad that the captain had not ordered negative flooded, we came left to 340. This would clear the coast of Bougainville and its many promontories, which we would pass after dark. We heard no further explosions or other man-made noises as we moved quietly beneath a sharp temperature gradient. Had there been any, a major part of its sound wave would have been reflected back to the surface, always giving a secure feeling.

In spite of what had transpired, sinking two enemy ships, one of them a warship, had made this patrol. Understandably, the same elation

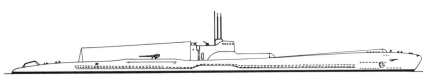

I-15 submarine, 356 feet in length.

that the crew had displayed after the freighter's sinking was lacking. In part, there was no combat pin or additional star involved, but the greater reason was the knowledge that the tables could have been turned. Perhaps not likely for us in daylight, but we thought back to Chan's first sighting of a periscope and the later screw noises that had speeded up and then faded as from a diving submarine. This I-boat, which the captain had identified as the I-15, could have been hunting us.

10

Wahoo returned to periscope depth an hour before sunset, and then surfaced routinely deep into evening twilight. For sure, our lookouts had needed no encouragement before coming to the conning tower, but knowing Pappy, they had been warned again of the gravity of their coming watch. On a fading but still distinct horizon, I brought down our stars. (To be exact, I preferred inverting the sextant first, and then, keeping the star in sight, bringing the horizon up to it. For the altitude reading, the sextant is turned right side up, and there's your star waiting for the final adjustment. It sounds like the hard way, but the moving star is easily lost when brought down directly, while the horizon is never lost.)

A course change of 20 degrees to 320 and one-engine speed would take us to the point that the captain had selected and marked on the chart for tomorrow's patrol. It lay 10 miles off Kieta, a settlement with a harbor protected by numerous islands. From there, we could close the islands to spot any ship, and wait a couple of days for her to exit. Morning twilight of December 15 found us in position. Tall, white radio towers, extending up from abrupt hills, caught the first morning sunlight, but were the only sight to shoreward of interest here, now about two-fifths of the way along Bougainville's north coast.

Back on course 340, a sweep-around showed two masts on our quarter. They were well separated, indicating a course parallel to ours and the island's coast. Had we stayed on 340 she would be overtaking us; we would have needed only to pull off to port or starboard and shoot. But all was not lost, for the masts of any escorts should now show; there were none, and now below the masts, great goal-posts signified the size and importance of this ship. She was surely heading for Buka Passage, and there was nothing to prevent *Wahoo* from making a surface dash to get ahead of the enemy and moving onto her track. I stepped off the freighter's positions on the chart, giving her 12 knots. One hour at full power would reach a position for a submerged approach. With only 4 days left in our area, this could be the last opportunity to turn this from a so-so into a good patrol. It seemed so sound and logical that I presented it with some confidence to my captain.

"Why, they'd have planes over us in minutes!" he scoffed, while indicating the direction of the radio towers, now well back on our quarter.

If the radio station, presumably near the towers that were actually located atop the 460-meter peak of Bakawaki Island, had lookouts, they would still have to spot and identify *Wahoo* as a submarine. Then, according to the Japanese monograph at Pearl, planes would have to be summoned from the enemy's base at Rabaul, about 200 miles distant. Giving the enemy an equal capability, its planes could not reach us in time to return before dark. Even if a plane could be dispatched from Shortland, we could dive before it could attack. This we had proved in *Argonaut* the morning after Pearl Harbor. We had been trying to charge near-flat batteries when a Marine bent on scoring his first kill of the war dived from high astern. At submarine school, we had been informed that there was no such thing as a "crash dive"—that was strictly Hollywood. We had found it quite descriptive. *Wahoo* could dive a good 10 seconds faster, so the captain's rebuttal was just another way of affirming his belief that in daylight, submarines belong beneath the sea. In conversations at the Royal, I had found that *Wahoo* was not alone with this problem, but in those few boats, none had our other restrictions.

11

After tracking exercises during the predawn hours of December 17 and 18 on a patrol and a fisherman, *Wahoo* dived for the day. Our crew suddenly remembered the course books for their next rate. December 19 arrived without further contacts, and undoubtedly, all hands gave silent cheers as *Wahoo* left her area to round Buka and then head for Brisbane, Australia. A third engine went on the line; the midwatch had taken over, and 30 minutes later, two blasts took us down.

Seaman Appel, our port forward lookout, heard a buzz like that of a plane close overhead. George confirmed it, pulling the plug. This was the first indication of aircraft activity in or near the area, so such a contact at night did not seem likely. But when there is doubt, sounding two blasts is a good policy. *Wahoo* stayed down an hour, checked the area with the SD, and then came on up to proceed on her way. The buzz was still there, caused by the lookout's rail that had broken loose from the periscope shears. In another place, it could simply have been welded at dawn, but in this area we were subject to attack by our own planes, and had to run submerged until we had reached 10 degrees south. Pruett, with the duty chief's watch, took care of this by sending up an old shoe heel. The rail was forced out and then allowed to spring back onto Pruett's heel placed between it and the shears. No longer could the pipe vibrate in resonance with our diesels.

Though Dudley had brightened the atmosphere in the wardroom for some time, he too had lost some of his joviality. But being on our way to Brisbane had lifted our spirits a bit. So when George appeared, having slept in after his midwatch and a bit late for breakfast, we called him Buzz. Always a good shipmate, George entered into the spirit of the ribbing, but the captain frowned a bit, and as the day wore on we knocked it off and went about the serious business of getting Jack and George Misch qualified. So Dudley and I took the afternoon watches, while Roger and Hank stood by the junior officers with the dive.

Though our course of 170 was leading to Australia, it was also crossing the tracks of possible shipping between Rabaul and the Short-lands, which would pass along the southwest coast of Bougainville. Just after 1600, our searches paid off—not with a ship, but with the next best thing, puffs of smoke coming up from over the northern horizon. They were drawing to the right; the enemy's course had to parallel Bougainville's coastline, and we changed course to intercept. Instead of drawing to the right, the true bearings of the new puffs of smoke drew left. At our cruising speed of 5 knots, *Wahoo* would pass ahead of the enemy. No change of base course could save that ship; a change away would run her into the island, and one towards would hasten the attack. To do just that, we went to standard speed to insure reaching a firing position before dark.

With an approach in progress that could not fail, I had the captain awakened, and Seaman Dooley on the wheel had the privilege of swinging down the handle of the general alarm. The captain came before the bonging ceased, perhaps being aware of the change of course, which would have shown on the gyro repeater in his cabin. I explained the situation orally, while pointing out the relative positions and the tracks on the chart. Then, as expected, he slowed to one-third to see for himself. This time there was not the great urgency, but he seemed to be taking undue time. Perhaps it was just me; after all, I was not holding a stop-watch on him.

The captain surprised me by taking only one bearing, lowering the scope and resuming our previous speed. He then pored over the chart. Time passed without comment, but during this period, *Wahoo* was drawing ahead of the enemy. It was coming up 20 minutes since his periscope observation when he picked up the dividers and commenced stepping off distances on the chart. More minutes passed, and then he straightened up, ordering, "Secure from battle stations," and then explained that *Wahoo* would be within *Grouper*'s area before the attack.

I had known that, but surely our charge to do our utmost to sink any ship took precedence over any boundary line. I could not disguise my fury, and Dudley, facing me behind the captain, could see a crisis brewing. He shook his head slightly and then looked down. Following his gaze, I saw his right hand at his side with fingers extended and palm facing the deck, all being quickly rotated at the wrist. It was the universal "cool-it" sign, but to me it said more: On approaching a tanker, yes, but for the puffs of a smoking *maru,* no.

And we resumed the first leg of our route to Brisbane.

12

Regardless of the final destination, returning from patrol is like "Sailing Down to Rio," and in this case Australia would be new to the whole ship's company. The events of the day seemed to have been put behind by the troops, but I was finding such to be increasingly difficult; for me, they had been accumulating, with some of them degrading the position I held and insulting to me. However, the sight of Richie checking over Jack and George Misch's Qualification Notebooks brought me up to the present and all that had to be done in the four remaining days. But nothing was so urgent that I could not accept a challenge from Dudley, who already had the pegs in place on the cribbage board.

It was the second night since George's plunge, and now on the midwatch, two blasts sent us down again. This time it was Seaman Ater (probably a boot camp buddy of Appel's) who had first seen a flash and then a plane's running light, and George had confirmed it. The bearing and altitude checked with that of Jupiter, still close to the horizon. I would doubt that there is any wartime submarine that hasn't dived for this planet, which can show white, red, or green, sometimes changing or in combination, and what plane would display running lights?

At breakfast, George was greeted by his new nickname, Flash. All seemed to enjoy this, including Flash, but excepting the captain who frowned a bit more than on the previous occasion. Fortunately, perhaps, George had business with his engines, so the new nickname was not given the acid test.

Wahoo had now left Rossel Island 50 miles on her starboard beam (Krause would swear to this) and was steady on course 185, crossing the Coral Sea, where the great carrier-air battle had been fought early last May, before the Battle of Midway. From here on, we should be immune from attack, but late in the morning of December 23, a British Albemarle bomber showed up that hadn't been told about that. It may have been our new mortar-type launchers that called her in (it had happened to *Argonaut,* our flares bursting so high that the pilot had really thought his plane was being attacked). We dived.

Entering this plane contact completed my needed sheets for the patrol report. The others concerning weather, tidal information, and navigational aids had already been completed, but with one exception. Krause and I had found that Buka was tilted about 10 degrees too far to the east on our chart. We could now concentrate on bisecting Cape Moreton light, our first landfall in Australia, on December 26.

Having more time let me consider *Wahoo*'s dilemma, and to be completely truthful, my own, since from my point of view, they were inseparable. Though holding lesser positions, I had been through this before, but then senior conflicts, not operations, were involved. In both cases, I had remained aboard while my captains and execs were detached. Now in that top echelon, I was not going to let this happen to me. I loved this ship and the challenge of her full potential, but could not go to sea again with my present captain when a blowup would be inevitable. I had been mulling this over during the day, when a glance at the clock showed it was time for an afternoon sun line.

I was a bit early, for Krause was always punctual, and the captain was there on the cigarette deck. I was about to give my usual greeting, ''Good afternoon, Captain,'' but he spoke first.

''O'Kane,'' he said, ''I don't know what I'm going to do with you.''

Except for substituting my name for his rank, he had spoken the exact words that were on my mind. And what had prompted this statement? I had not long to wait, for after pausing, the captain continued.

''I have just been checking the ship and aircraft contacts that you tabulated for the patrol report, and you have failed to include the plane that buzzed us and the one with running lights!''

''I had believed that neither was a bona fide contact, Sir, but if you think otherwise, I'll include them as soon as I've taken this sun sight.''

''Please do,'' said the captain, and then, relenting a bit, commented more to the wind and sea than to me, ''You'd probably make a good submarine captain.''

For me, taking star sights is always accompanied by a bit of wonder, and on Christmas Eve with reverence too. This would be my second on war patrol, and like others, my thoughts were far away. Rowls, showing foresight, had eased the situation by having turkeys thawing. Usually, the senior cook or chief commissary steward is informally referred to as belly robber, but for good reason I had not heard this in *Wahoo*. In our Christmas dinner, he "done himself proud."

Cape Moreton light sits atop a bluff and is visible at sea level for 26 miles. From our bridge, we could add another 15 miles, and from the raised search periscope, its loom could be seen from at least 50. Our evening stars were followed by another round at midnight. The loom showed dead ahead on schedule. The captain came to the bridge and ordered stationing the special sea detail. Believing he might still be half-asleep, I pointed out that Cape Moreton was still 5 hours away. He repeated the order. The time was 0300.

The pilot boat, waiting in the open sea off the cape, put her bow to ours, and the pilot, wearing a black suit with bowler, and with a black folded umbrella in hand, hopped nimbly aboard. Intentionally, I believe, he had met us about a half-hour's run from the sea buoy, for after directing the course, the pilot went below with the captain for coffee, and maybe breakfast too.

Pappy had been quietly rotating the watch so the special sea detail could get their breakfast, and now Krause took care of ours by returning with two special turkey sandwiches that had been put together by Rowls. Normally, this would not have been my first choice, but having been up all night, the sandwiches and a mug of crew's coffee were perfect.

Returning to the bridge just in time, the pilot conned *Wahoo* into and then across Moreton Bay. Having this open water gave us an opportunity to adjust to the pilot's orders of "Right a spoke" or "Left two spokes," which would have given us increasing rudder angle. Quickly, we interpreted this as 5 degrees right or 10 degrees left rudder, and the pilot readily agreed.

The total run to Brisbane would be 90 miles, and the fun began on entering the 60-mile, truly serpentine river. Here, the pilot faced aft, giving "spoke" orders when buoys or other markers that only he knew came in range (lined up). Chan, Krause, and I tried to keep *Wahoo*'s actual track plotted on the chart—good only for the court-martial that would follow a grounding! That necessitated my spending most of the time on the bridge identifying objects and the occasional buoy number.

Our progress was slowed by the current created by the summer rains, but we finally reached civilization, marked by a cement works on our starboard hand, where people could be seen working in the river. A few more turns and the river opened into a large basin, almost a bay, and there ahead to starboard lay *Sperry* alongside the quay.

Part Four

THIRD PATROL
Brisbane to Palau and Pearl

1

As is customary, the pilot had turned the conn back to our captain. Taking full advantage of the current, he used just enough speed and rudder to move *Wahoo* sideways into her berth alongside *Sperry* at New Farm Wharf in Brisbane.

It was 1215, Saturday, December 26, 1942, and the special sea detail had finished a 9-hour watch. I had expected them to head for their bunks, but the same relief crew *Wahoo* had first enjoyed at Pearl Harbor was coming aboard. Our troops knew the way to the showers and the disbursing office, so in relays, with hamburgers in hand, and packing their gear, they were off to the awaiting busses. Their rest camp would be a reserved floor of the downtown Hotel Canberra; hardly a camp, but I dare say no one would object.

Adm. James Fife, Jr., ComSubSePac, and Captain Styer, about to make admiral, came aboard and congratulated our captain on the two sinkings, the required number for the recommendation of a Silver Star medal. With one of them a warship, the decoration was practically certain, and for sure, no skipper could have been under greater strain. Surprisingly, this had been the best patrol in that area for some time.

There was a house, complete with cook and steward, reserved for skippers, and I saw my captain, so exhausted that a consecutive patrol seemed unlikely, off to his awaiting transportation. Jack was waiting too, with a car and driver to take us to an apartment house without mess attendants, which was more than all right with us. Of the two suites, ours on the second floor was the more spacious. There was another advantage, we were quick to learn: none of the windows were screened, and the flies and mosquitoes preferred the first floor.

We had stopped for a dozen cold, tall bottles of Australian ale, and now, with our feet propped up and with glass in hand, since the bottles were too big to hold, we were truly relaxing for the first time in nearly 2 months. I had not and would not be discussing my visit with Commander Grenfell, and neither had any of *Wahoo*'s officers considered that Dudley's orders were anything but routine. So we were again talking of the separation of the captains and how it could affect our patrol, when Dudley suddenly appeared in the doorway and called, "Do you mind if I shack up here?"

We had a quorum, but after another round of ale, all conversation turned to food, since none of us had eaten more than a few sandwiches during the last 24 hours. All of our officers had now rallied around, so Dudley phoned for a lorry. The dispatcher must have been tempted to send a delivery wagon, but probably judging from the background noise, had a taxi with jump seats at the apartment in minutes.

It was too dark for a sight-seeing tour, so the driver took us directly to what he said was the best restaurant, adding, "You might as well go to the best; they're all the same price." That seemed to be a strange statement, but it was forgotten as we entered an old-world restaurant with its deep mahogany paneling, generous tablecloths, and the aroma of a dozen entrees being carried to guests already seated. This took some of us back to our midshipman cruises, and just as then, we were ready to try two or three entrees. At our table, however, was a card, plainly printed so there could be no mistake; each person could spend a total of three shillings six pence for food. So that's what our cabby had been telling us—it did seem a simple and just means of rationing.

While others were stewing, a waiter passed close by with a generous platter of fried oysters. It was one of the modestly priced entrees, and permitted the selection of a salad, one vegetable, and dessert, all within the allowance that was equal to about ninety cents. Then too beer or ale was not rationed; I guess the Aussies wouldn't have stood for that. So this part of our rest and recuperation looked good, at least for me and the oyster eaters.

Few of us had had any sleep during the last 24 hours, and now pleasantly filled, we commenced nodding. When two went to sleep, we were surely creating the impression of Yanks passing out on ale. I'm not sure who did the urging, but we all tumbled into one cab and were delivered back at the apartment house door. Two flights up, turn left, and then straight ahead took me to my bunk. The others' navigation must have been successful too, for they were there when I started frying ham and eggs that had been kindly left in the refrigerator by our immediate predecessors; at least they had smelled fresh. The breakfast got us off to a good day of walking and relaxing, our first in about 2 months without scheduled demands, giving an exhilarating sense of freedom. Our four duty commanders—George, Roger, Chan, and Richie—had experienced the same, and taking a practical step, had rented a beach cottage, and all but Chan, with the duty, were off with their gear to catch the last narrow-gauge train. As a water polo player, that would suit George to a T, but the very thought of moving again, even going out to a restaurant, made me feel weak.

Rummaging around the kitchen, I found the makings of a good supper right at hand, thanks again to the former occupants, and an important ingredient from *Wahoo*. Immediately, I had takers in Dudley, Jack, and George Misch, maybe because they were too tired to eat out. The entree would be tuna delight, which is tuna on toast, smothered by cream sauce, but with a twist. I made the cream sauce with lots of fresh creamery butter, flour, and milk, while Jack drained and heated the tuna and prepared the hot, buttered toast. The tuna went on the toast, but just before passing the cream sauce, came the twist: Four small bottles of depth-charge medicine (still LeJon brandy) were stirred in at the last moment so as not to lose the alcohol to the atmosphere. It even added to the sauce's golden color. String beans on the side, and canned peaches for dessert seemed to satisfy everyone, and it fulfilled the color code requirements from the Steward's Manual. Perhaps mindful of the moose story, there were no complaints.

After another breakfast and time for reading the latest letters from home, Dudley and I again started a long walk towards the countryside. We had established a good rapport on patrol, in part because Dudley was able to view the somewhat taut situations more objectively. Now, we spoke more fully and found that we were of a mind in all submarine fundamentals. Out from under a command echelon, at least for the following days, our conversations were uninhibited.

Dudley talked at length of his first patrol while commanding the *R-5*, which he fondly called the "Nickel Boat." (She had been one of my school boats at New London, so mechanical explanations were unnecessary.) Late one afternoon, off the Virginia capes, the periscope watch had sighted a surfaced Nazi submarine at long range and presenting a large angle on the bow. *R-5* had approached till her can was flat, reaching a range of 4,000 yards before it started to open. At the last moment, in the increasing dusk, he had fired a spread of four torpedoes that missed. In the endorsement to the patrol report, Dudley had been criticized for not searching for the enemy after dark, when any hunter would recognize that in so doing, *R-5,* moving on the surface, would have become the target. In return, I told of *Argonaut*'s first patrol.

Late in the morning of the last day of 1942, without ceremony, Dudley W. Morton took command of *Wahoo.* Back at the apartment, my new captain told of the PCO school he had attended just before coming to Pearl.

"Commanders Patterson and Hensel were our underway instructors, and while I was on the scope calling angles on the bow, reading the telemeter scale for the range, giving orders to the steersman for rudder and speed, whirling the ISWAS, and checking plot for the new course, the instructors would be making entries in their notebooks. After the approach, they'd compare my actions that were recorded in the Quartermaster's Notebook with their recommendations. Because they could concentrate solely on conning, they almost always arrived at better submarine maneuvers and more quickly."

Captain Morton paused, but only long enough to bring over a bottle of ale, and then continued.

"Now you're going to be my co-approach officer, not my assistant. You'll make all of the approach and attack periscope observations, or on the TBT if we're on the surface. I'll conn *Wahoo* to the best attack position, and then you'll fire the torpedoes."

He paused again, and his serious countenance changed to the usual engaging smile as he added, "This way I'll never get scared."

This opportunity and sharing of responsibility was new within our submarine forces. I answered with a simple, "I appreciate your confidence, Captain," and told him that I was off to the *Sperry* to make a lazy Susan for our ship models. I would need them to sharpen the ability to call angles on the bow quickly and accurately.

There'd be no fried oysters or tuna delight this evening, for we had all been invited to a New Year's Eve party. In anticipation, I had taken my shower on board after providing *Sperry*'s carpenter's mate with the azimuth circle from a mooring board plotting sheet. He would saw a wood circle to fit, with dowels to take our models, and pivot its center on a square fitted with a brass pointer. Back at the apartment, the captain had rated first call on the tub, and any others could look forward to a cold plunge. A leisurely bottle of ale got us on the road, and our hosts, in full Australian tradition, took on from there. Away from home and excited about my singular opportunities in *Wahoo,* my thoughts remained elsewhere. If I verged on being a wet blanket, however, the junior officers more than made up for it, since apparently the party had continued most of the night, maybe longer.

We had a leisurely breakfast aboard *Wahoo;* the phone would have buzzed to relay the word from *Sperry*'s bridge of any ship movements. All seemed to be quiet in the harbor, so willing hands from the relief crew manipulated the lazy Susan perched on the sideboard at the after end of the wardroom. Through one barrel of a pair of 7 × 35 binoculars inverted, I called angles from the pantry scuttle on a realistic target. In part to keep interest, but also to rest my eyes, we'd exchange places. It thus became a game of trying to beat me, and gave my assistants an appreciation of the task. They were at a disadvantage, for to the inexperienced, a half ship's length looks like a 60 to 70 degree angle, but it is only 30 degrees (the sine of 30 degrees is one-half).

The captain had not been idle, for the dehumidifier holding tanks had been replaced by personal lockers, and the ship close-ups were gone. Should a ship be that near, either she or *Wahoo* would already be on her way to Davy Jones's locker. In their place, one to each compartment, hands were placing page-size cards containing the statement by General McNair that had been met with violent objection by the clergy. The printing on the cards was similar to that on an ophthalmologist's chart to be read from across the compartment. None of our troops, who would return in a few days, could avoid these words:

WE MUST FIGHT
WE MUST SHOOT TO KILL
FOR OUR ENEMIES
HAVE POINTED THE WAY
TO SWIFTER SURER
CRUELER KILLING

There were still two vacant card holders in each compartment, three in the crew's mess, and I wondered what the skipper had in mind for them. I would preempt the one in the crew's mess that had the central location, for a photograph of Olivia de Havilland, autographed to the crew of USS *Wahoo,* with love, had come from home. Perhaps the skipper was saving the best for the last, but for sure, *Wahoo* was off on a broad reach.

At lunchtime on January 11, 1943, I was called to headquarters and shown a relayed message. On the previous day, a returning Australian bomber had observed a submarine attack on a small Japanese convoy and the following counterattack. After repeated depth charging, the submarine's bow had emerged at a sharp angle and was shelled until it disappeared. One destroyer-type ship had exploded; two other ships appeared to have been hit. It was sad news, especially for me, since the submarine had to be my dear *Argonaut,* and was made more difficult by her recent history.

Admiral Withers, ComSubPac, had been the only force commander to have all of his ships (not in upkeep) at sea or on war patrol at the time of Pearl Harbor. He had definite ideas concerning the use of the V-boats *Argonaut, Narwhal,* and *Nautilus* to raid the Japanese coastal installations: *Argonaut* to lay mine fields and then join the other two for bombardment with a combined firepower of a light cruiser and from a greater range. *Argonaut* could have done so, departing from Midway; it was the humidity from 50 days of all-day dives that caused her fires, and this wouldn't have happened in cruising to and from the Empire. The admiral insisted on this immediate use, but lost the argument and his job.

With new engines and air conditioning, *Argonaut* was even more capable to carry out her original missions as a minelayer and raider. But after the successful Makin raid, Admiral English visited her and agreed that her mine gear was much too noisy for use close to enemy shores, and authorized its removal to convert *Argonaut* to a Marine transport.

All of the years of work, the three consecutive 100% mine plants prior to Pearl Harbor, the official sound testing including one off Pearl Harbor in which her mine gear could not be heard by the listening barge with its sophisticated equipment just 200 yards away, had all been ignored or was unknown in making this snap judgment.

As it turned out, there was then no further use for *Argonaut,* and ending up in the South Pacific at Brisbane, she was finally allowed to go on antishipping patrol into the hot area south of Rabaul. If a fleet boat were stripped of one battery, two engines, six torpedo tubes, and could use no more than 15 degrees rudder, she would still have greater torpedo attack and evasion ability than *Argonaut.*

It was well that a ship was coming up the river to demand my attention, though the initial angles were difficult to see. But what better way could I add meaning to this loss than by sharpening any expertise brought from *Argonaut*. From the thought came dedication, and from the calendar, urgency, for in 6 days, *Wahoo* would be getting underway.

Sterling had come back a day early to get ahead on the paperwork, but inherited a short job from his new captain first—an armful of placards to be placed in the spare 8½-by-11-inch card holders in each compartment. Printed in the largest size block letters the cards would accommodate, and in bright red, they said:

S H O O T   T H E
S O N S   OF
B I T C H E S

And in case anyone didn't know what the spare card holders were for, the one in the crew's mess already had an autographed favorite pinup.

During the forenoon of January 13, our crew returned, some singly, others in groups, and many with pretty dolls to dockside. Avoiding the usual, and unnecessary mad rush to quarters was my contribution. *Grouper,* on leaving her area, had reported attacks but no sinkings, so most of the young ladies with tears would be smiling in about a week when *Grouper*'s crew relieved the watch.

An asset for *Wahoo* was the reporting of Ens. John S. Campbell, who had fleeted up from chief machinist's mate. Of medium size, with dark-brown hair, and still feeling his way, he would be our assistant engineer.

Serving at lunch were Manalesay and Jayson (pronounced Hisen), both MA1c (mess attendants first class). The change in our wardroom was heartening, perhaps best described as a combination of pleasant, proper etiquette, with an overriding camaraderie. Morton was the president of the mess and set an example by recognizing the junior officers, so they were no longer hesitant about entering into any of the conversations. Topped off with correct and polite service, *Wahoo* now had a wardroom mess to be proud of.

Loading for patrol continued, and so did my efforts at calling angles, with Jack assisting in the wardroom and Krause in the conning tower. This worked well, giving each time for their other tasks in communications and charts. Everyone was busy.

In the morning, the captain spoke briefly to all hands, stating simply that *Wahoo* was going to investigate every surface contact, and if it developed into a legitimate target, we would stay with her till she was on the way to the bottom. He said if there were any who didn't want to patrol that way they could report to Sterling, who would take care of their transfer without any aspersions whatsoever appearing in their record. This was what the crew wanted and Sterling had no takers.

Loading proceeded with such enthusiasm that the duty section could handily keep the schedule. So early liberty, helped by belated mail from home, eased the transition from friendly Australia. After the *Sperry*'s movies on January 15, I reported to the captain, "All hands are aboard and *Wahoo* ready for patrol, Sir."

Commencing my presailing turn through the boat, I found everything in order, with the Westinghouse washing machine quietly sloshing away, and waiting laundry bags stenciled by compartment. The detail seemed to be enjoying their task, and I could see that this would be a popular assignment on a stormy night. Completely satisfied, I turned in with a good feeling towards *Wahoo* and confident about the coming patrol.

2

The nest of submarines had breasted out from the tender to give *Wahoo* extra space for backing clear. Even then, our maneuver would have to be fast for the current would push the nest in quickly when the bulge of our hull ceased to act as a fulcrum. Any damage would be to the starboard propeller of the inboard boat, but it would be a rather inglorious departure for *Wahoo*. The lines were singled up, ready to be taken in by *Sperry*'s deckhands when the captain returned with the pilot. In his business suit, bowler, and with umbrella in hand, he looked more like an English businessman than a seafarer, but we were already aware of these pilots' skill. The diesels were rumbling quietly but impatiently when I reported our ship in all respects ready for getting underway. The brow had been snaked aboard the tender, and now most eyes topside were on Morton, who ordered, "Cast off all lines," for this would be his first actual maneuver before this crew. The captain was accustomed to maneuvering at New London, however, where the combined current of the Thames and the tide would exceed this and where the piers were perpendicular to the flow. I anticipated his action, but believe most others were taken by surprise when they heard a loud, "All back full."

Wahoo hesitated a moment, still held by the force of the submarines and the tender against the fenders like giant pliers. The wash from the screws boiled alongside our hull till it literally spread the jaws, and our ship shot out of the "V" as if from a catapult. "Port ahead two-thirds," and "Left twenty degrees rudder," started our turn out into the river; the current caught our bow, accelerating the turn. "Rudder amidships, Starboard ahead two-thirds, Steady as you go" pointed our bow between the channel markers, and the pilot, with a nod of approval, took over. If there were any in *Wahoo* who had thought their new captain's friendly manner was indicative of a carefree approach to seamanship, the last few minutes had squared that away. To me, it meant that he would not hesitate to use the 5 million watts at his disposal to close the enemy.

The captain had gone ahead standard, after a nod from the pilot, and turned the conn over to George. Morton would still remain responsible, intervening if necessary, but George would receive conning instructions directly from the pilot. Taking a lesson from our trip up the river, I would be advising the captain from a folded chart in hand on the bridge. Our position on this chart might not be quite as accurate as one plotted below, but it would be timely and of practical use. Again, we had to explain our action to the orders of "Right a spoke," or "Left a spoke," and I wondered if all wouldn't have gone just as well anyway, and if the pilots weren't just holding to salty sailing terms.

Now entering a wider part of the river, we could relax a little, and the pilot lighted a cigarette, though still keeping an eye aft at points lined up or in range. On the port hand were the cement works that I had noted 3 weeks ago, but now through 7 × 50s, I could see people wading, some of them seemingly chest deep. Curiosity got me; it was a quiet moment, so I asked the pilot what was going on over there. "Oh," he replied with some pride, "that's the city's sewage disposal plant, and they're gathering our fine oysters. Did you try them?" I may have gulped a bit, but answered that yes indeed I had, and that I had been brought up on the Oyster River in New Hampshire. It rather cemented a relationship, for he had been raised on an Oyster River in England. But hovering over all of this was the happy thought that my typhoid shots were up to date.

With the following current, *Wahoo* raced along the great, sweeping curves of the channel, while the pilot, already using his umbrella to ward off the summer sun, conned with "spokes" and an occasional, "Steady as she goes." From my plotting, he could not have done better had there been a white line. Thus at 1030, only 90 minutes after getting underway, we entered the upper reaches of Moreton Bay, now pronounced "Morton" Bay in *Wahoo*. The way ahead was clear, except for two shoal areas which the pilot indicated on my chart as he went below to enjoy some Navy coffee, perhaps more than I would now like his oysters.

Off in the distance lay the destroyer USS *Patterson*, with whom we would work this day in conducting underwater sound tests. These required the quiet waters of the bay, clear of the surf, and would be of mutual value in peaking our similar equipments. We would make the first run, and after laying down a track that would leave her 4,000 yards abeam, and observing Richie and the third section take over the watch, I took a quick turn below.

Lads were still gathered around reading the brief details of our operation order, though they must have been aware of its probable main features as soon as Krause had drawn the pertinent charts from the pool in *Sperry*. Perhaps it was the confirmation, or more likely the fact that they were allowed to read this confidential order; I liked Morton's approach to this—"All in the same boat, why not." It read in brief:

When in all respects ready for sea on or about 16 January proceed to Moreton Bay for sound tests and such other maneuvers as time permits during daylight.

When both ships are satisfied, proceed to sea in company and set course for the Palaus Islands via Vitiaz Straits.

Conduct DD-SS exercises along route as conditions permit until 1800 January 17, when PATTERSON will return.

Adjust speed, if possible, to permit daylight reconnaissance vicinity Wewak Harbor, New Guinea Lat 4°S-Long 144°E.

On crossing the equator, commence guarding Fox schedule and pass to control of ComSubPac without dispatch. Enter Palau Area 10E on January 30th or as soon thereafter as practicable.

There were amplifying instructions, but the meat of the whole order lay in the assigned area, for Palau was in reality the western terminus of the Carolines and, next to Truk, Japan's second bastion of the Pacific. But for the present my primary task was navigating, so after checking and initialling the menus that Sterling had typed for the captain's signature, I rejoined Krause in the conning tower. A bearing and range confirmed our position; *Patterson* would be abeam in another 15 minutes, and Richie called the captain as directed.

At the end of the first run, the captain took the conn and put his new ship through her paces as she opened the range: first working up to full power and then running the turbos to see if their constant stream of bubbles would lessen *Wahoo*'s skin resistance and give her extra speed. It did, a bit over a knot, and since the speed was checked by ranges on *Patterson,* who was subjected to the same current as *Wahoo,* the reading of 21 knots from plot and the Bendix log should be correct. As a double check, like the race drivers, we repeated the procedure on the return run with the same result. One knot wasn't much but it could count, and the troops knew it and loved it.

Patterson made her runs during lunchtime, and then we each conducted static listening tests of the other to see if any single piece of machinery could be heard outside of the pressure hull. It would be important for *Patterson* to know if an evading submarine might thus hear and track her when the destroyer was proceeding at dead slow speed, and for us when rigging for silent running on evasion. As expected, our dual-piston drain pump was our only real culprit, but other machinery, which we could hear within the boat, would also be secured, but more for reasons of saving juice and improving our listening capability than in any apprehension the enemy might hear it. By midafternoon all tests were completed, and since we had been working down the bay towards Cape Moreton, a 2-hour run brought *Wahoo* to the pilot boat. Our gentlemanly pilot walked across as if he were just stepping off a curb, and in company with *Patterson* we proceeded to sea.

The captain had taken a step in support of his exec by passing all appropriate instructions by me. The first administrative report that had bypassed me was firmly redirected, and he was otherwise helping to establish the authority and prestige that normally accrue to my office. By my unique assignment in *Wahoo*'s torpedo fire control, he had done even more. In this, I already had the confidence of my two assistants, Jack and Krause, but the proof would await the first ship.

Morton was not one to waste time. We had barely settled on my recommended course of 010 to pass well clear of Fraser Island when two blasts took us down. It was just the customary trim dive, but we also manned our battle stations as a warm-up for our night surface operations following the evening meal.

From dark to 2300, I manned the TBT, calling bearings on *Patterson,* first just a blurb out in the night, and then including angles as the range closed, giving her a distinct shape. Morton conned to the best firing position, and then I fired each simulated torpedo to hit a specific point on her side. It was his system, combining the best of the old and the new: the extra accuracy of instantaneous firing when the point of aim touches the steady vertical wire was maintained, and was combined with the accurate lead angle from the TDC's angle solver section. The mechanics of carrying this out were very simple. For the firings, I would announce, "Stand by for constant bearings," swing the vertical wire ahead of the desired impact point, and give a "Mark," leaving the wire absolutely steady. The TDC operator would set and hold that bearing constant in the computer, calling, "Set." When the impact point touched the wire, I barked, "Fire," and Krause hit the plunger on the firing panel. We had practiced and were able to get the succeeding Mark, Set, and Fire for additional torpedoes completed handily in the normal 5-second firing interval. This may have been the first time that Morton had seen his system actually work; he didn't say so, but expressed his approval with the thumb and index finger OK sign when I joined him in the wardroom after setting the course for the night. Cape Moreton light had dipped below the horizon just before I came below, giving a fair position, but stars would still be needed in the morning and I excused myself after a single game of cribbage.

The morning star fix, run ahead to our 0800 position, showed *Wahoo* already 200 miles along the line, and as is customary when cruising in company, we sent the latitude and longitude over to *Patterson*. During this second day of DD-SS training, the target ship would race ahead before the start of each run so the group could continue a good speed of advance. The more accurate angles one can call in daylight, combined with the captain's conning, brought our submarine to a favorable attack position on each approach. After a short break for lunch, Morton removed all restrictions; *Patterson* would now charge our periscope if she spotted it. She didn't until the last run, when the captain had me keep the scope raised. We then went through the down-the-throat procedure we had rehearsed orally in the wardroom, in which each would attack the other head-on. *Patterson* roared in; we simulated firing four torpedoes, then she swerved right and headed for the barn. We surfaced to receive her "Godspeed," put her astern, and headed for the Vitiaz Straits, the narrow passage between New Guinea and New Britain. Hunter pointed the Aldis lamp at *Patterson,* now little more than a blurb, and relayed our captain's oral message, "Thank-you and well-done." Out of the night came her receipt and instructions, all contained in the single, five-letter group, R S K U M. *Patterson* had been a whirlwind—no wonder she had been cited for her actions in the battles for Guadalcanal. We wondered if she might not think the same of *Wahoo*, for our DRI showed us already over 400 miles on the way to our patrol area, an unprecedented position for the close of training.

After the evening meal, our two mess attendants cleared the table quickly and spread the green poker cloth in seconds, as if they had grown up together. Actually, Manalesay was a Chamorro or Guamanian, while Jayson was a Filipino from the island of Cebu. They had a common bond, however, for they knew only that their homes had been overrun by the Japanese. Each of them had welcomed our captain's overture to come and fight the Japanese in *Wahoo*. Quiet, pleasant, and efficient, they were more than welcome.

We had finished a three-handed cribbage game and coffee when Krause appeared with the conning tower chart and instruments. We pushed the cards aside and gave attention to Morton's remarks. He looked over our situation, now clear of Fraser Island, and approved of the course change to 350 at midnight, as shown on the chart, and with *Wahoo* continuing at two-engine speed. Formally, he penned the instructions in his Night Orders book, a 5-by-8-inch hardbound, green cloth-covered notebook. In addition to the tactical instructions, he had written a caution to all hands, noting that we were on patrol, on our own, just as much as if we were in Empire waters, and for every watch to conduct itself accordingly.

3

Now on her own, *Wahoo* was on patrol. Chan and Jack, wearing red goggles, initialled the captain's Night Orders and proceeded to the bridge and conning tower. Whoever had the bridge would be the OOD; the assistant or AOOD in the conning tower would be the operations officer to interpret sound or radar, serve as assistant navigator, and take care of anything that would distract the OOD from his primary duties. Both men being thoroughly familiar with the status would permit the exchange of positions at any time—for putting on rain clothes, or getting a cup of hot coffee—without the distraction of a formal turnover.

There was now no such thing as an officer not qualified to stand a watch in *Wahoo,* and this, with the flexibility of our new OOD arrangement, was paying dividends this night: Upon surfacing in midafternoon, the exhaust valve on No. 2 main engine had been opened prematurely, before sufficient exhaust pressure had built up, so the seas had flooded some combustion chambers. Nothing can be built that's totally "sailorproof," though Fairbanks Morse engines came close, but not close enough. Water doesn't compress; something had to give, so the shear plate in the vertical shaft that connects the upper and lower crankshafts had carried away, just as it was supposed to do. George and his engineers were replacing the shear plate, but the shaft might be bent as well as their pride.

Our new captain had his submarine over a day's run ahead of schedule, the time he planned for the reconnaissance. It's the dream of any submarine skipper to have a ship down before reaching the patrol area, but the lack of one engine could spoil this chance for *Wahoo,* since we did have a deadline for reaching Palau. When I went back to the after room, the port engine was practically crawling with motor machinist's mates and machinist's mates. Chiefs Lenox, McGill, and Keeter had all attended school at Fairbanks Morse, and if it could be fixed at sea, they and their assistants could do it. I could add nothing to their efforts, and went forward with the knowledge that no single engine would ever receive greater attention. More than a matter of pride, it was for their new captain, with whom they enjoyed a unique relationship.

The evening Fox carried a message for *Wahoo* and *Grouper,* and now our coding board, composed of officers not on watch, ran it through the machine. Our submarines would pass tomorrow night, but considering our advanced position, that could mean tonight. We would not break radio silence to correct the situation, but in his Night Orders, Morton penned a caution to sight the *Grouper* first and take evasive action if our tracks were close. It was near dawn when her black shape and then thin silhouette came in view, giving our lookouts a realistic drill. Radar or not, they must sight another submarine before it reaches torpedo range, and this they did. Having an operations officer in the conning tower had made this possible, for George Misch had plotted her position by radar on our chart, and quietly informed the OOD, the captain, and me that *Grouper* would pass well clear. We exchanged recognition signals by Aldis lamp, and I wondered if she had intercepted the *Smoky Maru* that we had tracked towards her area. Of one thing there was no doubt; she would surely believe that the staff was sloppy in plotting positions.

With the new hands, and perhaps a bit rusty ourselves, we went through all of the emergency drills. As before, with seasoned hands to coach, the drills went well, but another round on another day would make each procedure automatic. We then conducted drills that were new in *Wahoo:* old-fashioned gunnery drills for the crews of our deck gun, the 20mm machine gun, and Browning automatic rifles. This was manning, loading, and pointer drill, not firing; that last would come when we spotted a suitable target.

George and his engineers were now ready to fire off their refurbished engine: The detached lube oil pumps had brought the pressure up to normal; the lever was thrown to admit high-pressure air from the starting bottles into four cylinders, and the engine started to roll. Then the starting lever admitted diesel fuel to the injectors of the other cylinders. They fired and then all cylinders fired; the customary blue smoke from the excess lube oil ceased, but a black smoke followed. The upper and lower crankshafts were slightly out of phase or the fuel injection was out of time, and our engineers rolled up their sleeves again.

Wahoo's progress through January 19 had been good, but not good enough to suit the captain, so after battery charging, the three good engines went on propulsion with the 500-kw diesel generator carrying the auxiliary load. En route south, no one had dreamed of suggesting ceremonies on crossing the equator. None the less, the whole crew considered themselves shellbacks. There were exceptions, the bona fide shellbacks, including me, who had been properly initiated. But we were in such minority that the despicable pollywogs scoffed at our threats. On the next morning trim dive, Morton privately passed the command to me, "temporarily," he said, and expected by none but the shellbacks, the ceremony commenced with the captain first to be initiated. Meekly, the pollywogs in the crew followed—how could they do otherwise?— but in truth, they loved the captain for it.

Back on the surface in a bit over an hour, *Wahoo* was on her way, and, counting the 4 knots while submerged, had dropped only 10 miles off her schedule. None of George's leading engineers would be needed, so we proceeded with another, and meaningful gunnery drill, the battle surface. First were the directions and then a dry run: The deck gun crew will man through the conning tower's after door, firing ready ammunition until otherwise supplied. The ammunition will be supplied through the mess-room hatch. We then went through the orders that they would hear addressed to the diving officer, who would be holding the boat at 64 feet: "Blow safety," and the diving officer would hold her down with planes and speed against the increasing buoyancy; "Battle surface," when the boat had started to rise; and then "Blow main ballast," and the diving officer would shift his planes to hard rise. *Wahoo* would almost bounce to the surface. The captain will then order, "Man your gun," and "Commence firing." When safe, you will hear, "Open the mess-room hatch," and the ammunition train will keep the supply moving. After the order, "Cease fire," you will be directed to strike ammunition below or to clear the deck.

The crews went through the procedure including casting the gun free and passing the ammunition, with the gun pointers getting some practice in chasing the horizon as we rolled in a modest sea. The next time, they could get their feet wet, for stepping out into ankle-deep sea is not unknown. When trained, the time from 64 feet to the first shot could be less than 2 minutes, so repeated drills would be needed.

The engineers were ready for another try by late afternoon, and this time there was no black smoke. The captain increased the load on three engines to 80/90, and the refurbished No. 2 engine continued to perform satisfactorily, but he was advised by Chief Lenox not to try more on this engine unless it was an emergency. Morton did him one better, deciding to leave well enough alone, for we could do everything planned with our other mains and the auxiliary.

4

By dawn, *Wahoo* had entered that "no-man's-sea" where she was fair game for friend or foe. Australian bombers could not identify us, nor could they afford to let a surfaced enemy submarine have a free passage. So, as always, we were responsible for our own safety, but also had the additional restriction of remaining submerged during daylight. Certainly, no one was going to check on us out here, and for practical reasons we could steal a couple of extra hours at dawn and before dusk since bombers couldn't be here. That meant an extra 40 miles a day towards possible shipping lanes, Wewak, and Palau.

In the between hours, we were trying out our new periscope search procedure and policy: After the initial all-around horizontal and elevated sweeps, the scope could remain up as long as someone was searching. This was practical, since a plane would be sighted while distant, long before it could disappear above the elevation of our scopes, and ships could be sighted earlier too. Further, unless conditions dictated against its use, a second scope clearly enhanced *Wahoo*'s chances of an early acquisition. To this, we would add periodic high-periscope searches as appropriate. So it was Simonetti on one of these searches who spotted some flotsam that included one large piece of wreckage as it raised atop the modest swell.

A suitable target was just what Roger, Richie, and Carr were hoping for. Morton ordered the word that went out over the 1MC, "Stand by for Battle Surface."

This was the crew's show in the firing of a converted four-pipe destroyer gun. Now I had spent 2½ years with these guns, two of them as gunnery officer and pointer on the officer's string on our cited "E" gun. So I had talked to Carr about the pointer's (elevation) cranking towards the horizon as the submarine rolled, and kicking off (firing) at the moment of steadiness at the top and bottom of each roll. Boatswain's Mate Rogers, my gun director and "E" gun pointer, had shown me, and I believe that alone had convinced Carr. With Richie, who would be spotting the shell splashes to hit, I had spoken of the "hecto-yard" method of spotting (leaving the zeros off), and saying simply, "Up-two," instead of the clumsy, "Up-two double-O." Then I mentioned the necessity of spotting down immediately till a short (splash) was seen, and then up to hit. This had been my total contribution.

The gun crews and ammunition train were lined up immediately, with the captain's specified ten rounds in their cans. To avoid a traffic jam, the 20mm crew would man through the conning tower. The procedure was followed precisely, with George giving at least three times the normal high-pressure blow, for using our screeching hyenas to bring the decks up from awash would have been too slow and would have blanked out orders to those below. *Wahoo* hit the surface on a nearly even keel and settled a bit, but with her decks above the sea. Roger was on the bridge with the captain who gave, "Commence Fire!" Richie would be spotting from the lookout platform, but otherwise, Gunner's Mate Carr was in complete charge.

I watched a creditable performance through the search periscope. The initial range came from Carter on the SJ; the pointer fired at the moment of steadiness; and Richie followed the spotting doctrine that we had discussed (he may have known it anyway). The vibration of the scope had steadied by the time the projectiles splashed in about 3 seconds, and I watched the large chunk of wreckage as it was reduced in size by at least three hits. The gun's trainer (in azimuth) had been on at the instant of firing too.

We closed the flotsam for the 20mm and Brownings' firing. Not to be outdone, they reduced the remaining chunk to the size of the other flotsam. The captain liked what he had seen; the crew loved it. Where had the men found time for the training that must have preceded this shoot? While I was calling angles seemed the only answer.

The guns were quickly secured and the brass cases, except for a couple that had been kicked over the side, were returned to their cans and struck below. The brass would be welcomed by the next tender or base foundry. In the security of night, the guns would be cleaned and greased. We would probably not be using our guns in this manner, but rather after considering a target from long range and then closing in cautiously. But this was one of the capabilities we might be called upon to use, and besides, it was a lot of fun.

Our evening star fix, plotted and run ahead to 2000, showed that we had dropped behind our DR position by a good 12 miles. We looked over the chart as usual in the wardroom, and rather than increasing speed, the captain decided on another 2-hour dash after dawn. The first hour passed; another hour would have us back on schedule, but we were now closing in on the enemy's flyways. Pappy cautioned each lookout, having them look at the chart on their way to the bridge. That view would impress them more than could any words. I was in the conning tower prior to the expected dive when the cry came from above, a blood curdling, "Clear the bridge! Clear the bridge!"

The diving alarm sounded; lookouts were tumbling below, while over the squawk box from control came, "SD contact 4 miles closing," and then, "It's a Mitsubishi bomber with its bomb bays open coming out of the sun."

I recognized Chief Lenox's voice, sometimes quite expressive, but this time it was straight from the shoulder. It was not of much help, for Wahoo was charging down as steeply as she ever had. Any larger angle would merely keep our stern closer to the surface longer, and our angle was increasing. At this, Morton, who had taken the conn, backed down—backing screws will always make a submarine squat— and ordered George to blow bow buoyancy. The trouble—our stern planes jammed on hard dive—had just been remedied by Chief Lenox, who pushed the circuit breaker's reset button. The planes shifted to rise with the combined effect of sending Wahoo into a sharp up angle. The backing screws would make that worse, so they were stopped, but our submarine charged on up and broached before submerging bodily like a foundering hulk. We had not forgotten about the bombs or depth charges that had been expected, so when broaching was imminent, the captain grabbed one scope and I the other. We searched around and up and down, but saw not a trace of the Mitsubishi.

We had done the unusual on this transit while neglecting fundamentals, so after Wahoo had settled down to periscope depth and was headed along our route, we spent the day in changing depth, shifting to hand on ship controls, and learning the location of the overload reset buttons. Instead of being perturbed, the captain learned them too, and so did I.

The Japanese undoubtedly had good charts of New Guinea's northeast

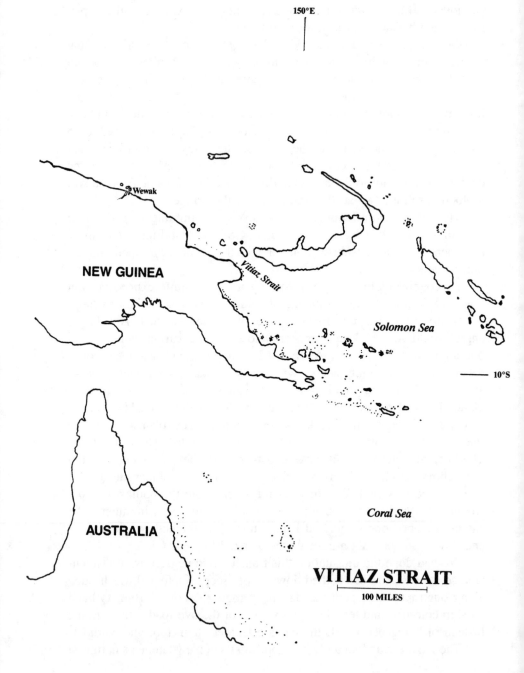

150°E

Wewak

NEW GUINEA

Vitiaz Strait

Solomon Sea

10°S

AUSTRALIA

Coral Sea

VITIAZ STRAIT

100 MILES

coast, but if so, they had not shared them with the rest of the world. Our chart simply showed a somewhat ragged coastline, with bays, islands, and reefs, without even the name Wewak appearing. Air reconnaissance had reported considerable shipping there and had provided the latitude and longitude of 4° south and 144° east. That might be all right for a view from the air, but a square 60 miles on a side, or even a circle with a 30-mile radius is hardly suitable for coastal piloting. The *Sailing Directions,* a series of books giving detailed information on most coasts and harbors, did little to locate Wewak; it just assumed that you had a suitable chart or wouldn't be at sea.

The captain was sitting down with Krause and me, while thumbing through the *Directions* for a possible clue, when Pappy Rau appeared at the wardroom's after door and reported that the crew had a possible solution. Specifically, it was Motor Machinist's Mate (MoMM1c) Dalton C. Keeter who might help, and Pappy ushered him in. In Keeter's hand was an Australian school atlas he had purchased to take home to his children. It contained a large, foldout map of northeastern Australia and southeastern New Guinea. There on the latter lay Wewak with good harbor and island outlines.

The outline of Wewak was much too small, but if we could draw an accurate enlargement, we might find where it fitted on our chart. George came to our rescue with his Graflex camera. We kept continuous tracings of our movements in patrol areas, so had the best tracing paper at hand. While Simonetti and Krause copied the map accurately, George set up his camera as a projector, pointing down between two separated wardroom table leaves. Raised by a book on either side, it focused perfectly on the deck as viewed on the ground glass. A careful tracing took less than an hour, and when taped in place of a film, with the Aldis lamp for light, they had a perfect projection. Hunter and Keeter shifted the chart around on the deck until they found the location, then George raised the camera with pages of two other books until the image was the right size. The lines of the projection were traced on the chart; *Wahoo* was in business, and all hands knew where she was heading.

At dawn of January 23, we were deep in the Solomon Sea and approaching the Vitiaz Strait. Off our starboard bow lay New Britain with its Japanese airfields only 30 miles away. Normal prudence called for submerged cruising, but the situation was not normal. We needed an extra 30 miles along our track for a full day's reconnaissance at Wewak. The captain's answer was two more lookouts, one of them with binoculars fitted with protective lenses, to guard in the vicinity of the sun. George had assumed the forenoon watch as usual, and after an hour sent for his sunglasses. Another hour passed, and *Wahoo* was now about 20 miles from the airfields. This time the request came down for his suntan lotion, and still we continued on. However, Morton checked the chart, and after another 15 minutes for insurance, called, "All right, George, you can go ahead and take her down now." Two blasts practically punctuated the captain's statement, and *Wahoo* slipped quietly under the sea.

Alerted as we were, there was no doubt that *Wahoo* could have dived before any plane could have attacked, and only the element of surprise for our coming operation was in jeopardy. However, such surface running was new to all of us, and we welcomed the security below.

5

The submerged run at 6 knots, followed by one and then three engines on surfacing, put *Wahoo* off Wewak at 0300, Sunday, January 24, one week after leaving *Patterson*. A half hour later, we dived 2½ miles north of Kairiru Island and proceeded around its western end to investigate Victoria Bay. Sufficient light for our periscope disclosed a small tug with a lighter alongside, and then smoke near the low rocks of the right-hand promontory at the entrance to the mile-wide bay. The tug had passed clear and I gave the scope to the captain.

"That's a Jap coast watcher cooking his breakfast on that rock," he announced, and then called Pappy up from below to take a look. Hunter raised the scope; Pappy grabbed the handles, took one look, and ordered, "Down scope!"

"Captain," he said, "that may look like a coast watcher to you, but it looks like two *Chidori*s to me!" We had seen these midsized antisubmarine destroyers in pictures only, but already in patrol reports they had gained a nasty reputation. It was not Pappy's good vision versus our poor; he had just remembered to twist the left handle shifting the scope to high power for his look—a bit embarrassing to both of us. The Bells of St. Mary's bonged throughout *Wahoo*.

At the captain's nod, I took the periscope for the following water-lapping angle calls as Morton conned *Wahoo* clear of their track. At the entrance to Victoria Bay, the *Chidori*s turned right towards the very position where *Wahoo* would have been had the captain not made our mad dash. Only then would the captain take the proffered scope to watch them go. I believed it was his way of showing confidence in me, and I would not let him down.

Chan had been cutting in our position regularly, leaving the bearing lines on the chart to identify the landmarks for our return. Buckley, on sound, had been providing bearings where swells rolled onto the beaches, and these too Chan plotted as we went around the southwest tip of Kairiru to observe the strait between this island and Mushu Island, a foul-weather anchorage. The final *u* was quickly removed from the latter island's name.

There were no ships in the anchorage, but the tops of a heavy tripod mast showed on or beyond Karsu Island at the other side of the anchorage. A tug or patrol prevented our direct investigation at the time, so Morton conned *Wahoo* westward, hoping to round still another island, Unei, which is connected to Karsu by a reef. That should let us observe the masts from the mainland side of these islands. Swells from the sea increased steadily, and after a half-hour's run I could see a reef with seas breaking over it that would completely block our way.

Another try through the anchorage seemed the only approach, and the captain reversed course slowly to help George, since depth control had become difficult in the swells. Chan's permanent marks on the chart received their first test and worked beautifully, both those on land and Buckley's on the beach, as we retraced our route. Back at the foul-weather anchorage, the tug or patrol had disappeared, which was good, but the heavy tripod masts were no longer in sight. We continued on, and in another mile forgot the masts when a distant object resembling the bridge structure of a ship came into the field of my scope. On the chart, the periscope bearing, converted to true, placed it in the bight of Mush Island, a good 5 miles farther into the harbor.

The time was 1318. We had been standing easy at battle stations, with normal meals for most having been served in groups as they could be spared. Rowls reported only a few stragglers at the mess tables, so they were given 20 minutes. In half that time all battle stations were reported manned.

Wahoo no longer had ready tubes with the attendant prolonged flooding of torpedoes. Instead, the torpedomen's watch schedule was so arranged that there would always be an available torpedoman in each room. So the captain simply ordered all tubes made ready for firing on what now appeared to be a tender with small ships alongside.

I continued to provide Chan with bearings of peaks and other promontories of the islands as he requested; Buckley gave bearings of the beach noises whenever they were prominent; and a glance at the track Chan had plotted was reassuring indeed. We would not leave a telltale periscope feather at our approach speed of 3 knots, but on each observation, water was lapping the lens of the scope.

As the range closed, the primary ship looked like a smaller warship with RO class submarines nested, resembling those with canvas hatch hoods and awnings that Lindhe had found in ONI-14 (Identification of Japanese Warships). Positive identification was not possible with our water-lapping observations, and neither was it necessary. We would sink them whatever they turned out to be.

The captain had selected a firing position 3,000 yards from the enemy. It would allow us to remain in deep water, which would help in clearing the area. Just prior to the next observation, Roger called the TDC's generated range of 3,750. That agreed closely with Chan's plot.

I called, "Destroyer underway, angle ten port." Hunter called the bearing and then the periscope stadimeter range, 3,000 using 90-foot masthead height, just as he had on *Patterson*. Could we possibly have been sighted? I thought not, but the captain had no option; he had to attack this destroyer lest his submarine be put in a deadly position. We commenced turning left when Buckley caught a probable zig by the temporarily muffled sound of the destroyer's screws. A water-lapping look: he was correct, and I called, "Starboard fifteen"; Morton ordered, "Shift the rudder"; and Simonetti reversed our swing, settling on the ordered course for a 110 track. The torpedoes would strike from 20 degrees abaft her starboard beam. From the second sound position, Carter's turn count on the destroyer's props (the rapid swish-swish-swish) converted to 13 knots on our tables, and this ratio should be comparable. Any correction would quickly be noted by the bearings of the destroyer's foremast that I was supplying.

All torpedo tube outer doors had been opened and 6-foot depth set. I wished only that there could have been more time for tracking.

"Any time, Dick." The captain's voice was firm and confident.

"Stand by for constant bearings," and Hunter raised the scope.

"Constant bearing–Mark!" Hunter read the bearing, 345.

"Set," came from Roger as he held that bearing constant on the TDC. The Mark had been on the after gun mount. My hands were removed from the steady scope. The impact point, her stern, was about to touch the wire.

"Fire," and Morton hit the firing plunger, instantly sending the torpedo on its way with a shudder, zing, and momentary poppet pressure.

Two more fish were on their way to hit amidships and under her bow, all in an elapsed time of 15 seconds. Buckley reported, "All hot, straight and normal," but I could see the faint, blue smoke of our last torpedo heading towards, not leading the enemy. They would all miss astern. We fired another torpedo with the destroyer's speed on the TDC increased to 18 knots, but now alerted, she turned away just in time to avoid it.

The destroyer continued her turn, completing three-quarters of a circle, and then headed down the still-visible fan that had been left by our torpedo wakes. Their apex marked our firing position, and the enemy would know that a submarine could not have traveled far.

"That's all right," said the captain. "Keep your scope up and we'll shoot that SOB down the throat."

For a fleeting moment, I thought of the prewar orders covering like situations. At this range, if the angle were 20° or less, we went deep and fired on sound information. But only a week ago, I had gone through this with the *Patterson,* except for the final shot. The requirements were quite simple: If the firing range were greater than 1,200 yards, the destroyer, on seeing the torpedo's wake, would have time to maneuver off its track. If the firing range were less than 700 yards, the destroyer would meet the torpedo before it had run far enough to arm. Presuming that the destroyer would be at 30 knots, she would traverse the 500-yard hitting space in 30 seconds. That is the total time we would have for our firing, but that should not be difficult; we had only two torpedoes.

I watched her come, already showing a white "V" bow wake, and marked bearings. Converting them to true, Morton instantly gave the new courses to Simonetti. In a minute, the destroyer was dead ahead and they kept her there. Now calling the scope's telemeter divisions from waterline to masthead, Chan converted them to ranges continuously. The "V" of her bow wake had now reached the anchors, while her image filled my lens. Shifting to low power to continue had an additional advantage: the smaller image of the destroyer was much less disturbing. I had to call no angles; they were all zero, and only an occasional bearing when the wire wandered off.

When Chan called 1,400 yards, the captain passed the conn to me. It consisted of coaching Simonetti with "Right a hair," or "Left a hair," to keep the periscope's steady wire bisecting the destroyer's bow.

Only seconds later, when the range was 1,250, the captain said confidently, "Any time, Dick."

I coached Simonetti with a "Left a hair," and then another. My wire steadied, dead center on her bow. "Fire!" and one-half my job was over. Continuing on the scope, I was barely aware of the pressure and shudder, nor heard the zing. Timewise, this torpedo could not hit before our last torpedo had been fired. The quiet seconds were still tense, but may have offered many the opportunity for a prayer.

Our last torpedo would not be fired until closing the minimum range, when the narrow destroyer would offer the widest target. The enemy was charging our scope; Chan called the ranges and I coached Simonetti. It was up to the three of us; no one else could help, except the captain with his confidence. Instantly, on the call of 850, came Morton's welcome "Any time, Dick."

I coached Simonetti twice, and then a third time. The captain became impatient, for after all, his was the total command responsibility. Mine was purely mechanical, to make this torpedo hit. I coached Simonetti again and the wire was steady-on. "Fire!" and we headed for the bottom, rigging for depth charge.

The range on firing had been 750, which was the best, especially since the time for our first torpedo to hit had now gone by. The props of our last torpedo had been blanked out by those of the destroyer, which were now roaring through our hull. There was no other noise, only her screws now menacingly close. We were passing 80 feet, and men commenced bracing themselves for the coming depth charges; though still confident, I chose the spot between the scope and the TDC.

The first depth charge was severe, but only to our nerves, and we braced ourselves in earnest for the pattern that would follow. A mighty roar and cracking, as if we were in the very middle of a lightning storm, shook *Wahoo*. The great cracking became crackling, and every old salt aboard knew the sound—that of steam heating a bucket of water, but here amplified a million times. The destroyer's boilers were belching steam into the sea.

"We hit the son of a bitch!" rang out in unison from the whole fire control party, and doubtless throughout the boat. Never could apprehension and despair have changed to elation more abruptly. Already, George had an up angle on the boat in anticipation of the captain's order, and with speed to help, had *Wahoo* back at periscope depth.

There was our destroyer, broken just forward of the stack, with the bow section canted down into the sea. Her crew, in whites, were climbing the masts and onto the top of the gun mounts in anticipation of another torpedo. Our captain gave higher priority to *Wahoo*'s camera bugs, and for every official picture with the Kodak Medalist through our scope, our troops took at least ten snapshots, and this included George with his Graflex.

The destroyer's bow was now deeper under water, and it appeared that she would sink, at least half of her anyway. The rest wasn't going anywhere in this war. Six torpedoes were enough; we could use the seventh for another ship, and besides, we faced the problem of getting to sea, all below periscope depth, and 9 miles away.

6

Using the notations he had made on the chart and my bearings, Chan fixed *Wahoo*'s position and Hunter lowered the scope for what we hoped would be the last time in Wewak. A single sounding showed a surprising depth of 150 feet, so the captain ordered 100 feet for our exit. At that keel depth, *Wahoo* would have maneuvering room, and touching bottom down there would not push our bow above the surface. Chan remained on plot; he knew his own markings, the ones from my periscope as differentiated from Buckley's, and the scratchings that noted varying intensity of beach noises.

We moved with careful dead reckoning at a steady 3 knots, and though I was responsible, primarily my part was only to advise a little more clearance when beach noises seemed too loud. Chan was able to advise Buckley where to search next, and sometimes Buckley would have the sounds first. They did a masterful job, and I was always able to inform the captain with confidence. It was 1900 when all beach and surf noises were abaft our beam, but the captain decided on another half-hour run to seaward as insurance.

Carter had taken over sound and made a careful sweep around before we returned to periscope depth. It was too dark for all but our search scope, and even with that I could see only indistinguishable lights astern. But that is what Morton wanted, and three blasts sent us to the surface into God's clean air. It has a fragrance, but it takes a day submerged in a submarine before that can be appreciated. Four engines were rumbling and in minutes would take over the load from our battery, which was driving *Wahoo* to the north. Back on our port quarter were huge fires about the harbor, probably lighted to silhouette that submarine, should she try to escape.

All remained clear on the SJ, especially astern, so after a half-hour dash we slowed to our usual two-engine cruising speed. Not much out of our way to Palau lay the pass between Aua and Wuvulu Islands. Convoys had been sighted there, so the captain ordered a base course through the pass, with searches to port and starboard. Starting with a half-hour run 30 degrees to the left, and then hourly legs crossing the base course, would reduce our advance by only 10%, and with the SJ searching would intercept any shipping on at least a 30-mile front. I was heading to the conning tower to lay down the track when Morton interceded, saying, "George, you take over navigation for a day, and Dick, you hit your bunk."

It was an order, but I offered two modifications: a game of cribbage first, and that Krause be relieved of duties too. In the excitement we had not particularly noticed it, but we had not turned in for 35 hours.

George and Hunter had quick verification of their morning star fix, for the duty chief's messenger reported islands in sight to port and starboard. Louder sea noises, beyond the hull and ballast tanks, told that *Wahoo* had increased speed in accordance with the captain's Night Orders. That would include a change in the base course too. Properly, a report of the change was made to me as well as to the captain across the passageway—my days of being the last to know were over.

The next report, a sighting, called me to the bridge. It was 0800, and our zigzag course had brought *Wahoo* to a sampan. Becalmed, the crew tried to row away, but a burst from Carr's tommy gun across her bow brought the sampan alongside. The crew of six looked half-starved, and one of them appeared to be blind. Jayson and Manalesay tried to converse with them, but did little better than had Roger. However, the three of them, mostly by sign language, learned that originally there had been nine, all of them fleeing from the Japanese. Three had died; another was sick; and a third, we could all see, had apparent scurvy sores. Our crew pitched up oranges, fresh and canned food, part of our day's supply of bread, and filled their water breakers. Just in time came Krause's penciled chart to go with a can opener, and we sent them on their way with a wave and a prayer.

Wahoo went on her way too, searching continuously with normal lookouts, and raised periscopes to extend our coverage. Those on the scopes were volunteers, many of them engineers and just as capable as those with experience. It was a matter of motivation, and they had shown that by their presence.

A turn through *Wahoo* in late afternoon showed a changed ship's company. Men were scrubbing up and shaving prior to the evening meal. Others were using the showers—wet down, soap up, rinse off—and those already heading for the mess room wore clean dungarees and freshly laundered skivvy shirts. Morton had been brought up to believe, as had I, that cleanliness is next to godliness. It had taken only a word to Pappy Rau, for after the experience on two patrols, this was a privilege, rather than a requirement.

Continuing aft I received many thumb-to-finger OK signs, though understandably some might be wondering just what was coming next. They were not alone. In the after torpedo room, the senior torpedoman's mate, Johnson, with McSpadden, had withdrawn one of the fish from its tube. This would be done one at a time, and checked by them and Roger. Especially after yesterday, they would not take the chance of a torpedo failure due to a flooded after-body. I liked what I had seen coming aft, including the traditional eyes painted on the torpedo's war-head. On leaving, I gave my assurance that, if possible, their torpedoes would be fired next. There is always great competition between torpedo rooms, and that adds its bit to torpedo performance. While proceeding to the bridge for evening stars, I experienced for the first time a truly warm, confident feeling for our submarine and her future.

The authorities had been concerned about maintaining our physical fitness while on patrol, so they provided us with sunlamps and rowing machines. These probably caused more harm than good, however, since without stowage space they were prone to trip anyone moving in the semidarkness. Empty torpedo skids had provided a stowage space, but at the expense of a crewman and his bunk. The crewmen won, with some of the machines slipped over the side, though many of the devices made it to the tender or base.

Now, some old salts who had never had to cope with the necessity of taking star sights without a twilight horizon presumed that it could not be done. Probably because of her catchy name, *Wahoo* was selected to try out the latest developments in aircraft bubble sextants. In them, a tiny, illuminated bubble will ride in the center of concentric circles when the sextant is absolutely level. The aircraft navigator asks the pilot to hold her steady and he gets his sights, which will give a triangle about 15 miles on a side. But the only moment of steadiness on a ship at sea comes at the end of each roll, and that doesn't include pitch. Taking the sight at that exact moment, and having the bubble centered too, took some doing. After our normal stars, Krause and I struggled with the bubble sextant, and finally had five more sights to work out and plot. We had plotted the fix from our own stars, and put off the Navy Department's until after breakfast. But George's voice bellowed from the control room speaker, "Smoke on the horizon, broad on the port bow!"

The time was 0757, this Tuesday, January 26, and the Bells of St. Mary's rang out in earnest for the second time on this startling patrol. The next puff of smoke was farther to the right, and the captain had *Wahoo* boiling through the seas to reach a position well ahead of the enemy. Topmasts poked over the horizon, their separation indicating a fairly broad angle on the bow, not over 50 degrees. In minutes, Hunter, hanging from the rungs halfway up the shears, reported two more masts similarly separated and confirming the angle. I went to the conning tower to search with the scope. It disclosed nothing more than Hunter had reported, which was good, for missing were the expected thin masts of an escort. *Wahoo* continued racing for a position ahead, and closer to the enemy's track, which Chan had plotted on the conning tower chart. At 0845, nearly an hour after the sighting, our skipper was satisfied, and two blasts sent *Wahoo* under the seas. Only a change in the convoy's base course could save it, and I was glad that Jack and Krause had continued working on angles with me.

Submerged, we went through the sighting of smoke and masts all over again, but once sighted, the ships came on quickly. First, angles on the bow and then estimated ranges flowed to plot and TDC, all on the leading ship to avoid confusion. Roger and Chan had the convoy's base course as 095 steaming at 10 knots. This was a bit puzzling since it led to no known port. However, this fact and the continued absence of any escort could mean that the destroyer we had sunk had been on her way to meet these ships, and that they had been rerouted on a circuitous course bypassing Wewak. If so, it was the captain's ordered search to each side of our base course to Palau that had found them.

The analysis had taken only a minute or so, and gave us confidence that the convoy would continue zigging along Chan's projected track

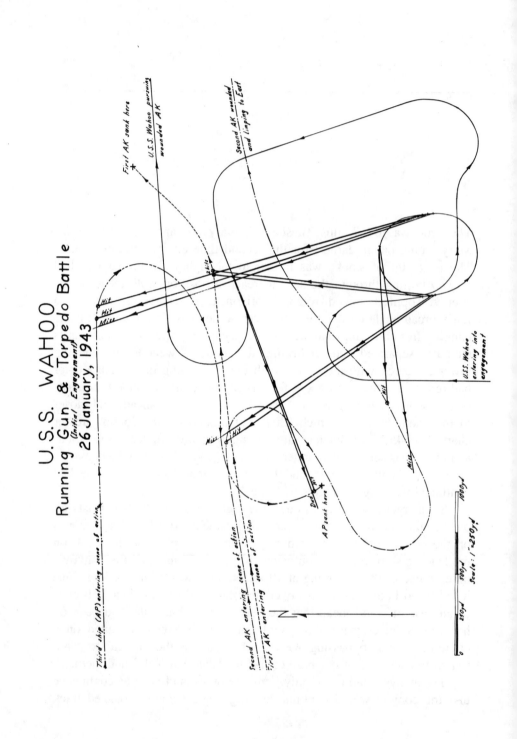

U.S.S. WAHOO
Running Gun & Torpedo Battle
(Initial Engagement)
26 January, 1943

Third ship (AP) entering scene of action

First AK sank here

U.S.S. Wahoo pursuing wounded AK

Second AK wounded and limping to East

Hit
Hit
Miss

2 hits

Second AK entering scene of action

First AK entering scene of action

Miss   Hit

Miss

Dud Hit

AP sank here

Hit

Miss

U.S.S. Wahoo entering into engagement

N

0   250 yd   500 yd   1000 yd
Scale : 1" = 250 yd

that he had run ahead on the chart. All tubes had been made ready before we slowed for the next observation. Our submerged speed of 5 knots had nearly kept pace with the convoy, for *Wahoo*'s run to the point where our respective tracks would intercept was only half that of the enemy's. Considering that the last half mile or less would be accomplished by our torpedoes at nearly 47 knots, this coming attack seemed to be in the bag.

The leading ship's superstructure was now in sight, so stadimeter ranges followed angles on the bow. After the scope was lowered, I described to Lindhe, at hatch level, the details of the ship: mast; tall bridge structure; tall, straight stack with superstructure behind; another mast; and poopdeck structure. That should narrow the ship to a class, and next time I would supply more.

The captain was now conning his boat to a position 1,300 yards on the leading ship's beam at our previous approach speed. Buckley had reported a 60 turn count while we were at 3 knots, and could now hear the beat through our own screws. There was no change, and we slowed again for what could be the next-to-final look. Simonetti called 3 knots; Hunter raised the scope; and I reported a zig towards, with the angle sharpened to 40 starboard. The range was 1,200, and the captain had

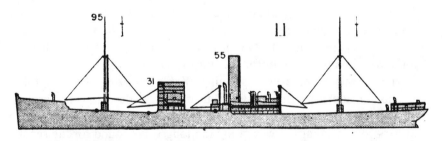

ALASKA MARU
ATLAS MARU, DAKAR MARU, DELAGOA MARU, DURBAN MARU

Tonnages:		Constructed:	
Gross: 7,148–7,378	D. W.: 10,560–10,916	1919–20	Japan
		Propulsion:	
Length:		Machinery:	Reciprocating
W. L. (B. P.): 420′	O. A.:	Screws: 1	N. H. P.: 574 I. H. P.: 3,100
Beam: 56′		R. P. M.: 60	@ Knots: 11
Drafts:		R. P. M.: 80	@ Knots: 15.2 (test)
Loaded: 28′	Light: 9′	Fuel: Coal and oil	Capacity: 2,600 tons of coal; 2,350 tons of oil
Speed:			
Normal cruising: 12	Max.: 14½	Radius: 18,000 miles at 12 knots	

Potential naval value: AP, AK.
Remarks:

already called for full speed and right full rudder. *Wahoo* would have been too close, resulting in excessive gyro angles and poor tracks. To Lindhe, I reported her plumb bow. We had a *Dakar Maru* class freighter.

Wahoo was turning in the direction of the convoy's advance to gain time and would continue diagonally away at convoy speed to the originally planned position. Almost prophetically, the after torpedo room was now opening their torpedo tube's outer doors. Morton was watching the tactical development with Roger on the TDC, and ordered one-third speed as we approached the firing position. Simonetti called our speed at each knot, now five, then four. Hunter brought the scope to my crouched eye level and followed me up about another foot.

"Bearing–Mark." Hunter read 175; the leading ship was crossing our stern broadside to us. "Any time," said the captain.

"Constant bearing–Mark." Hunter read 179.

"Set," came from Roger. Her mainmast was about to touch the wire.

"Fire!"

The second torpedo was marked and fired to hit under her foremast. We shifted immediately to the trailing ship, and with identical procedure sent torpedoes to hit under her masts. The time was 1040.

A reassuring report from Buckley—"All hot, straight and normal"— was punctuated twice by torpedo hits in the leading ship, but only once in the trailer. A glance at the quartermaster's log showed why: Only 17 seconds had separated the two firings, and the gyro setting mechanism hadn't had time to catch up for the third torpedo.

The captain commenced swinging *Wahoo* to bring our bow tubes on, and I made a periscope sweep to check on our targets. The first freighter was listing and sinking. In the confusion of both submarine and periscope's swings, I was going the long way around for the second freighter, but she came in view, big and fat.

"You're on the wrong bearing," advised Morton.

"That may be, but I've got a big one coming at us with a zero angle!"

"That's all right, we'll shoot the SOB down the throat," he said.

I had hoped never to hear those words again, much less in just 3 days. Now on the firing line in rifle practice, you never say shoot or fire unless you mean it. Krause and I had practiced my sharp bark when I said, "Fire," and his hitting the firing plunger; soon it had become instantaneous. It was instantaneous on the captain's, "Shoot," too, and Krause had his own $6,000 torpedo charging out into the South Pacific.

I watched the torpedo's wake leading straight away from our bow's position at the instant of Krause's firing. It was missing the ship so far that her skipper would be laughing if he even saw the wake. But wait— the ship apparently had seen it, but it was so far out they couldn't tell if it was coming or going. She was doing the safe thing, turning right to get the hell out of there, and would pass nicely within torpedo range. Buckley and Carter were reporting propellers ahead and to port, so after a single setup for Roger and Chan on Krause's ship, I continued the sweep around. The first freighter was about to sink, but the second ship was heading toward us, though not dangerously close.

Back to the ship at hand, now presenting a broad angle, I could see that she was worth the other two put together, for we had a large passenger freighter or transport in our grasp. I called her angle port 70, and Hunter read 1,800 yards. Plotted on her true bearing, she was still making the convoy's speed of 10 knots. The captain was satisfied and at 1047, we fired Krause's two companion torpedoes, one to hit under her foremast and the other under her main.

Buckley was keeping us posted on the torpedoes, both running hot, straight and normal, for our attention had now shifted to the second freighter. Though showing no bow wake, she was menacingly close, and had probably spotted my scope on the last firing. Buckley had our torpedoes' props blending with those of the transport, and the captain called for two torpedoes down the throat of the menacing freighter. The firing was momentarily delayed by the welcome "whack and thunder" of our two fish as they hit the transport, but then proceeding with the down-the-throaters seemed almost routine. It was probably the contrast, for the freighter was closing at no more than 6 knots and her beam was a good four times that of the destroyer. We went through the procedure precisely, and at 1053, *Wahoo* had two torpedoes on their way. Carter reported the thud of the first torpedo's hitting, but there was no detonation. The second fish announced herself with a tremendous explosion, but the freighter just shuddered a bit and kept on coming.

For the first time since Wewak, *Wahoo* was on the defensive, and the captain ordered 100 feet. George took us down, while our skipper maneuvered at full speed to get out from under the freighter's possible positions, lest she carried defensive depth charges. That was Morton—

be on the offensive or defensive, never in between. But that didn't include standing easy at battle stations till the situation above became clear. It took Buckley 8 minutes to sort the ships out, and that gave enough time for hands from battle stations to bring back coffee and the sandwiches Rowls and Phillips had prepared. Without request, Jayson and Manalesay took care of us, and *Wahoo* headed up ready to shoot.

A periscope sweep showed the freighter on our port quarter, heading away, and the transport about 2 miles ahead, apparently dead in the water. Our first freighter had now gone, and her turbulent sinking had caused some of the noises so confusing to Buckley and Carter. There was nothing confusing about our next target, and the captain increased speed to close the transport. A series of true bearings on her stack did not change; she was a sitting duck, and we maneuvered for a precise shot at her vitals. She was putting up a fight by shooting at my periscope, and I found myself ducking when the small-caliber shell splashed close ahead, since mentally my eye was at sea level. At 1133, after the captain's "Any time," I called, "Fire." This time, it was the captain who hit the plunger.

The torpedo's wake streaked towards the point of aim, amidships. It hit in 45 seconds, but there was no explosion. A second torpedo, with an identical depth setting of 8 feet, followed. Its track jogged a bit to the left and then settled down towards a point halfway between her stack and bridge. The fire control party was cheering it on, as if it were a horse with their money on its nose. It was more than that: American lives could be riding on the result. This torpedo did not fail. Pappy on the search scope and I on the attack both watched a tremendous explosion blow the structures aft of her bridge higher than a kite. Momentarily we saw a gigantic hole in her side bigger than a Mack truck, until she listed towards us.

Immediately, Morton headed for the crippled freighter, the second ship attacked with a single hit, and as soon as we had steadied, the camera bugs took over the search scope. The transport was launching boats, and troops were jumping over the side as she settled forward. We would not need Lindhe's identification, a *Seiwa Maru* class transport, but it would be good for the patrol report.

In a surface chase, with about a 3-knot differential, a stern chase is a long chase, for you are closing at the speed of a walk. Submerged, with little more than a knot's advantage, our prospects did not look good. We were taking cautious observations so as not to have our scope

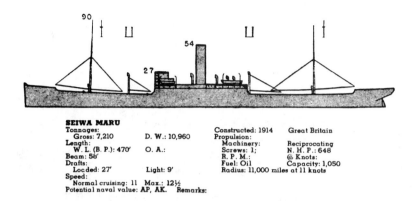

SEIWA MARU

Tonnages:		Constructed: 1914	Great Britain
Gross: 7,210	D. W.: 10,960	Propulsion:	
Length:		Machinery:	Reciprocating
W. L. (B. P.): 470′	O. A.:	Screws: 1;	N. H. P.: 648
Beam: 58′		R. P. M.:	@ Knots:
Drafts:		Fuel: Oil	Capacity: 1,050
Loaded: 27′	Light: 9′	Radius: 11,000 miles at 11 knots	
Speed:			
Normal cruising: 11	Max.: 12½		
Potential naval value: **AP, AK.**	**Remarks:**		

sighted, but frankly, it would not have made any difference. Having seen her two companion ships head for Davy Jones's locker, she would know that her turn was next. Her engineers were undoubtedly doing their damndest to get more turns on her screws. The stadimeter range remained steady and then started opening slowly. To add to that, Chief Pruett came waist-high into the conning tower to report that both batteries' pilot cells were down to 1,060. Though with that specific gravity we could cruise at 3 knots, *Wahoo* was no longer capable of the high speed that could be required in an approach and the following evasion.

It was time to charge *Wahoo*'s batteries and our own, for after all, we had been making approaches and attacks since breakfast, and it was now past noon. The freighter called a break for us by managing to put another boiler on the line, and slowly increased speed to her original 10 knots. George Misch manned the search scope in tracking her, and Hunter passed the bearings to Chan. We would plot this ship's track for later pursuit. To our surprise, George reported another ship coming over the far horizon and closing the freighter. The new ship's thick masts, almost in line, made her look like a warship. She could be coming to the rescue of the Japanese troops, and if so we were already in an intercepting position. But the ship turned right, joining the freighter, and displaying a large stack aft. She was a tanker, and we still had torpedoes for both of them. As they headed north, I was able to provide Lindhe with the final details he needed to identify the freighter's class. He had already recorded her plumb bow, the old-fashioned counter stern with structure above the poop deck, and exceptionally tall midships stack. I was able to add a forward king post, another in her forward

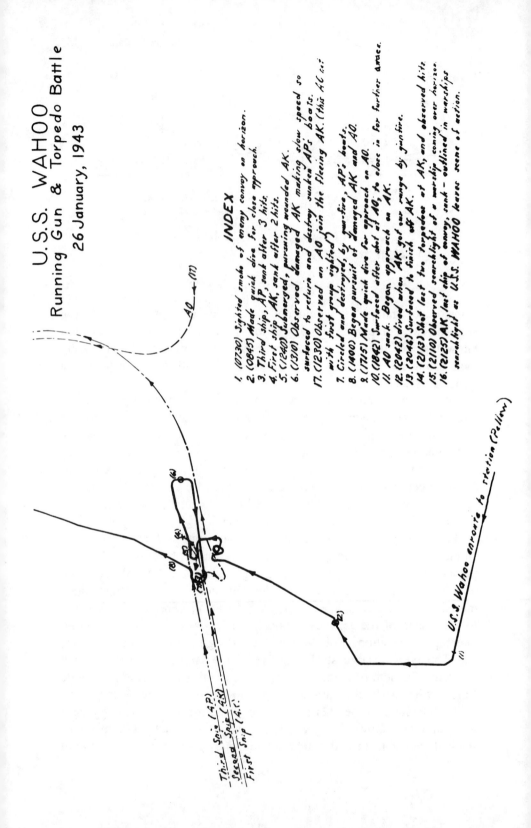

U.S.S. WAHOO
Running Gun & Torpedo Battle
26 January, 1943

AO → (17)

INDEX

1. (0730) Sighted smoke of many convoy on horizon.
2. (0845) Made quick dive for close approach.
3. Third ship, AP, sank after 3 hits.
4. First ship, AK, sank after 2 hits.
5. (1240) Submerged, pursuing wounded AK.
6. (1310) Observed damaged AK making slow speed so surfaced to return and destroy sunken AP's boats.
17. (1230) Observed an AO join the fleeing AK. (this AO in with first group sighted.)
7. Circled and destroyed by gunfire, AP's boats.
8. (1400) Began pursuit of damaged AK and AO.
9. (1715) Made quick dive for approach on AO.
10. (1842) Surfaced after shot of AO, to close in for further attack.
11. AO sank. Began approach on AK.
12. (2042) dived when AK got our range by gunfire.
13. (2046) Surfaced to finish off AK.
14. (2113) Shot last two torpedoes at AK, and observed hits.
15. (2110) Observed searchlight of a warship, coming over horizon.
16. (2125) AK, last ship of convoy, sank — outlined in warships searchlight as U.S.S. WAHOO leaves scene of action.

Third Ship (AP) ————
Second Ship (AO) —·—·—
First Ship (AK) ——··——··

U.S.S. Wahoo enroute to station (Pallaw)

and after well decks, and a small mast between her bridge and stack. Within minutes, the party had settled on the *Arizona Maru* of 9,684 tons, a larger ship, but not as important as the transport with her troops.

Rowls's noon meal was served as usual, with those not at a sitting remaining at their battle stations. With enemy ships in view, the crew would not have wanted it otherwise. But now, with only mastheads in sight, the captain ordered, "Secure from battle stations and prepare to surface." Five minutes later, at 1310, three blasts sent *Wahoo* up to a quiet, empty sea. Our three good engines all went on charge while the turbos were bringing our submarine up to cruising trim; then one main engine went on propulsion to take us back to the scene of the transport's sinking. It would be over a 6-mile run and, at our present speed of 9 knots, would require more than 40 minutes. That was too much time, and Morton ordered another engine on propulsion at about 15 minutes into the run.

When about 3 miles off, we could see a minimum of twenty boats loaded with Japanese troops, the craft ranging in size from scows to a small cabin cruiser. In a serious, considered tone, the captain ordered, "Battle stations. Man both guns." Morton must have seen my questioning expression, for "Dick," he said, "the army bombards strategic areas, and the air corps uses area-bombing so the ground forces can advance. Both bring civilian casualties. Now without other casualties, I will prevent these soldiers from getting ashore, for every one who does can mean an American life."

He was, of course, correct and had no option. To do otherwise, with islands and the coast of New Guinea within reach to the southwest, would be aiding and abetting the enemy, a court-martial offense.

With Roger, Richie, Jack, and the gun captains assembled, Morton gave explicit instructions. "I'll order a single four-inch round at the largest craft, and we'll continue in to see if we draw any return fire. Keep your crews in any protected area until I order commence firing. Machine guns, it'll be your job to chase the troops out of their boats, and Chief Carr [speaking directly to the four-inch deck gun captain] you smash up the boats. There's only time for a single pass, so use maximum rate of fire." Besides the deck gun, we had one 20mm machine gun and two Browning automatic rifles; all were manned and ready.

The single four-inch deck gun round splashed just short of the largest craft, probably ricocheting through it. All of the troops seemed to have dived into the sea, but about 2 minutes later, the craft returned a long burst from a machine gun. Immediately Captain Morton ordered, "Commence fire!" The time calculated from surfacing (at 1310) was 1342.

Wahoo's fire, all to starboard, was methodical, the small guns sweeping from abeam forward like fire hoses cleaning a street. The Japanese troops, in khaki with shorts and all wearing life jackets, sought safety in the sea as the deck gun demolished their boats, pausing only once when Carr fired his 45 toward a nearby Japanese soldier who was about to lob an apparent hand grenade toward the gun crew; both missed. Not seeing the reason, Captain Morton gave a sharp, "Knock it off, Carr!" Some Japanese troops were undoubtedly hit during this action, but no individual was deliberately shot in the boats or in the sea. The boats were nothing more than flotsam by the time our submarine had completed a broad half circle and Morton ordered, "Cease fire!" before 1400 as seen on the chart.

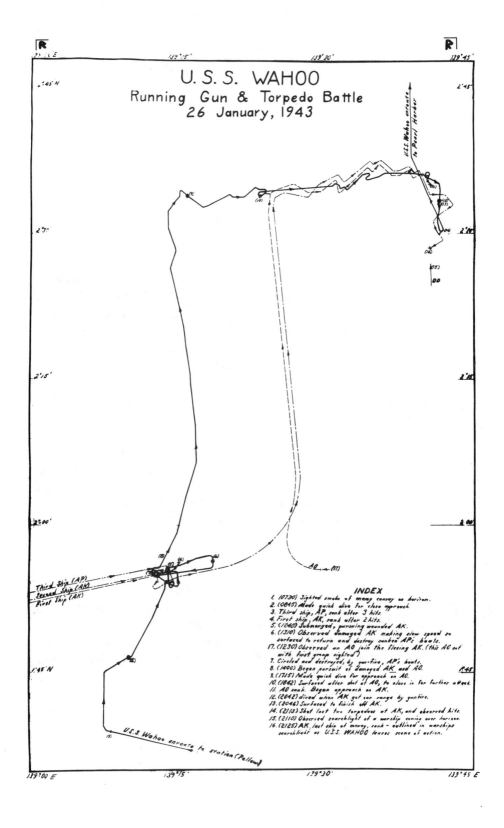

U.S.S. WAHOO
Running Gun & Torpedo Battle
26 January, 1943

INDEX

1. (0730) Sighted smoke of enemy convoy on horizon.
2. (0845) Made quick dive for close approach.
3. Third ship, AP, sank after 3 hits.
4. First ship, AK, sank after 2 hits.
5. (1240) Submerged, pursuing wounded AK.
6. (1310) Observed damaged AK making slow speed so surfaced to return and destroy sunken APs boats.
17. (1230) Observed an AO join the fleeing AK. (this AO set out with first group sighted)
7. Circled and destroyed, by gun-fire, APs boats.
8. (1400) Began pursuit of damaged AK and AO.
9. (1715) Made quick dive for approach on AO.
10. (1842) Surfaced after shot at AO, to close in for further attack.
11. AO sank. Began approach on AK.
12. (2042) dived when AK got our range by gunfire.
13. (2046) Surfaced to finish off AK.
14. (2113) Shot last two torpedoes at AK, and observed hits.
15. (2110) Observed searchlight of a warship coming over horizon.
16. (2125) AK, last ship of convoy, sank – outlined in warships searchlight as U.S.S. WAHOO leaves scene of action.

Third Ship (AP)
Second Ship (AK)
First Ship (AK)

AO

U.S.S. Wahoo enroute to Pearl Harbor

U.S.S. Wahoo enroute to station (Palliau)

8

Our course was 025 to regain contact with the enemy, even though we had seen the two ships heading due north. If we had headed farther northward to intercept them, and they had resumed an easterly course, we could miss them altogether. On 025, our flank speed would reach a position where their tops would still be in sight no matter what course they had steered. It was another example of basing your strategy or tactics on enemy capabilities, not intentions.

Below, Lindhe and George were taking care of our two casualties, which had only momentarily affected *Wahoo*'s gunfire. The piping hot, 20mm gun barrel had jammed and was quickly replaced by a spare. About a minute later, the projectile exploded, blowing the cartridge out the breach, and igniting the powder. Fireman Glinski, who was making his first patrol, suffered two mangled toes from fragments of the cartridge case, and Torpedoman's Mate Tyler received a piece embedded in his shoulder. Both of them and Doc Lindhe, who had been standing by, had some powder burns.

The doctors had succeeded in keeping any operating instruments off our allowance lists, though our grand senior pharmacists, I believe, were on a par with many hometown doctors of a generation ago, and right up to date in medical reading. The lack of one instrument was solved by Motor Machinist's Mate Chisholm, *Wahoo*'s new auxiliary-man, who produced a brand-new pair of wire side cutters from his toolbox in the pump room. Rowls boiled them along with a suitable knife. After a numbing shot, Lindhe removed the remnants of the dangling second toe, but decided that the third toe might be saved. Sutured, splinted, and well doused with sulfa powder, Glinski's foot gave the impression that a major operation had been performed. Tyler, looking on, had not been forgotten. The dark outline of the fragment, or at least the blood, could be seen, but lacking instruments, its removal would await Pearl, especially since we had targets for our remaining torpedoes just over the horizon, and *Wahoo* could almost certainly check Palau off her list. A padding to prevent bumping the wound and a sling to reduce mobility were Tyler's badge of combat.

Volunteers were in line for a turn at the scopes, and Fireman Whipp reported smoke from the fleeing ships at 1530. The single puff was on our port bow, and we changed course to intercept. In minutes we had mastheads indicating their course of north. We had intercepted the enemy the long but sure way and had ample daylight hours to gain an attack position.

Morton conned his submarine parallel to the enemy's track on courses I provided from the mooring board plotting sheet. My information came from Chan on the search scope and we would alter positions. Backing us up was George Misch, perched like King Kong atop the shears. The courses would keep us just beyond the enemy's horizon—unless George should stand up—giving *Wahoo* a tremendous advantage. Roger and the fire control party were not idle, and had the enemy zigging along a base course of 350 and still at 10 knots. George Grider, with Lenox and Keeter, had all mains carrying their maximum load, even the one with the twisted vertical shaft, and at 1721, *Wahoo* was dead ahead of the fleeing ships. After my final look, confirming that the masts were in line, the captain pulled the plug for our submerged approach and attack.

Wild zigs by the enemy ships, sometimes in unison (which is usual), but at other times in column movements (ships turning in the same water), taxed our fire control party and our battery. At times, our log showed speeds up to 10 knots, but by 1830, the captain had *Wahoo* in a good position on the tanker's, or engine aft freighter's, port beam. We would attack this undamaged ship first.

"Constant bearing–Mark." Hunter read 016.

"Set," came from Roger; her stern was coming on.

"Fire!" Morton hit the plunger; the shudder, zing, and momentary pressure told that all was well. The second and third torpedoes went to her midships and bow, but our own screws drowned out the torpedoes' propeller noise. The captain was swinging *Wahoo* with full speed and rudder to bring our stern tubes to bear on the freighter. I was passing bearings to him when a great flash enveloped the tanker, followed almost instantly by the whack of one torpedo's detonation. The freighter turned away before reaching our firing bearing. But we still had those torpedoes. Three blasts sent *Wahoo* up and after her. To our surprise, the tanker was still going, now close on the freighter's port quarter. Instead of four torpedoes aft for the freighter, they must now sink both ships.

Staying with the tanker, our first approach to another good firing position went well. Turning to bring our stern tubes to bear put us broadside to the enemy for a moment. That was all the tanker needed in order to spot us, and she was turning away before we could bring our stern tubes to bear. We tried from various positions, but now alerted, the tanker was even faster in her evasion. Perhaps she had all extra hands on lookout, or had better binoculars than ours. But our captain was not at a loss: He simply turned *Wahoo* around, and ordering all back full, we chased the tanker down going backwards. All did not go exactly as planned, for as we neared full speed late in the approach, the force of the sea against our rudder was greater than that of the hydraulic steering rams. The rudder swung right, looking aft, taking us into a sharp turn. That served to confuse the enemy more than it did us. We barged ahead at full speed on the convoy's next zig and were in fair position when the ships zigged back.

Accepting a range of 1,850 yards, the captain's, "Any time, Dick," came over the TBT's speaker. I checked my binoculars again to be sure that the hinge pin was firmly wedged in the "V"-shaped receptacle, and then called, "Constant bearing–Mark." The wire was amidships, and now her engine spaces aft were coming on.

"Fire!" The second torpedo was marked on her bow and fired to hit under her bridge structure forward. The tanker was apparently waiting for us to make our move, but two curving phosphorescent wakes were doing that for us. Morton came to the bridge in time to see the wakes disappearing into the night, but with lead angles that appeared correct. We had not long to wait, for the torpedo run would take only 72 seconds according to the word over the speaker. A flash aft of amidships and the instantaneous whack below our feet made the time academic, and the captain called, "All ahead full," as we went after the remaining freighter. The course took us by the sinking tanker, but only in time to see her after section canted at about 30 degrees. The details in silhouette checked with Lindhe's party, the *Manzyu Maru* of 6,515 tons.

We had spent an hour and a half putting this last ship down, and would have to do better on the freighter or we would be attacking in partial moonlight. It would give enough light for her to spot us, but

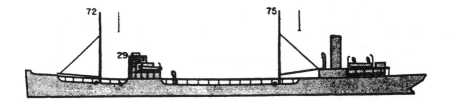

MANZYU MARU
TATIBANA MARU

Tonnages:		Constructed:	
Gross: 6,515–21	D.W.: 9,336–45	1921	Japan

Length:		Propulsion:	
W. L. (B. P.): 420'	O. A.:	Machinery:	Reciprocating
Beam: 54'		Screws: 1	H. P.:
Drafts:		R. P. M.: 57	@ Knots: 10
Loaded: 26' 6"	Light: 9'	Fuel: Oil	Capacity: 1,250 tons
Speed:			
Normal cruising: 10	Max.: 12	Radius: 10,000 miles at 10 knots	

Potential naval value: AO.

Remarks: Oil-carrying capacity: 71,400 barrels (42 gallons).

not sufficient for our scopes. The time was 2036, just 11 minutes after firing on the tanker, and we commenced an approach on the last ship of the convoy. Our plan was simple—present only our sharpest silhouette when within her sighting range—and that meant an abbreviated end-around. Her zigs were frantic, but far from bothersome, for they slowed her progress along the base course. Her gunfire, however, was something to behold. A dim, reddish flash, no more than from a flashlight, would be followed by thunder and the thump of a shell splash. It was the same flashless powder that we had observed in *Argonaut* off Midway on the night of December 7, 1942. But here, we, not the island, were the potential target.

The gunfire was obviously at random, but became a bit disconcerting when a nearby splash was the first indication that we had been spotted. They weren't supposed to be able to see us at this range. The "convincer" was a shell splashing dead ahead that ricocheted over our shears. The gun had our range and the captain pulled our plug.

In the security at 90 feet, we thought this one over as the wumps of shell splashes resounded through our hull. It was dangerous up there, and a dawn attack at periscope depth seemed the answer. We were, after all, a submarine. But the captain decided to size up the situation on the surface before making his decision. The intensity of the wumps had now diminished, and three blasts sent us up.

The surfacing procedure was normal; lookouts manned their stations, the engines were firing, and the turbos would screech for about 5 minutes. Above it all was Seaman Wach, our port forward lookout, pointing and shouting, "Searchlight broad on our port bow!"

Richie hopped up with Wach; the beam was just coming over the horizon, and with full power, *Wahoo* would be able to intercept the freighter should she close it. Morton had already presumed that she would, and that this was a destroyer sent to rescue this remaining ship. Chan had plotted the freighter's position with a radar range and my bearing from the forward TBT, and now we did the same with the destroyer. The captain directed plotting the destroyer at 20 knots to go with the known 10-knot freighter's speed, so Chan solved graphically the algebraic problem of their meeting point. Morton picked a point on the freighter's track 5 miles before the junction, and then a firing position 3,000 yards off the track. Chiefs Lenox, Keeter, and Pruett got us there with minutes to spare, and after reversing course with full rudder, we slowed to steerageway.

I commenced almost continuous bearings on the freighter's stack from the after TBT, not calling angles, for on a known course TDC's would be better than mine. The captain kept our stern pointed directly at the freighter, which was now steering a steady course. A reassuring, "Checks with TDC," or "Checks with plot," followed my bearings and the one angle I had just called, "Port ninety!"

Perhaps grasping my impatience, "Any time, Dick" came immediately.

"Constant bearing—Mark!"

"Set," came over the speaker. Her stack was coming on the wire.

"Fire!"

The second and last torpedo followed 15 seconds later to hit in exactly the same spot, for the captain wanted no cripples. The shudder and zing, followed by Buckley's report, were normal for each torpedo, and I reported their phosphorescent wakes on course. The range was longer than had been our custom, but everything else looked good, and after all, our torpedoes could hold a course within one-half of a degree. All of this gave me confidence as Hunter called the seconds over the 1MC for the troops. There was more than a freighter involved, for if these torpedoes hit, a return to Pearl and a ticket to the Royal would be assured. Morton came to the bridge and then aft to watch the freighter from beside the TBT. Two minutes had passed and there was less than a minute to go. In the speaker's background, we could hear George exclaiming over the torpedo run. He must have moved over to the chart desk, next to the 1MC, and seen Chan's plot, for in his measured, southern voice, the following words came over loud and clear: "Paine," he said. "If those torpedoes hit, I'll kiss your butt."

About 15 seconds later came the first of two detonations that shook *Wahoo* a mile and a half away. A quarter hour after the detonations, the destroyer was sweeping a clear sea with her searchlight. The freighter, long since identified as of the *Arizona Maru* class, had sunk. The time was 2128, still Tuesday, January 26, and we set course 358 for Fais Island with its phosphorite works, and just off the route to Pearl.

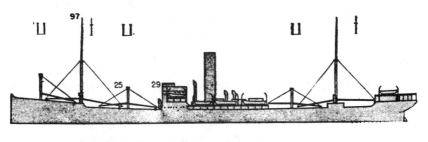

ARIZONA MARU

Tonnages:		Constructed:	
Gross: 9,684	D. W.: 11,100	1920	Japan

Length:		Propulsion:	
W. L. (B. P.): 475'	O. A.:	Machinery:	Reciprocating
		Screws: 2	N. H. P.: 995
Beam: 61'		R. P. M.:	@ Knots:
Drafts:		Fuel: Coal and	Capacity: Coal,
Loaded: 28'	Light: 11'	oil	1,300 tons; oil, 2,000 tons

Speed:		
Normal cruising: 14 Max.: 16	Radius: 8,000 miles at 14 knots.

Potential naval value: AP, AK.

Remarks: Sister of AFRICA MARU class except has kingposts on forecastle.

Except for George and Jack with their customary watch, and the captain, we were gathered in the wardroom. After a word and friendly smile through the doorway, Morton started forward to seek out every hand and personally thank and congratulate them. As far as he was concerned, this was their day, but I believe they felt just the opposite. For sure, our captain had lived up to his statement to all hands after taking command, and he had the wholehearted respect of every one of us. Naturally, there was only one subject in our discussion: none of us had heard of any other submarine sinking her first ship before reaching her patrol area, to say nothing of a convoy of four more ships. These were the things submariners daydreamed about but never expected to happen. Like some other boats, we had long possessed the capability, but it had taken Morton to cast aside unproven prewar concepts and bugaboos. Dead serious during battle, he still commanded with a flair that captured the support of all hands.

The fighting was over, but not the flair. Returning to the wardroom, the captain called for a pad of lined paper and started composing a message for ComSubPac. Crossing out words and adding others, the final version read:

SANK DESTROYER IN WEWAK SUNDAY AND IN FOURTEEN HOUR RUNNING GUN AND TORPEDO BATTLE TODAY SANK CONVOY OF ONE TANKER TWO FREIGHTERS AND ONE TRANS-PORT DESTROYING HER BOATS TORPEDOES EXPENDED PRO-CEEDING PEARL HARBOR VIA FAIS ISLAND

Handing it to Chan for encoding by the board and transmission, he reached for the cribbage board. While I was dealing, Morton raised his forearm diagonally in front of his chest, and with his finger pointed for emphasis, like a preacher, he said with a smile of satisfaction, "Tenacity, Dick. Stay with 'em till they're on the bottom!"

The success of this patrol, of any patrol, was in that statement. The captain had made his own luck by starting already 400 miles en route, and with some well-planned daring. His luck didn't hold for crib-bage, however, and after the rubber game, I joined Krause for midnight stars. While on the cigarette deck, he related the captain's having assured him that taking over the firing panel had nothing to do with Krause's lucky torpedo; he had just realized when in that position he could hold up a firing at the last second should it be advisable. Then the captain had added, "It's fun too!"

Our midnight stars had shown us in the ball park, and dawn stars on the money. Wahoo would make a dawn landfall on Fais Island, 24 hours hence, and have the day for a submerged reconnaissance. All was going well, so I changed the Plan of the Day, making it a rope-yarn Sunday. No action would be required; the duty chief would simply run the schedule accordingly. But the call, "Smoke over the horizon!" took precedence.

9

The time was 0720, January 27, and John Campbell had made, perhaps, his first wartime sighting in submarines. He had called an initial TBT bearing, the required first action. Standing watch with Chan, they had already brought *Wahoo* to an intercepting course. This would provide a good drill for our tracking party; they were called, and I told the captain what we were doing. At 0801, the topmasts of three ships poked over the horizon. Plot had a mean course for the enemy of 146, and we pulled the plug for a truly realistic drill.

A half hour into the approach, upon reporting the masts of three more ships, the captain could stand it no longer and took the conn. With 10 feet of scope exposed, I gave him the picture: Four large freighters in column, followed by a large tanker, and then trailing by about two ship lengths, a small freighter. For one of the few times, the captain took a look for himself, sweeping past the major ships and then concentrating on the small freighter before lowering the scope.

"Dick," he said. "We're the only ones who know we don't have any torpedoes; the enemy doesn't know that. Supposing we were to battle surface and make a run at them. Wouldn't they likely run off leaving the small freighter behind for our deck gun?"

Having seen big guns on the leading ships and none on the trailer, I was all for it, but with one slight modification—that while the gun crew got ready, we move out to about 9,000 yards from our present 7,000, to put us outside their guns' expected range.

Chief Carr had jumped the gun and had his crew ready before we were. The battle surface went smoothly, but this time, only Carr with his pointer and trainer went out to cast the gun loose, and then returned through the conning tower's after door. The captain headed *Wahoo* diagonally towards the convoy to see what would happen, and all engines went on the line. It had taken the enemy a couple of minutes to assess the situation, but now black smoke belched from their stacks, and flag hoists were being run up to their yardarms, and the signals executed (hauled down). Zigs and column maneuvers ensued, giving the impression of general confusion. Perhaps they had been warned of a mad-dog submarine on the loose. Quite suddenly, however, a column reformed and laid down quite respectable gunfire.

The splashes of the shells remained short, and we headed for the trailing ship as planned. When the smoke, pouring down the length of the convoy, cleared, we found that our small freighter had been replaced by a tanker. That did not change the captain's plan; she might be carrying gasoline, and our deck gun could blow her up, or at least set her on fire. All looked good as we raced towards an initial firing range of 6,000 yards. Buckley on the SJ called 7,500, then 7,000.

"What's that?" said Morton. "Right beyond the middle ship!"

In seconds, two thin masts slightly canted to the right came into the clear between ships. Their relative movement, opposite that of the convoy, gave the impression of high speed. They had to belong to the convoy's escort, which had been off on a morning search somewhere on the convoy's port bow. As her hull came in view on rounding the tanker's stern, our captain reluctantly put her astern using full rudder. Already at four-engine speed, we handily left her behind as she shoveled on more coal, leaving a black cloud of trailing smoke.

"Why, that antiquated coal-burning corvette!" chided Morton. "What a hell of a thing to have escorting a six-ship convoy. Why, the Emperor deserves to lose every ship he's got."

Within 20 minutes, *Wahoo* had opened the range to 14,000 yards. The "antiquated coal-burning corvette" by now had stopped her profuse smoking; all of that smoke could have come from lighting off more boilers. Exhorting our engineers, we continued to gain another 3,000 yards. Motormacs can always find an extra knot or so at a time like this. But now, looking aft with our 7 × 50s, we tried to convince ourselves that the escort was not gaining. The SJ had taken this delightful time to act up, but it doesn't take much of a seaman's eye to recognize the tips of a bow wake's "V." They appeared to be even with her deck, and very slowly the "V" filled in as her bow came over the horizon. She would know that coming much closer would put her within torpedo range, and it was with some relief that I observed her turning slowly to the right.

The captain had different thoughts, saying, "Hot dog, she's giving up. Why, we've dragged her a good thirty miles from her convoy, counting its run. She can't afford to leave it unprotected."

We were both wrong. As the escort continued to turn, her appearance changed to that of a full-fledged destroyer, at least the equivalent of the *Asashio* or *Fubuki* in Wewak. When broadside, she seemed to lay over to starboard as she let fly with a salvo that gave the impression of a battleship shooting at us.

"Watch for the splashes," said Morton, still undaunted and keeping his binoculars towards the destroyer.

Now I had spotted shellfire in gunnery practices—from the firing ship, not from the target. But if the captain thought this was the only salvo or that it was going to fall way short, then I would spot the splashes with him. About 3 seconds later a mighty clap of thunder to port and starboard sent me towards the hatch with ringing ears. I saw the shell splashes a half ship's length ahead; she had straddled our shears horizontally. In the excitement, the captain sounded five blasts instead of two, and I had to drag him down the hatch when he stopped to check on his lookouts. Hell, they had dived for the hatch on the flash of gunfire. It was *Wahoo*'s fastest dive, and well so; the next salvo whacked overhead as our shears went under.

The speed log still showed 15 knots, with *Wahoo* at a 15-degree down angle as she passed 250 feet.

"What depth, captain?" called George, who had already blown negative.

"Just keep her going down," was the reply. It was obvious that *Wahoo* was going to exceed test depth, so George used his best judgment and caught her somewhere below the last numeral on the depth gauge.

"Rig for depth charge" was apparently an unnecessary order, for Pappy reported back immediately, the troops having taken that for granted. Morton conned our boat through a fishtail to get us off our original track, but that was the only maneuver possible, for the destroyer's screws were already resounding through our hull. In a minute or less, they would roar menacingly overhead, and then would come the tense wait as the depth charges sank to the preset depth for detonation.

There were two theories concerning minimizing damage from depth charges. One was that a boat under strain from excessive depth needed only a moderately close charge to cave her in. The other, probably believed by fewer of us, was that at greater depth the increase in total force on the hull is minimal (100 pounds per square inch when going from 200 to 400 feet), while the chance of even receiving a lethal charge when at twice the depth has been reduced to one-eighth, for depth charging is three-dimensional bombing.

I was not rehearsing these figures as the destroyer roared overhead, but as long as *Wahoo*'s hull didn't mind, George's depth suited me fine.

"Now we're going to catch it," said the skipper, softly, as the screws roared above. The tense waiting was longer than expected; the destroyer had set the charges' firing hydrostats deep. Six tooth shakers cracked and whacked, dumping seeming tons of bolts into our superstructure. Our stout ship suffered no damage, but I doubt that anyone could ever become used to these taut moments.

The destroyer's screws did not slow, probably wanting nothing more to do with a submarine that would attack on the surface in daylight, wondering what she might do submerged. It was a mutually agreeable withdrawal. In the wardroom Morton reached for the cribbage board and sent for Lindhe. It was a legitimate time to dispense some depth-charge medicine, and our pharmacist, in charge of the medicinal grain alcohol, would likely supplement the small, individual bottles of brandy.

After losing the first game, the captain pushed back his chair, saying, "Dick, I think we've been stretching things a bit. Let's stay down here and relax for about 30 minutes or so." Down here was now 200 feet, where a minimum watch was required, and 30 minutes was about the time that would be required for him to win the next two games. Chan's arrival with a message that had come on the Fox before dawn changed our plans. It was ComSubPac's answer and read:

ADMIRAL HALSEY LIKES YOU FOR GETTING DESTROYER SUNDAY X WE ALL LIKE YOU FOR GETTING ALL FOUR SHIPS OF CONVOY YESTERDAY X YOUR PICTURE IS ON THE PIANO XX

The message seemed a bit mild to me, but the arrival of Jayson and Manalesay bearing bowls of fresh-frozen strawberries to go under our depth-charge medicine changed our conversation, and shortly thereafter, we changed our depth. We did, after all, have a contact report to send and a rendezvous tomorrow with Fais Island.

All was clear on scope and sound, so three blasts sent us up and on our way. Again, three engines were on the line, for the destroyer had driven *Wahoo* in the wrong direction. As plotted from the DRI, the setback could be made up handily. We would know for sure in another hour, when a sun line in the west would give a better longitude line. Until then our bow was slicing modest seas towards the island.

The time was 1415. Chan had encoded our contact message, and was having his radiomen go up and down the scale in harmonics of our basic frequency of 4,155 (8,310–16,620 and so on); they could not raise NPM at Pearl, so they transmitted the message blind several times. We'd try again at night.

The evening Fox brought the following messages:

COMMANDER IN CHIEF PACIFIC FLEET SENDS WELL DONE TO WAHOO THE SHIPS YOU HAVE SUNK WILL DECREASE THE ENE-MYS CAPACITY TO CARRY ON THE WAR XXX

FOR WAHOO FROM COMTASKFOR 42 QUOTE ADMIRAL HALSEY SENDS CONGRATULATIONS FOR WEWAK JOB ALSO FROM TASK FORCE 42 FOR NEW EPIC OF SUBMARINE WARFARE COM-PLETE DESTRUCTION OF LOADED CONVOY UNQUOTE X INFO ALL HANDS X WAHOO LT COMDR MORTON COMMANDING TWO DAYS AFTER SINKING DESTROYER AT WEWAK ENCOUN-TERED UNESCORTED CONVOY WHILE ENROUTE PALAU X WA-HOO SANK ENTIRE CONVOY TWO FREIGHTERS TANKER AND TRANSPORT DESTROYING HER BOATS AND EXPENDING ALL TORPEDOES DURING FOURTEEN HOUR BATTLE X TWO MEN WOUNDED X

These dispatches were more to the captain's liking, and one jump ahead, Sterling had typed a copy for the crew's mess, with carbons for spare card holders. For sure, they would remain a part of *Wahoo*'s history, but there was now more to the story. The captain called for the plain-language copy of our contact report and the pad of lined paper from his desk. Omitting the padding words that are placed before and after a message to increase its length and security, he copied the facts of what, how many, where, and what doing. On the line above and below, he toyed with his own padding, though using those words to convey a message was frowned upon. When satisfied, he pushed the pad out to the center of the table for the rest of us to see. On decoding, the total message would now read:

ANOTHER RUNNING GUN BATTLE TODAY CONVOY FIVE AK
ONE AO LAT FOUR DASH FIFTEEN NORTH LONG ONE FORTY
DASH THIRTY EAST COURSE ONE FOUR SIX SPEED NINE WA-
HOO RUNNIN DESTROYER GUNNIN

For sure, the captain had not lost his flair, and exact translation or not, a copy would be tacked to the white-painted cork insulation in the crew's mess; they'd love it.

Our dive off the depth gauge had served another purpose, for it confirmed that our new TBT installation by *Sperry* was indeed watertight. It had a selsyn-type electrical transmitter forward and aft on our bridge, so we could fire torpedoes at night while already on an evasion course. This was a big improvement over my simple mechanical one, which had worked well in sighting Tol Island and for initial bearings of the ship we had sunk; it was replaced by the Sub Base with an electrical system that flooded during the deep evasion at Bougainville. The cable, acting as a hose, had even flooded the conning tower receiving unit. But any doubts concerning our new system had now been set aside.

10

Thursday, January 28 had arrived, and we dived at the gentlemanly hour of 0850 on the circle 10 miles from the center of Fais Island. While closing at 4 knots, our regular soundman took single-ping soundings at 10-minute intervals as coached by Simonetti. If there were a listening station, as had been reported, the enemy's operator would consider the pings as just another fish noise, and so also the occasional single-ping echo range toward the charted reefs. On soundings, these echo ranges produced bottom reverberations, so would tell little unless a reef were truly close, but knowing of a close reef is what we wanted. The soundings and periscope observations of landmarks checked with those on our chart, so we went about the rest of our reconnaissance confidently.

We saw no evidence of the sound listening post, but the trading station was just as shown. Proceeding around the southwestern end of the island at 1½ miles from the beach, the phosphorite works, with its warehouses and refinery, came in full view. Immediately, Morton proposed his plan for shelling it under moonlight. I expressed my full agreement, especially with the moonlight feature, and we withdrew to the selected firing point to make preparations and to avoid the chance of being sighted.

Now free from possible periscope sighting, the crew queued up for a look at the island and snapshots for our photographers. Ten seconds apiece kept the line moving, and it was Fireman Anders who sighted the tops of a ship heading for the island. The line unqueued as we conducted a fire control drill on the ship, now identified as an interisland freighter. We watched her moor. Broadside she displayed two efficient-looking guns. Her crew quickly installed canvas gun covers and started lacing them in place, but stopped after one or two grommets. We waited;

if they laced the covers further, the guns could be inoperative for several minutes, depending upon the type of lacing. This offered a possibility, but perhaps fortunately, the canvas covers remained at the ready. Recalling that this ship was similar to, though longer than, the Q-ship (antisubmarine decoy) reported by *Gudgeon* and could have additional surprise armament clinched the decision to leave well enough alone. The idea of an across-the-island bombardment lingered, but our remaining ammunition could do little damage. So we settled on picture shooting with the Kodak Medalist that would give Intelligence a negative large enough to play with.

At 1800, well clear of the island, three blasts sent *Wahoo* to the surface. There was now one priority, to reach the Submarine Base safely. Rather than a letdown, there would be concentration, and three diesels were doing their part as we set course for Pearl Harbor. Below, there could not have been a happier ship's company. We were proud of our captain, of *Wahoo,* of our shipmates, and believing that I can speak for all, proud of ourselves.

There would be a change for morning stars as George and Hunter had relieved Krause and me. Since George would likely have orders as an executive officer and navigator, the experience of navigating to Pearl Harbor would be advantageous. The captain had an ulterior motive, however, for this would give me time to work on the patrol report. The real winner would be Krause, for he would head the quartermasters' watch list.

Sprucing up our ship proved to be no problem, for hands turned to as if they were working on their hot rod at home. Already, the best from our freezer room had been segregated for consumption, and for that we had the whole ship's company as volunteers. Roger and Richie had turned in their reports on torpedo and gunnery attacks, including that of the gun casualty. George had long since submitted his on the engine, and all of these came to me typed by Sterling. He was now typing the stencils as I turned in my sections upon their completion. Should anyone feel rushed, there would be two Tuesdays, each February 2, as we crossed the international date line, and I would enjoy the unique experience of two birthdays.

I was on the homestretch as I proofread the captain's narrative of the patrol. I had been reading patrol reports for almost exactly a year, and Morton's narrative was the first that devoted a separate paragraph to his officers and men, the senior by name. But he was a new breed of captain to us, one who exercised the adage of reprimand in private, commend in public. Because we felt the same of him, and my pride in his words, I include the exact paragraph from the patrol report here:

> The conduct and discipline of the officers and men of this ship while under fire were superb. They enjoyed nothing better than a good fight. I commend them all for a job well done, especially Lieutenant R. H. O'Kane the Executive Officer, who is cool and deliberate under fire. O'Kane is the fightingest naval officer I have ever seen and is worthy of the highest of praise. I commend Lieutenant O'Kane for being an inspiration to the ship.

Our rendezvous with *Litchfield* was set for 0730 Sunday, February 7, with mooring an hour later. But George and Hunter, who had seemed a bit disdainful of our midnight stars and such, had *Wahoo* on a track that had missed the escort altogether. Yet we could hardly miss Oahu, whose mountains showed high above the horizon. With seaman's eye, the captain conned his submarine towards the channel while Jack tried desperately to get off a message stating that we were proceeding independently. Unescorted, we were fair game for a fledgling aviator, so Morton told Jack to use a higher priority. Inadvertently, Jack had then used the Operational Emergency designation reserved for enemy threat and the like, and in return had received a bawling out by CinCPac's communications supervisor, who considered that this error took precedence over the message. Jack had returned topside to find *Wahoo* entering the channel and *Litchfield* boiling up astern. She had undoubtedly been through this before and was taking pains to see that we were not embarrassed.

On rounding ten-ten dock, we saw the Base crowded with people, very much like a peacetime Navy Day, and on closing, we found Pier 1 reserved for dignitaries and the press with the band drawn up across the shoreward end. The crew had not had time to make up a flag or pennant decorated with red meatballs or rising suns to designate merchantmen or warships sunk. But some prophetic hand had borrowed one of the large Australian brooms used to sweep the dock, and the captain had Lindhe tape it to the very top of the attack scope with bristles up. It told the whole story—a clean sweep—and raised high above restricted radar and such, it quickly became the most photographed broom in the world, all to a deafening rendition of the "Hawaiian War Chant."

Third patrol, first attack: in Wewak harbor, Asashio *destroyer broken in two by a "down the throat" torpedo. (White spots at top of the mast are Japanese sailors.)*

Giving food, water, and chart to starving Malayans fleeing the Japanese.

Transport stopped by two torpedoes, listing to port and sinking after taking a third hit just aft of the bridge.

Returning from third patrol: O'Kane and Morton upon mooring at Pearl Harbor.

Mail call after third patrol.

Fourth patrol: Seiwa Maru *sinking at dawn.*

Nitu Maru *heading for Davey Jones's locker.*

Wahoo *makes deck gun attack on* Sinsei Maru, *afire and sinking after 90 rounds.*

Hadachi Maru *on fire and sinking after taking 80 four-inch rounds.*

Clearing the area after the two gun-attacks.

Trawler stopped with 11 four-inch rounds, now under attack by Wahoo's *"Commandos."*

R & R CENTER — MIDWAY

BEER RATION CHIT ★ **3**

GOOD FOR ONE BEER

Midway refit after fourth patrol. The sign on Gooneyville Lodge reads, "The Best Submariners in the World Recuperate Here."

Mare Island's greeting to Wahoo *on arrival from fifth patrol.*

Admiral Friedell congratulates Captain "Mush" Morton, flanked by his father and wife Harriet.

Lieutenant Commander O'Kane greets family.

Last photograph of Wahoo, as she departs for sixth patrol. Note cut-down bridge and conning tower fairwater.

_____Part Five

FOURTH PATROL
The East China and Yellow Seas

1

The Base had provided brows for forward and aft of the conning tower fairwater, so the admirals and captains came aboard and departed as though they had gone through a receiving line. Waiting sedans whisked them away except for Capt. John H. Brown, the senior squadron commander and acting ComSubPac. Over a quick cup of coffee, he broke the sad news that Admiral English and senior members of his staff had been killed in a plane crash near San Francisco. Adm. Charles A. Lockwood, who had been relieved as Commander Submarine Forces Southwest Pacific Fleet (ComSubSoWesPac), was en route from western Australia and would take over in a few days.

Mindful that the wardroom would be needed as a disbursing office, and because of a briefing at the commander-in-chief's conference room, Morton took Captain Brown on a quick tour through the boat. Even if late, he would not have let the crew's work in polishing their ship go unnoticed. I was to attend also, so promptly turned over to George the business of getting the troops off to the Royal. It would be no great imposition, since he would be at hand for testing his engine before its dismantling. Topside, the press and our crew were having a field day with photographs ranging from Glinski's foot to Keeter's baptism before donning his chief's hat, and more photographs below had been specially authorized.

Friends and onlookers had taken over the dock, and the band played on as we left for Captain Brown's sedan. Altogether, it seemed that *Wahoo* had put a crack in the silence of the "silent service." This was not lessened upon seeing those in attendance at the conference; I believe every type commander or his deputy was among those present, and several wore dolphins.

The captain touched briefly on the highlights of the patrol and raised an eyebrow among some submariners when explaining why he had me on the scope or TBT and firing the torpedoes. Only a nod followed his description of destroying the Japanese boats, but a vice admiral, commander service forces, I believe, asked pointedly, "When *Wahoo* was traveling at high speed astern, what would you have done if you had to dive?" Without hesitation, Morton replied, "Oh, we already had our battle station's bow planesman on the stern planes and vice versa, Admiral." The reply had been so matter-of-fact that the admiral didn't ask if we had ever tried it. For sure, in the space of about 20 minutes, they had learned of unexpected submarine capabilities when under a truly strong command.

The captain was going on to lunch, and though I was invited, appropriately I had to return to *Wahoo,* for this was Morton's day. On board, George had taken charge handily, for only he, Chan, Sterling, and Lenox from our ship's company remained aboard. The relief crew, skippered by a salty warrant officer, had taken over with extra enthusiasm since some of them would join our regular ship's company. It was the way to get the best performance from the relief crew and to get the best of them to fill our vacancies.

The captain had already signed the forwarding page of the patrol report, and now Chan and I checked the stencils against the typed, green pages. Sterling was standing by for any corrections, and understandably seemed a bit smug when we could find none. All three of us were the winners. In addition to the patrol report stencils and the usual tracing of the submarine's track to small scale, our package included the detailed, inked charts covering the actions against the convoy. One of them contained the complete legend from the Quartermaster's Notebook, showing the exact times. The first chart, showing the initial firings, did not correctly show Krause's torpedo or the two subsequent ones that hit the transport. His should have been about 20 degrees off to the right, and the hits should have been shown where the torpedoes crossed the transport's continuing turn below. A glance at the notebook gave the answer; there were no entries during this confusion, and Hunter had put it together as best he could. There was an advantage as it was shown, however, for this way the captain would not be faced with saying ill of any member of his crew, something that he would not do. Sterling left with the complete package for the division commander's office.

Chan and I left too, picking up Sterling on the way, and arrived at the Royal in about a half hour. Asking for accommodations in the captain's name, as he had suggested, I received an emphatic, "Yes, Sir," and we had a suite. A small rotunda, reception room, two bedrooms, and a lanai to seaward seemed like a mansion after our cramped living spaces, and we put the lanai to work as soon as our packets of mail had been delivered. The refrigerator had been left stocked with beer by the last tenant, and we would do the same on leaving. So, with bottles in one hand, the latest letters in the other, and feet propped up on the lanai table, we were at peace with the world. But soon, assured that all was well at home and at Mare Island, we sought our shipmates in the surf.

It took only minutes to locate them; they were the swimmers with white skins from two patrols and with little chance for sun at Brisbane. Just as after *Wahoo*'s first patrol, they had congregated on the shoreside of the second reef. It was a secure area for relaxing; the sun was too low for burning, so I floated in the varied positions with my head back and lungs nearly filled, letting the ocean currents take me where they wished. This, and swimming to the outer reefs, had been an almost daily enjoyment when *Argonaut* was in port, for we had lived only a few streets back from the beach. Since the seas, the reefs, and the beach would remain the same, I wondered if similar times could return.

Meals were still served almost continuously; there was no hurry, but the thought of fresh vegetables and green salads brought us ashore.

We had anticipated exchanging patrol experiences, but copies of all the dispatches, paraphrased so as not to compromise a code or our tactics, had been posted for all to read. There was no exaggeration in our answers to the almost continuous questions, nor did I withhold some opinions: Down the throat is certainly not a tactic to be sought, but is rather a desperation shot. And as for entering harbors, unless there is a compelling reason to do so, choose a likely spot well off a harbor entrance where there is maneuvering room. If the enemy doesn't come out, you've stopped his commerce while you're there.

Until this time, when discussing patrols with contemporaries, primarily we had learned what not to do. This discussion was different: Morton had demonstrated, in one patrol, the very tactics some of us had been urging. While a few other boats had used some of these tactics, it was *Wahoo* under Morton that had turned the corner completely from the prewar submerged vessel of opportunity to an aggressive raider, even on the surface when conditions would permit. In round figures, we had been submerged over 500 hours on the second patrol, and just under

50 hours on our third. This would never be the norm for submarine patrolling, but it should demonstrate to any boat that at times she can surface close to the enemy for a good, high-periscope search, and then dive again.

The captain did not join us until the second day, and even then his schedule was dotted with official commitments. However, he did relax with us at cribbage and we joined the others in the surf. So within a week we all were physically and mentally ready for another patrol. *Wahoo*'s engine had been repaired by replacing the slightly distorted vertical shaft, so it would now carry a full load. All other work was nearing completion, and then, just days before departing, came George's orders to *Pollack* as executive officer. *Wahoo* would miss him, but other boats were losing officers too, and we had been fortunate in keeping our original watch officers this long.

Prompted by this transfer, the captain started a program that would retain certain key men during his expected command of *Wahoo*. Already, Chiefs Lenox and Lindhe were departing for the States on leave and would rejoin *Wahoo* before her fifth patrol, when two others would go on leave. Though it was not the best time to lose leading engineers, the reporting of Comdr. Duncan C. MacMillan as a PCO eased that a bit. He had completed graduate studies in diesel engineering, and his advice would be available.

Our third patrol had been the shortest on record, 24 days including the training period, and so also had been our refit, completed in 8 days. *Wahoo*'s readiness for sea had been set for Wednesday, February 17, so loading of torpedoes, ammunition, and provisions commenced immediately. Four days of underway training, especially for the six new hands and our PCO, were followed by an emergency docking to repair a sticky shutter of No. 5 torpedo tube. Of almost equal importance was the opportunity to scrub and paint bottom, most of this being done by the shipyard with high-pressure hoses and then paint guns. But our hands welcomed the opportunity to man punts and scrub off spots as the water receded, for the new paint would give us an extra half knot on *Wahoo*'s coming voyage. Undocking before dark gave all hands a full day to catch up on loose ends, and befitted Washington's Birthday. At 2200 that night, a half hour after the Base movie, I was able to report, "All hands aboard and ready for patrol, Captain."

Returning to the wardroom, I talked with Commander MacMillan, who had been my second executive officer in *Argonaut*. Though 8 years my senior, with slow peacetime promotions he was only one rank above me. Now with two ranks, it seemed best to address him as commander, and I would set the pace in this. Though we were aware that he had been slated to be *Wahoo*'s first captain, I thought it best not to mention this, and after a pleasant updating of our respective families, I excused myself for a full night's sleep, perhaps the last for a month or two.

2

The lines were singled up for *Wahoo*'s scheduled 1300 departure. She would thus reach Midway Island at dawn of the fourth day. Well-wishers who had come to see us off stepped aside for Vice Admiral Lockwood as he came aboard. He had assumed command of Submarine Force Pacific Fleet while we were at the Royal, and since then had talked with our captain. I had known him when he wore three stripes and commanded the *Bass, Bonita, Barracuda* Division, and rode *Pruitt* when she had served as target for their torpedoes. His contemporary, William H. P. Blandy, had been our division commander and rose to be Commander Atlantic Fleet. The two of them could keep any OOD hopping, and I had found it a challenge to be one jump ahead. He greeted both the captain and me by our first names. In a short conversation, he asked only one question: at what running depth had we set our torpedoes, and nodded when Morton said, "As shallow as the situation permits." I believed that we had a force commander who was going to get to the bottom of the dud torpedoes all boats were experiencing.

Rumbling diesels served as an "All ashore who are going ashore." Topside, their exhausts were spitting steam and cooling water from the mufflers, as if impatient to get on with their task. The admiral wished us Godspeed, and then stood at attention with the line handlers, but with all of them covering their ears during the prolonged blast as our submarine backed clear.

Morton conned her through the harbor, with Commander MacMillan on the bridge. Most of the hulks were still present, if anything a bit rustier, and I knew what this first sight was doing to our PCO. Missing, however, were the battleships *Tennessee* and *Nevada*, which I had previously thought to have been sunk upright and resting on the bottom. They had been only damaged and were now being modernized at Bremerton Naval Shipyard. In continuing respect for the men who had died in all ships, we had a full section, which included our six new hands, at quarters in clean dungarees and facing each hulk. As before, there would be many misty eyes.

Passing the sea buoy, we turned west to clear Barbers Point light, which marked the end of the long point of land and reef extending southwest from Oahu. Roger and George Misch, whom we could now call just plain George, took the watch. The special sea detail was relieved by the first section; below our submarine had been rigged for dive; and *Wahoo* was on her fourth patrol. Our escort till dark, a PC, took position ahead and turned with us to course 290, the heading for Midway Island, 1,300 nautical miles away. Head seas required a third engine to maintain the speed of advance for the dawn landfall, and our escort found it heavy going, as did some of our new hands. Pappy solved that by sending them up, two at a time, to relieve our leeward lookouts, and the captain took care of the PC by suggesting that she take position astern or on our quarter. Following there served just as well, for her main purpose was to identify *Wahoo* as a friendly submarine.

Unfriendly were the seas to Rowls, who came forward to request a change in the menu. This would be our Washington's Birthday dinner, and it would be impossible to keep the filling in the cherry pies. Now, once signed, the menu for the week is sacrosanct; only the captain can change it, which he would do with great reluctance since hands look forward to a specific meal (and in port, bachelors may regulate their liberty accordingly). So Morton simply suggested thickening the filling with cornstarch or such. After an "Aye Aye, Sir," Rowls went aft, slowly shaking his head.

The overcast sky would probably continue and preclude evening stars, so the final visual bearing and radar range on Barbers Point light would be *Wahoo*'s point of departure. Below, I met our new hands, all of them having specifically requested *Wahoo*. This had been an unexpected spin-off from our last patrol. Eager volunteers, they remained only to be trained. But already schooled in *Wahoo* by their Chief Redford and Petty Officer, Second Class Holman, this would hardly be necessary. With such replacements, the captain's leave plan would indeed work, and the lingering doubts that we might put to sea shorthanded were pushed aside. Continuing with a quick turn aft, I found our ship well secured for sea, for if such had not been so, gear would already have been adrift. Proper securing had become routine, but would never be taken for granted. Not routine was the enticing aroma from the galley, where turkeys for the first sittings had just been removed from the ovens. The pleasant thought that without stars, Krause and I would enjoy a piping hot instead of a warmed-over holiday meal sent me forward.

No Thanksgiving, Christmas, or other holiday meal could have been better. A part of this was the quick, polite serving by Jayson and Manalesay. All dishes were hot until the pies, which had been removed from their tins and served on two round dinner plates. Morton struggled with the pie knife and then called for a carving knife. With the two, he removed a precise, generous wedge. After passing the plate, he tried for the first bite, but the edge of the fork wouldn't penetrate his slice; even the tines had trouble. Picking up the wedge, the captain shook it in front of Jayson, saying, "What do you call this?" as the slice continued to vibrate like a piece of resilient rubber. "Captain, sir," Jayson replied, "I just serve it, I don't cook it." Morton burst out laughing and said, "Well, I asked for it."

As far as I could learn, the crew had taken the dessert in stride, though some had cut a part of their pie into chunks for pogy bait on the midwatch and such. Frankly, I believe that they would eat, in one form or another, whatever their captain, now privately called Deadly Dudley, had ordered.

En route to Pearl and in keeping with his nickname (though I doubt he had yet heard it), the captain had nominated George Misch to lead *Wahoo*'s Commandos. The largest and strongest aboard, he was to pick five others—six being the largest number our rubber boat would accommodate. While at the Submarine Base, the prestige that accompanied this designation had made it easy to outfit them all. Serious and methodical about this, George had consulted the Marines for recommended equipment. The Base sailmaker had sewn individual belts, with loops and pockets to hold what each man would carry. I did not see the complete inventory, but it ranged from wrecking bars through small compound bolt or wire cutters to machetes, while at least half of the belts had deep, narrow pockets that could hold submarine sandwiches or sticks of dynamite. I believe that the whole was somewhat more than Morton had in mind, but so as not to quell such enthusiasm, he suggested only that each member keep his belt loaded and ready. They did him one better, lashing them to their bunks. Like it or not, *Wahoo* had an elite corps.

A complete round of emergency drills allowed us to put them on the shelf for this patrol; from now on the alarm would signal the real thing. Daily dives and battle stations took up any slack, and at dawn of the fourth day a Navy utility plane met *Wahoo* on the 30-mile circle from Midway. This was a twist, at least for me, since threatening planes from the island had kept us down when on patrol just a year ago. Only the 10-degree course change to the right, as shown on our track, was necessary to reach the point 5 miles due south of the channel. Ours had been the cautious approach, since it takes only a speed error in a direct approach to an atoll to put your ship on the reef. And there was another advantage; *Wahoo* would be heading straight for the slot through the reef, already on the range markers.

We could observe the seas breaking, except for a narrow space. That would be the dredged, or probably blasted, channel into the lagoon. With seas from astern, *Wahoo* was yawing to either side of the directed course. Under these circumstances, the steersman cannot keep the lubber's line steady on the directed compass-card course, but must dampen the yaw with just the correct rudder. This was not the time for Simonetti to learn; he could do that in any good following sea, and Hunter took the wheel. The seas were smashing over the reefs to port and starboard when the captain and Hunter threaded the slot into the quiet lagoon. Now we knew the reason for an air escort; it was too dangerous for a small surface escort. The fuel pier lay to port, off the main channel, and in minutes we were moored alongside the USS *Tarpon*.

It was 0830, Saturday, February 27, 1943. The fuel lines came over from the new dock immediately, while Duncan and the captain left with Submarine Division Commander (ComSubDiv) 44, the submarine command here. We had left Pearl with one job still outstanding—the replacement of the scope with the pitted tube. Half in jest, Morton had said, "We ought to have the dentists fill the damn things." It hadn't sounded like a bad idea to me, but at dental quarters, no one believed such a solution was practical. Here at Midway, 1,300 miles closer to the enemy, they might think differently. They did—the dentists shaking rocks and scissors to see who would get the job. Simonetti cleaned the pits, appropriately with old toothbrushes; a corpsman mixed the amalgam; the dentist filled; and Krause polished, as soon as it had set, using double-aught emery paper. Joined by the second dentist, who had apparently closed the clinic, the whole job was completed before noon, with the scope as smooth and shiny as the other one. A sumptuous submarine meal was their unexpected reward, and they would have a story for their grandchildren.

George had not been idle, and after visiting the Marine detachment, had a story to tell his captain. The Marines had shown him and other commandos the latest technique in making surefire Molotov cocktails. A small, sealed tube of nitric acid is cemented to the inside wall of a quart whisky bottle, which is then filled with about a half cup of sodium— under diesel fuel so it won't contact the air and spontaneously ignite. Half the diesel fuel is then poured off and replaced with gasoline before sealing the bottle. Since manufacture would be difficult on board, the Marines had given George and his men two cases all sealed and ready for action. The flames are started on the bottles' cracking from the nitric acid, and then maintained by the sodium.

They were dandy weapons for a raiding party, but just imagine one of them in a submerged submarine during a depth-charge attack, or at any time for that matter. But there was a possible solution. Somewhere back in *Wahoo*'s design, it had been decided to install two torpedo storage tubes in the conning tower fairwater. These torpedoes could supposedly have been struck below on a quiet night. Perhaps so, but this would have required the rigging of the torpedo handling mast and boom and other skids from the superstructure. No skipper would have his submarine unable to dive for a period of 2 or 3 hours. So the few boats with these tubes had long since converted them to other uses ranging from ready ammunition to spud lockers. Ours were the former, with racks to hold the deck gun's ammunition cans, and one deck storage tube for this would be enough. So George had the problem, the answer, and a smile broader than usual when he met with the captain. Molotov cocktails properly stored in the deck tube should ride all right, and at worst would do no more than blow the door off; besides, they might just be of real use. With the stipulation that each bottle must be wrapped in rags so as to fit snugly in one of the ammunition storage racks, Morton went along with George's project, and *Wahoo*'s Commandos left the ship on a rag hunt that had a deadline on *Wahoo*'s sailing in 1 hour.

When Morton returned from thanking those who had helped his ship, two diesels fired. A quick glance showed Duncan on the cigarette deck, *Tarpon* snaking in the brow, and then the remaining two lines as *Wahoo* backed into the dredged turning basin. Proceeding onto the range, a high rear and lower front marker, I looked aft like the Brisbane pilot, and kept the skipper informed as he conned our submarine through the slot in the reef and into the open sea. The angry coral heads, menacing a minute before, disappeared in the clear depths and we came right to course 293 true.

Four thousand miles ahead lay our operating areas, the whole of the East China and Yellow Seas. To help with the voyage and give us a fresh start, Midway had topped us off with 16,000 gallons of diesel and 2,500 of fresh water. It was like having SubBasePearl 1,300 miles closer to the enemy; more than that, for our attack periscope would no longer tear up the flax packing, and those Molotov cocktails were duly stored. In the crew's mess, Sterling's typed copy of the pertinent page of our Operation Order now occupied a spare card holder. Other boats that had excelled were frequently rewarded with Empire patrols in one of the four Pacific areas about her main islands. Our route by Midway had indicated this, but few of us besides Krause, Hunter, and Simonetti, who had drawn and corrected the charts, had even dreamed of patrolling as far as the China Station. The secrecy until after leaving Midway was necessary since someone returning to the States might talk, and that could give the enemy time to shift some of their antisubmarine forces before our arrival. It was our intention to remain one jump ahead of them.

We were now passing through the northern portion of *Argonaut*'s area, where we had patrolled for 2 months commencing 10 days prior to Pearl Harbor. Had we been to the north, sighting of the Japanese Task Force might have been possible. As it was, we were perhaps the last to know of the attack. At first, we didn't believe our CPO's, who got the word from the States on the shortwave band of their receiver at about 2000 our time.

On this night, *Wahoo* would cross the 180th meridian, skipping Sunday, but not on Rowls's calendar, for the menu had already been signed. Unchangeable, however, was the area we would traverse, the scenes of the famous Battle of Midway in June 1942. Japanese had decimated our torpedo bombers; the only survivor, Ens. Geórge H. Gay, was rescued by a Catalina patrol bomber the next day. But the action of these brave men had pulled down the enemy's Zekes, making possible our successful dive bomber attacks. Including the *Soryu,* sunk by our submarine *Nautilus* and witnessed by Ensign Gay, the enemy had lost four of her major carriers and two cruisers. Our only ship loss was the

damaged smaller carrier *Yorktown* sunk by Japanese submarine torpedoes, but such personnel losses could not be long sustained. Now, almost
three-quarters of a year later, it appeared that this battle might mark
the furthest incursion by the enemy.

Continuing head seas impeded our progress, but fuel was of more
importance than our arrival date. So the captain interpreted the phrase
"on or about" March 10 rather liberally, and we slowed to one engine
when the seas increased, rather than spending useless oil in fighting
them. This kept our new Oil King, Machinist's Mate Lemert, more
than busy, for his fuel consumption recordings would determine our
speed.

Roger's transition to engineering officer had been smooth, for he
had lived with and knew the job thoroughly; but at battle stations, we
would retain his skill on the TDC. And so it was on the next fire control
drill that he and Richie detected errors in the machine's gyro angle
solving section. We could still get the gyro angles from the Mark-8
solver, and by relaying the information by telephone, the torpedomen
could set them by hand; but most of the great flexibility provided by
the TDC would be lost. With books at hand, Richie spent his off-watch
hours of the following days checking the insides of this electromechanical
computer. It was a task second only to the uncounted hours that Chan
had spent on our SJ.

From March 4 to 6, enemy planes from Marcus Island to the south
were possible, and I listened to Chief Redford's instructions to the oncoming lookouts with approval. No planes, only birds were sighted, and so
it remained for the following week. In another 3 days, however, *Wahoo*
would pass through the Nampo Shoto. This is the eastern island chain
extending south from the Empire and which provides a somewhat protected shipping route to and from Tokyo. Ships would be possible, and
word from Richie that the angle solver was again operating properly
could not have been more timely. The trouble had lain in several insuffi-
ciently tightened electrical connections and maladjusted microswitches.
There was an offshoot from this trouble: we now had a knowledgeable
repairman who wouldn't hesitate in tackling the TDC's analyzer section
should it dare give us trouble.

Our route, as laid down on the chart, would take *Wahoo* through
one of the wider passes between Sofu Gan to the north and an unnamed
small island to the south. The former was also shown in relief as an
almost vertical pinnacle some 400 feet tall. We would use it for the

final tuning of Chan and Buckley's SJ, and then for checking our TDC by making an approach as if it were a stopped target.

The original radar contact on the island was at 13,000 yards; then leaving it astern, the SJ held it to 16,000. A part of this increase was probably the tuning, but once acquired, a contact can usually be held to a greater range. But we knew that our SJ was performing at its best, and similarly the TDC, which even detected the current to the northeast, shown by small blue arrows and figures on the navigational chart. Satisfied, Captain Morton ordered the course for the Colonet Strait, the major passage through the Nansei Shoto, and we came to course 274 true for the 600-mile final run to our first area.

Maneuvering answered the telegraph; the speed called for a third engine, and Chief Keeter's after engine room watch went through the procedure efficiently. Not the date, but the hour of our landfall was paramount, for it must permit a long afternoon submerged approach to within a few miles of the Nansei Shoto. From there, *Wahoo* would run the strait on the surface at night. Much of this plan depended upon the continued cooperation of the enemy air patrols, for to date there had been none. At first, this seemed unbelievable, with the south coast of Honshu, the Empire's major island, only 150 miles to the north. But their north-south shipping would be following one of the two island chains, while east-west shipping would run close to Honshu's south shore. We were in a no-man's-sea, so why patrol it? That was a theory, but the duty chief, in cautioning the lookouts, spoke only of the enemy's shoreline to the north; nothing more was needed.

By afternoon, we were south of the Kii Suido, the eastern entrance to the Inland Sea. Off that passage *Plunger* had received a thorough drubbing. Built before certain materials had become scarce, 9-inch-diameter vent risers in the torpedo rooms were made of copper, which could be more easily formed to follow the interior curvature of the hull. One very close Japanese depth charge found that they were more easily formed too, and expanded the after port riser with an enormous aneurysm. This jammed the hand-control shafting to the stern planes. *Plunger*'s skipper, Lieut. Comdr. David C. White, called this depth charge close to number 178, his boat's hull number. Would our stronger steel risers have cracked, and had *Plunger* survived because hers could expand? The way Captain Morton operated, I would expect *Wahoo* to leave most opposition and depth charges far behind, so we'd not put that to a test.

Bungo Suido, the southwestern straits into the Sea of Japan, was now back on our starboard quarter, and our passage continued to go unchallenged. At midafternoon on March 10, a call of "Land ho!" came from Torpedoman's Mate Bair, a volunteer on the search scope. There was probably a pool involved, and this was one way to keep the regular lookouts guarding their sectors and not favoring the area ahead.

The landfall was the peak of Yaku Shima, which *Wahoo* would round before entering the strait. "Right where it's supposed to be," injected Krause, implying a bit facetiously that any errors would have been the island's or on the chart; after all, Buka had been shown erroneously. The island continued to rise steadily out of the sea, and soon appeared much like pictures of Mount Fujiyama, near Tokyo, but with steeper sides. After another hour, a submerged run would reach Yaku Shima during evening twilight. Two blasts took *Wahoo* down and we were assured of reaching Colonet Strait undetected, and unless one should come in view of our scope, of not seeing even a plane since Midway.

KOREA OR **CHOSEN**

Sea of Japan

127°E

35°N

KO-TO

DAIKOKUSAN
GUNTO

HEN SHO

KAKYO TO

Tsushima

Strait

Shimonoseki

*To
Inland
Sea*

SAISHU TO

MARA TO

Sasebo

JAPAN

Nagasaki

ONIKI SAKI

KYUSHU

32°N

DANJO GUNTO

KAMI KOSHIKI

SHIMO KOSHIKI

Koshiki Strait

NOMA MISAKI

BONO MISAKI

KUSAKAKI SHIMA

TANEGA
SHIMA

EAST CHINA SEA

YAKU
SHIMA

Colonet Strait

SIXTY MILES

GAJA

TAIRA

NAKANO

SUWANOSE

Nakano Strait

NANSEI

SHOTO

*Pacific
Ocean*

3

Other islands that were shown on our chart rose above the horizon as *Wahoo* approached Yaku Shima. With true bearings of their peaks, we kept our position accurately plotted on the chart until well into evening twilight. Only a few fishermen and one trawler had come in view, and they had all passed clear before we surfaced into a black, quiet night. There were two options: to race through the strait and identify ourselves as a warship should the enemy have land-based radar; or to proceed at one-engine speed and, if spotted, to be identified as a trawler. The captain chose the latter, for the two engines that had already gone on charge could instantly be shifted to propulsion should speed be needed.

The dark, conical shape of Yaku Shima, now broad on our starboard bow, towered into the night, while her 6,000-foot peak still caught the sun's fading rays. Our attention, however, lay to port, where Kuchino Shima lay ahead and on the southern side of the strait. With time to spare, the island was positively identified, and continuing along the track, *Wahoo* entered the East China Sea. The time was 0110 on Thursday, March 11, and clear of the Nansei Shoto, we came to course 005 true, which led to the area our captain had selected for the first day's patrol. It lay on the natural Nagasaki-Formosa shipping lane, and unaware of any United States submarines, the enemy might use it this day.

The whole island chain, extending from Japan's westernmost island, Kyushu, to Formosa was labeled the Ryukyus on our chart. Although they were not clearly labeled, the Nansei Shoto apparently included the northern islands; the Sakishima Gunto those to the south; with other islands, including Okinawa, in between. Beyond the Bashi Channel south of Formosa lie the Philippines, so altogether, these islands gave Japan a somewhat protected shipping route to the areas that she had captured.

At dawn, *Wahoo* would be patrolling the northwestern terminus of that route.

A lookout, in his normal watch rotation, had a freshly baked roll between his teeth as he came up the conning tower ladder. Baking had followed a full battery charge on this first day in our patrol area, and was a couple of hours late. No longer absorbed with piloting, Krause and I suddenly felt hungry and headed on below while the supply lasted. He was fortunate, for many hands had stayed up for the transit and celebrated becoming China Sailors with Rowls's extra baking, but our chief cook had not forgotten him. Similarly, Jayson had sequestered two rolls in the pantry's warming oven and had only to turn on the switch. Such thoughtfulness always received my thank-you and would be reflected in his quarterly marks.

The time was 0610 when *Wahoo* dived for the first day of submerged patrol since Fais Island. To be factual, this was a day of reconnaissance rather than patrol, the first under Commander Morton. There would be changes that we had first discussed at Brisbane, and we both looked forward to the crew's reaction. The area had been clear on diving, so first we came up to SJ search depth as soon as Roger had reported, "Satisfied with the trim." At periscope depth a few minutes later, the search scope was kept up and manned continuously as long as sampans or other small craft remained clear.

Patrolling a line, rather than an area, we continued along the track from the strait towards Bono Misaki, the promontory on the southwest coast of Kyushu that all north-south Nagasaki shipping must clear. A half hour had passed with nothing in sight when the captain ordered a search with *Wahoo* at 50-foot keel depth. That would expose 17 feet of scope and treble the distance to the horizon. All was clear and we returned to normal search depth, which was now 64 to 60 feet. This would be a half-hourly procedure unless sampans or other craft were sighted, and then the captain or executive officer would modify it appropriately. It was a new and meaningful search that would detect any north-south shipping across a 15-mile front, with the visibility we enjoyed this day. The watch loved it, especially when they found that after the OOD's initial sweep-around, one scope was theirs with an initial sighting quite possible.

Searching through a periscope is not natural, and even though you can switch eyes, it soon becomes tiring. You are not just gazing at the sea, but literally examining every portion of the horizon and the clouds that jut up beyond but seem to be a part of the sea. It is there that a tiny cloud formation that doesn't change becomes a ship, or one that elongates can be a wisp of smoke above a ship that is still hull-down beyond the horizon. The experienced officer or quartermaster, even though spelling each other at the scope, will have flushed cheeks if they've been doing their best, and so it was with our seamen and volunteers. Though their combined effort had produced no sightings this day, a continuation surely would locate the enemy before many watches had passed.

Our daylight run had taken us 60 miles to the north, and probably to the west of any shipping, but that would not be the case tomorrow. On surfacing, two engines had gone on charge, while the other two were driving our submarine to the northwest towards the Koshiki Islands. Jutting out from the west coast of Kyushu, they formed an extended promontory. Since the *Sailing Directions* classifies the passage between the islands and Kyushu—the Koshiki Strait—as dangerous to navigation, we could expect major shipping to round these islands, and the captain selected a position to the southeast of the southernmost island for the morrow's patrol.

After surfacing, the crew had Tokyo Rose, the turncoat disk jockey, to amuse them in their mess room. Her remarks were corny, perhaps quite intentionally so, and cast doubt that she was really a defector. In either case, the records were all popular ones, the same that the crew would have heard stateside, and we found no objection.

More important to all hands was the evening Fox, for Buckley, always on the ball, hustled forward with an encoded message for members of the coding board. This now included any officers not on watch or without urgent business, and they gathered in the wardroom to use the ship's cipher. Since we would soon be in very salvageable waters, our secret electric coding machine had been turned in to the Submarine Base. Though breaking messages encoded in strip cipher takes longer, it is frankly more fun, much like a game: Twenty numbered strips each contain full alphabets, but with the letters in different scrambled order. The order in which strips are slid into grooves in the board is stipulated in a booklet, a different order for each day of the year. The letters from the message's five-letter groups are set against a vertical tape by sliding the strips to the left. Somewhere to the right, the plain language will appear in a vertical column. Including some padding, it took four setups to complete the decoding, but the message was worth the waiting:

LARGE SHIP DAMAGED BY SUNFISH MAY PROCEED RYUKYUS
NAGASAKI TOMORROW

According to the Japanese monograph, the damaged ship could just as well proceed eastward through the Bungo Suido and then via the Inland Sea to Kobe for repairs, but ours was a fifty-fifty chance. Morton considered a high-speed run back to the Ryukyus, but the Japanese current, or Kuroshio, setting to the northeast at 2 knots would make submerged patrolling amongst the islands difficult. So he chose a new position off the southern entrance to the Koshiki Strait where Bono Misaki would still be in sight to the northeast. Another engine went on propulsion, insuring that *Wahoo* would be on station waiting before the enemy could pass, and we moved on into the night, concentrating our searches in the sectors ahead and to starboard.

Lighted sampans, operating in pairs, gave our new lookouts practice in making the proper reports, and then before dawn the loom of the light on Bono Misaki showed over the dark horizon with characteristics, the seconds of light and occult periods, just as shown on our chart. The light's burning at all assured that our presence was unsuspected, and we dived at dawn confident that if *Sunfish*'s damaged ship were routed through this sea our scopes would spot her.

Sampans were in sight most of the day, and even two tall masts that seemed worthy of an approach. Beneath the masts, however, were two trawlers of about 60-foot length. But they served to check again Richie's TDC and to give the fire control party a moving target for its warm-up drill. On surfacing, we gave the area a thorough search and then headed for Saishu To, the great island that lies about 50 miles off the south coast of Chosen, or Korea. Within this passage, we expected to find shipping; for in his shirt pocket, following a final briefing at Pearl, Captain Morton had brought the various coordinates of a known shipping route connecting Shimonoseki, at the western entrance to the Inland Sea, to the great city and port of Shanghai to the west across the East China Sea.

The troops, as expressed by Pappy, had taken the minor disappointment of the day in stride, and would rather sink their own ship than share one with another boat. It could be that after just one day of participating in the periscope search they had a better appreciation of the work involved, but this in no way lessened their confidence in Deadly Dudley's ability to find ships and sink them.

At morning twilight, *Wahoo* was south of Mara To, a small island that shipping would round when passing to westward of Saishu To. This also included southbound ships from the small harbor on the western tip of Saishu To. Now 6 miles from the small island, the captain pulled the plug, and *Wahoo* would proceed to the known shipping lane, avoiding the possibility of being sighted. Ships were probably just as likely to pass within sight during this 25-mile run as they would if we were on the shipping lane, and we went to breakfast with a general feeling of confidence.

Mayberry, our new seaman, fairly burst through the wardroom's after doorway. Though seemingly out of breath from having raced 30 feet, he announced in a measured and clear voice, "We have smoke on the horizon, Captain." The time was 0814 on this Saturday, March 13. The captain saw me starting to rise, and nodded; this contact would be mine to investigate, and I went aft with a piece of toast in hand. By the time I had completed my first periscope observation, Manalesay had brought a cup of coffee.

The ship under the smoke became a will-o'-the-wisp: sometimes in sight, and moments later not, our changing identifications ranged from a circling, large, coal-burning trawler to a Q-ship. Whatever, she gave Richie and his fire control party conniptions. Captain Morton settled this by dubbing her a *Smoky Maru,* and we had to conclude that an atmospheric inversion layer was bending the light rays intermittently and thus giving us a wild fire control drill.

We finally gave up on this target, but she was not through with *Wahoo.* At 1640 the same *Smoky Maru* came over the horizon heading directly for us, and the Bells of Saint Mary's rang in earnest for the first time on our fourth patrol. The problem was simple; the captain conned his boat away from her path, and she came on to present us with a 90 track. She was worth one torpedo, especially if it hit, but not worth the two that could assure the sinking of a large ship. Accordingly, Morton ordered a single after tube made ready for firing; this would preclude a natural impulse to fire more.

The *Smoky Maru*'s angle had opened nicely. Richie and Chan agreed on an enemy speed of 12 knots; and on my call of port 70, the captain gave his assuring, "Any time, Dick."

"Constant bearing–Mark"; "Set," from Richie; and "Fire!" as her stack amidships touched the wire, sent our torpedo on its way. The smoke and bubbles seemed to be leading the small ship properly, but then the torpedo itself broached and disappeared just ahead of the enemy, who gave no indication that she had seen it or the wake.

We had used a masthead height of 75 feet in determining the range, but now on reviewing the books and *Gudgeon*'s sketch of her similar Q-ship, the height should have been 55 or 60. At the start of the approach, the ship was closer, and her speed to the firing point had been about 10 instead of 12 knots, so our TDC and its angle solver, performing as directed, had sent our lonely fish too far ahead.

4

Knowing our mistake lessened the pain of wasting a torpedo that we had brought thousands of miles, and this was further eased by the knowledge that our presence was still unsuspected. The whole day was not lost, however, for our extensive maneuvers had emphasized the limitations imposed by our failing storage batteries.

Back in the Bureau of Ships, the experts had surmised that depth charging might crack the conventional hard-rubber battery jars, so a suitable alternative had been proposed. Perhaps, once again, as in the case of the bubble sextants, *Wahoo* had been selected as a guinea pig. Our battery jars were laminated, having a rubber jar inside a steel jar, and then another rubber jar outside. The design must have withstood shock tests and such, but quite evidently not the internal temperature of about 120 degrees with the outer shell in contact with the colder, lead-lined battery well. The steel didn't crack, but the rubber, having a different coefficient of expansion, did. The acid then reached the steel insert, and when the outer shell cracked, that individual battery cell grounded to the battery well and *Wahoo*'s hull. Such cells had to be disconnected immediately lest the current impressed by partial or even total battery voltage start a fire. For this, we carried jumpers to bypass the affected cells and some healthy cells too in order to maintain the same voltage in the forward and after great batteries.

The failure had become progressive, an arithmetic one at present, and not considered vital by those behind the desks who had simply ordered a new battery. The problem of just where, when, and how it could be installed was apparently on the back burner, while *Wahoo* very nearly had a corner on the jumper market. Though we still had three-quarters of our original battery capacity, there could be little juice to spare for evasion following a long approach and attack. This would be particularly true to the north and west, where the depth of the sea is better measured in feet than fathoms, and where evasion would consist of a horizontal run for it.

These were our considerations as we crossed CinCPac Intelligence's recommended track, which Krause and Simonetti had neatly laid down as a dotted line on the conning tower chart. Another *Smoky Maru* came over the horizon for supper, a third for breakfast after we had dived south of Kakyo To light, and then two more before 0800. At least our extra periscope watches had things to see other than birds on this Sunday, March 14; in part as a reward for their diligence, Morton conducted an approach on a pall of smoke lying over the area where they had gone. The scopes soon had five SM's in sight, and then the one under the smoke made it six large commercial fishermen, perhaps gillnetting. Any large ship would avoid their nets, and so would *Wahoo* as the captain asked the course for Hen Sho. I picked 040 off the chart and received Morton's, "Make it so." (We were informal in our conversations, but always precise in orders affecting our ship.)

A submerged day off Hen Sho brought an innovation—a bona fide patrol. Her presence might foretell a ship, so rather than evade, we kept her in sight until she finally disappeared amongst the small islands to the east. This left only the passage inside the Daikokusan Gunto to complete our coverage of the provided shipping route. By the following midmorning, with horizon clear, three blasts sent us up for a surface patrol. We had done our part in finding where the ships were not, and now headed where they had to be, first due north.

Upon reaching the latitude where our submarine *Haddock* had found east-west shipping, the captain directed a course towards the Shantung Promontory, the great peninsula that juts out from China into the Yellow Sea. On Roger's order, Mayberry brought our bow smartly to port, met the swing with 5 degrees right rudder, and settled *Wahoo* precisely on 290. Our new seaman was a good steersman, which had been a requirement in peacetime, but now it came routinely with a trick at the wheel on every watch.

Stepped off on the chart, our run would be just over 200 miles, which was good, for the landfall would come after dark, permitting us to gain a likely dawn attack position. But that was tomorrow and today was Wednesday, March 17, Saint Patrick's Day, and those with Irish forebears outnumbered any other group in *Wahoo*. So Phillips, Rowls, and our new cook, Rennels, would be preparing the traditional corned

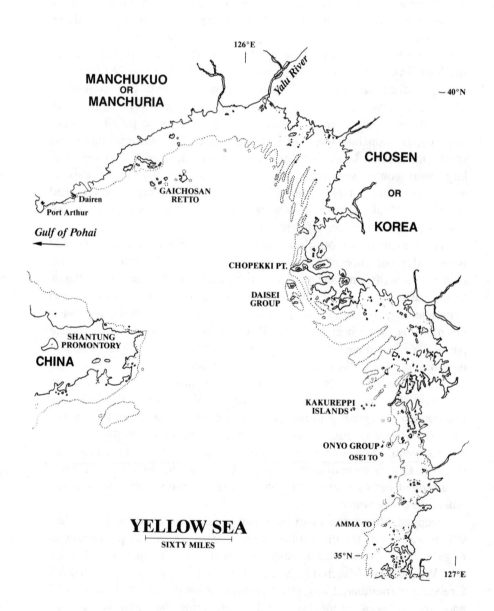

YELLOW SEA

SIXTY MILES

beef and cabbage with all the trimmings, while others, except for their watches, would enjoy a rope-yarn Sunday.

During *Wahoo*'s first two patrols, a key to transfer had laid in qualifying in submarines and making the next higher rate. Then shown in excess of our allowance for that rate, orders would be forthcoming from Force Personnel. So working on their course books and qualifications had required little urging by their division officers. Now, most of *Wahoo*'s hands were afraid of being transferred before they had the usual five patrols to rate new construction in the States. The captain had entered into this with his personal guarantee and went a bit further: They might be eligible for transfer if they *didn't* qualify or complete their course books. A turn through the boat showed the result. For every cribbage or acey-deucey game, there were a half dozen or so studying, some singly and others in groups—a performance usually seen only while returning from patrol. Truly, Morton had his crew eating out of his hand.

The holiday meal was moved to suppertime, when the crew's watches and all hands would be assured of a hot meal. The corned beef had been boxed and frozen, the same as all our meats. The cabbage must have been canned, but of finest quality. Like the whole meal, the boiled potatoes were piping hot and done till they'd just fall in pieces when pierced with the fork. It is said that you can't find real corned beef and cabbage outside of New York City. From personal experience, I'd add Durgin Park in Boston, and now the USS *Wahoo*. Cooks may not participate in the final mechanics of sinking an enemy ship, but I believe the final patrol results can well be proportional to the quality of their work.

Our plan of completing the transit for an evening landfall had been thwarted by three geese that certainly resembled a formation of fighter-bombers on an intercepting course. Commander MacMillan's two blasts had taken us down, and nearly an hour passed before a similar flight closed our periscope and we were sure. Another dash brought a horizon dotted with small masts, and below them our raised periscope watches called out the hulls of sampans, junks, and trawlers. On the latter, we could see antennas, which would probably crackle with messages if we ran through them on the surface, so our landfall was rescheduled for dawn.

The commander was standing Chan's watches while he worked with Buckley on our sick SJ, so he and Captain Morton bore the brunt of the tactics to avoid the fifty or so fishermen. We felt no thuds, so considered that their maneuvers had been successful. For sure, no submarine was ever conned through a fishing fleet by more rank or talent. The DRI should have taken into account all of their maneuvers, but I was just as happy that our track would clear the promontory to the northeast should we be ahead of our DR on the chart.

Our dawn stars on March 18 showed *Wahoo* 19 miles northeast of the promontory (51 degrees to be exact), and Jack's two blasts took us down for the day. Shortly, the morning haze turned to thick fog, and sound had to be our ears and eyes, for Chan and Buckley were still struggling with the SJ. The intermittent light screws of fishermen provided training for our new hands, and *Sailing Directions* provided training for me. Such fog was not usual this time of year in the Yellow Sea, so it must have been a local condition, and the captain picked Round Island light off Dairen as our next patrol spot. Lifting fog and successful SJ repairs came simultaneously in late afternoon and *Wahoo* was up and on her way.

The captain and I had continued to vent our frustrations and help the adrenalin subside after actions by a game or two of cribbage. And for more friendly reasons, an evening game after he had written his Night Orders had become routine. I am told that I learned to count on our cribbage board, so all of the intricacies of the game, the value of hands, and scoring had become quite automatic. So this night, when Captain Morton dealt me three fives and the jack of the missing suit, I instantly realized that my chances were approximately one in forty of cutting the remaining five of spades for a perfect twenty-nine cribbage hand. I let out a whoop, calling, "This could be it!" Hands going forward to the movies filled the doorways to watch the cut, and all protocol was brushed aside for such an event. I cut, and this time it was their war whoop, for face up for all to see was the five of spades.

Richie signed the five; the captain signed the jack; while Roger, Chan, and Jack signed the other fives. *Wahoo* being a cribbage-playing ship, we had constant visitors for a look, and later a repeat viewing after the movies. By then, remembering what we could from our math course in permutations and combinations, various odds—ranging from the hundred thousands to the low millions—filled our sheets of lined paper. The chief of the boat has singular authority in settling shipboard differences, and this time Pappy Rau produced a well-thumbed book of facts. Pappy read: "Some mathematicians figure the odds at one in a quarter million."

Twenty-nine cribbage hand held by Lieutenant Commander O'Kane and dealt by Captain Morton in the U.S.S. Wahoo *ten miles north of Shantung Promontory at 2030, March 18, 1943. Mathematicians Cedric G. Larson and Dick Cornwell independently figured the odds against this hand at 216,580; against a 28 hand at 15,028.*

A host of omens concerning ships and the seas has accumulated over the ages. Once taken seriously, most are given but a smile today. But if the greetings I received from a fair portion of the crew—the rubbing of their palms together at chin height, like a crapshooter—were an indication, they believed this twenty-nine hand was a good omen, portending success for our ship.

When Krause called me for morning stars, Jayson had a Silex of friendly coffee ready. (He and Manalesay now took turns at this.) With mug in hand, I had started aft when the Bells of St. Mary's chimed in earnest for the second time on this patrol. A glance at the clock on the bulkhead read 0422 on this March 19, and we raced for the conning tower to avoid the rush to battle stations that would follow.

Topside, George Misch and his lookouts had the silhouette of a fine freighter, and he had taken the immediate action required—to get ahead of the enemy. Already, our battle station engineers were pouring on the coal, and it was none too soon, for the crack of dawn was only 20 minutes away. *Wahoo* raced, now approaching full speed and laying down a trail of smoke. My TBT bearings and the SJ fixed our relative positions, and encouraging word came up from below: we would reach a good attack position.

At 0440 the first gray of dawn showed to the east, and fortunately helped to silhouette the enemy, not us. Her angle was now sharpening, and we surely must be close enough to her track for a submerged approach. I had advised only that it was getting pretty light topside. But Morton was set on gaining a position from which he could attack even if the enemy made a dawn course change.

At 0455 it was light enough to see through the scope, and finally two blasts took us down, pausing while a final radar range and periscope bearing fixed her position. Both Chan and Richie agreed on an enemy speed of 9 knots instead of 10. Captain Morton had readied two tubes forward and aft, and now ordered the forward doors opened; it would be a bow shot. Her port angle was opening as it should. I heard Richie advise, "750 yards from the track," as I called 90 port.

The captain waited for an approximate 120 track, the aspect that would allow maximum enemy maneuvers and still insure that our torpedoes would hit, and then said, "Any time, Dick. Fire just one torpedo."

"Stand by for a constant bearing," and the scope came up to my hands.

"Constant bearing–Mark!" Hunter read the bearing.

"Set," came from Richie. Her stack amidships touched the wire.

"Fire," and the captain hit the plunger simultaneously. The time was 0515. The shudder, the zing, and the slight pressure on our ears were followed by Buckley's, "Hot, straight and normal." Chan was calling off the seconds since firing. For the 750-yard torpedo run, it should hit in 49 seconds. It did with a crack, whack, and wallop such as none of us had heard, for the warhead contained the new explosive called torpex.

The freighter's midships and stern disintegrated, and Chief McGill, who had long awaited his turn, saw only the bow at a sharp angle and then flotsam as the steam and smoke blew clear. Chan timed the sinking at 2 minutes and 26 seconds. Three blasts sent *Wahoo* up and through the bits of flotsam. Our camera bugs had the first priority, but the smashed bottom of a small boat and surrounding debris were the only objects for snapshots. Just a few were taken since everyone found the finality of the destruction without possibility of survivors too sobering. A salty, "Sail ho," from the after port lookout sent the photographers below, and 5 minutes later we dived for another approach. First sighted in the morning haze, the target developed into a classic junk that proved to be more popular with our photographers anyway, and convenient since she was sailing towards Round Island too.

Rowls had seen the light and we all had breakfast early upon securing from battle stations. A ship down with two torpedoes fired instead of our one miss was infinitely better both mathematically and mentally, and it showed on every face. That every new hand would be on the list to receive the coveted submarine combat pin, and others would add a star designating another successful patrol, had its part in the general elation. And a few skeptics might have second thoughts about such omens as a perfect cribbage hand.

The singular wallop of the torpex warhead remained the main topic of conversation, but was soon replaced by ONI-208J. Pharmacist Kohl and party had flagged the pages of possible ships with numbered slips indicating the priority of their choices. I was surprised that they had even been able to do this from the meager information provided. Before I had a chance to look at the party's choices, the captain bent the slips over each of the four pages so I could not see the numbers on the slips. I quickly chose the *Nanka Maru* of 4,065 tons as the class most closely resembling what I had seen. It was the party's choice too, confirming their value, my continuing luck, or perhaps both.

The captain was finishing his bacon and eggs when the phone to his left buzzed. Our conversation stopped, and as he raised the receiver we could plainly hear, "Captain to the conning tower." Glancing at the clock, which read 0755, he left with a "Here we go again," and his usual friendly smile. In the conning tower, Richie already had *Wahoo* at standard speed on the normal approach course. The ship was another freighter, and it was already presenting such a broad starboard angle that gaining an attack position could be in doubt. Instead of slowing to confirm the situation, as some skippers would, Morton complimented Richie with a "Pretty good for a battleship sailor," and then confirmed Richie's judgment by increasing our speed to full.

It would be a long chase, with only the tracking party and talkers required at their battle stations, though the others would probably be close at hand. The situation would not allow slowing for normal observations; two would have to suffice. If the enemy ship continued on course, *Wahoo* would just reach an attack position; if she zigged away, we would not. Watching her zig would not help. I found myself looking at the conning tower overhead in the direction of the enemy and mentally urging our submarine on, just as I had done at the races. No doubt others were doing the same, for this race made any other seem insignificant.

At 0830 the captain stopped the screws for a possible sound bearing, and at his nod, I tried an observation. The scope was vibrating too much in the passing seas to permit details, but Hunter read my bearing at the middle of the blur. It checked with sound and was close to Chan's plot. *Wahoo* was maintaining a nearly constant bearing; an attack would be assured if the enemy continued on course, and the Bells of St. Mary's chimed for the second time this day. Simonetti had rung up full at the captain's nod; compartments reported manned, and the log showed 10 knots.

At 0905 we slowed and I reported her angle at starboard 30. When the angle opened to 45, I reported her visible details: She was a plumb-bow, mast-funnel-mast freighter, with long midships superstructure and high bridge forward. Kohl had head and shoulders through the hatch, so had the word. I watched for an exact 90 angle and called it when the forward face of her bridge came in line. Hunter read 2,000 yards a moment later.

I expected the captain's usual word, but he chose to close further for his favorite 120 degree track. The few minutes seemed to drag; the enemy might well be zigging, but finally Richie's dials showed 120 and a range of 1,850. Apparently noting my impatience, Morton changed his usual wording to, "All right, Dick, any time," but I still caught his usual smile as the scope came to my hands. This time there was no "Stand by."

"Constant bearing—Mark," called by Hunter, was followed by a "Set," from Richie, and my, "Fire!" Our captain hit the plunger, and the torpedo should hit under her stack. Buckley had called, "Hot, straight and normal," but from my scope, the wake seemed to be leading the ship too much. The captain directed the outer door opened on the second tube. The wake did not lie, but the result was not too bad, as a whack, wallop, and shaking detonation tore her side out abreast the foremast.

Within seconds, the next torpedo was on its way, similarly aimed, but with the ship's speed at 7 knots instead of the previous 9 set in the TDC. This wake appeared to be leading the ship properly, now falling behind the foremast and then the bridge. It hit exactly as aimed, with a plume of water thrown upon the ship's side by the exploding air flask. There was no detonation, but coinciding with this sight was Buckley's report of the thud of the dud.

Somewhat down by the bow, the ship turned away, so we could not confirm that she was sinking, but that would be the case if she did not have better-than-average athwartship bulkheads. We could not pursue her while submerged with our low battery, nor could we surface in the face of her large guns, but our torpedoes could and would reach her in less than 3 minutes. Two more went on their way; if she maneuvered to avoid the first, the second would have a broad target. The Japanese are good seamen, however, and her skipper conned his ship precisely, avoiding both of them. Then to discourage us, the after gun commenced shelling our scope. We obliged by dropping to 80 feet and clearing to the east. On the wardroom table were the pages from ONI-208J with our ships' silhouettes:

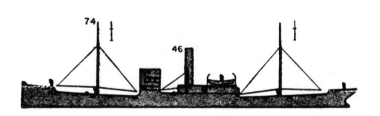

NANKA MARU

Tonnages:		Constructed:	
Gross: 4,065	D. W.: 6,650	1906	Great Britain

Length:		Propulsion:	
W. L. (B. P.): 361'	O. A.:	Machinery:	Reciprocating
		Screws: 1	H. P.:
Beam: 50'		R. P. M.:	@ Knots:
		Fuel: Coal	Capacity: 756 tons
Drafts:		Radius: 6,700 miles at 9 knots.	
Loaded: 22' 6"	Light: 7'		

Potential naval value: AP, AK.

Speed:	
Normal cruising: 9	Max.: 11

Remarks: Do not confuse canvas ventilators with kingposts.

KUWAYAMA MARU
Similar: **SIRAHA MARU, TATUHA MARU, TOKUSIMA MARU, TOTTORI MARU**

Tonnages:
  Gross: 5,725   D. W.: 9,500
Length:
  W. L. (B. P.): 423'   O. A.:
Beam: 56'
Drafts:
  Loaded: 25'   Light: 10'
Speed:
  Normal cruising: 10   Max.: 12
Constructed:
  1916   Great Britain

Propulsion:
  Machinery: Reciprocating
  Screws: 1   N. H. P.: 556
                       I. H. P.: 3,203
  R. P. M.: 88   @ Knots: 12
  Fuel: Coal   Capacity: 2,300
                                 tons
  Radius: 15,000 miles at 10 knots.

Potential naval value: AK, AP.

Remarks: TOTTORI MARU has two life boats to a side. TOKUSIMA—Believed to be carrying oil in bulk.

Ship similar to *Tottori Maru* reported by Japanese to have been sunk in same location.

5

We had a quorum in the wardroom, including the commander, who was enthusiastic about the attacks but did not voice an opinion about the last two torpedoes. To me, they were the captain's follow-through, the right cross after the left jab, and carried out his promise to the crew that *Wahoo* would go after every ship and do everything possible to put them on the bottom. I would not have had it otherwise.

We were turning our attention to the ONI sheets when Electrician's Mate Heiden, whom we would see frequently, pushed the wooden grill aside and emerged from the battery well abreast the wardroom. After closing its hatch, he presented the pilot cells' gravity readings of 1,060 and 1,062 to Roger at our table. Morton considered the situation out loud: we could continue at our present 4 knots until dark, but not so if we made an approach on another ship. Our course of 075 leading back across the Yellow Sea to a position just north of Chopekki Point on the Korean coast might well intercept another ship, and the captain ordered 3 knots and intermittent high-periscope searching.

Back to the ONI pages, we found the pictures poor but interesting. More useful were the accurate broadside drawings that contained all of the details to assist in identification and then the heights and lengths for use in the periscope stadimeter. One detail of *Nanka Maru* that I had not seen due to her sharper angles was her counter stern, which was clearly shown on the sketch. On *Tottori Maru* the same type stern must have been clearly visible, but I had failed to note and report it for Kohl. That type of stern almost marks a ship's age. Both originally British ships, *Nanka Maru* was built in 1906, *Tottori Maru* in 1916. Of more importance was the 2-knot speed error that had appeared on both Chan's plot and Richie's TDC. Had the last target slowed just before our firing, or was the input from our Pit log in error? To find out, Roger would check our average propeller turns, then Chan and Richie would run a previously recorded problem on the TDC. Before the next ship, we must know the answer.

If there had been a sailing junk astern, she would have passed us up, but for a change not even a fisherman came in sight. We must have been off the banks, for a single-ping sounding showed a comfortable 130 feet, leaving 70 feet below our keel. An 0310 sighting on March 20 served as an early star call for me and Krause, and we almost missed our sights during a half-hour approach on a trawler or patrol. A good position for our coming landfall took precedence over further investigation, so when clear we surfaced momentarily for stars. The fix showed that we would see the coastline by noon, giving a half day to observe any shipping and plan our operations for Sunday, March 21.

Tracking smoke during the early afternoon, followed by mastheads and stacks later in the day, outlined our strategy for us. The shipping to and from the large Korean port of Chinnampo had to round Chopekki Point. On the chart, the noted local currents seemed formidable for a submerged submarine. Rather than avoid them, we decided to try them out during the night with the thought of picking a dawn diving position where they could work to our advantage.

Without Chan, Buckley, and Carter with their SJ and fathometer giving peak performance, we could not have prowled the bays and promontories. But before dawn we had found a spot that should insure an attack and a subsequent retreat with the current to open, if not deep, seas.

Well cut in with bearings and ranges recorded on the chart, *Wahoo* would maintain station waiting for a ship till into morning twilight. Soon thereafter, we would dive, and if remaining in this location required an unacceptable drain from our batteries, we would move with the current and trust that our potential target would be affected similarly.

In such a situation, the captain or navigator would normally be at hand in the conning tower or on the bridge. Our organization, with an operations officer acting as an assistant navigator and sharing the responsibility, eased that situation considerably. I was able to take catnaps of a half hour or so and remain refreshed. (The ability to fall into immediate deep sleep was one I had acquired in destroyers and then perfected in submarines.) I was routinely called by Krause for morning twilight whether we were to take stars or not; thus I had time to learn what was going on before the captain did.

Topside, Jack and his four lookouts, all equipped with 7 × 50s, were peering out into the still-starlit night with the concentration of hunters, which indeed they were. In the conning tower again, Chan had our position plotted well within the circle that the captain had drawn on the chart. Yesterday we had seen ships during daylight; but none, we were certain, had passed during the night. Being prudent mariners, they would not pass close to Chopekki Point, or inside the Daisei group during darkness, and so would have planned their passage accordingly. With good visibility we could spot a ship before she sighted us, and with our SJ the same would hold in the frequent morning haze. But here there could be shore lookouts on the point just 4 miles distant, and we dived during morning twilight when our period of periscope blindness would last only a few minutes. After Jack had reported the horizon clear, I took the scope to find Chopekki Point right where it was supposed to be as we headed into the current.

On my way to the wardroom, I noted that the captain was awake, reading. I reported the situation above as all quiet, only to have it contradicted by Jack's excited voice over the 1MC: "Ship on the horizon! Angle on the bow thirty starboard," and the Bells of St. Mary's tumbled the remainder of the ship's company out of their bunks. *Wahoo* was already swinging to intercept the enemy when I took the scope from Jack. His call was correct, as I expected, for he had worked with me on angles since Brisbane. Another call was not necessary, only the range of 7,000 yards, our distance to the horizon; but in support of Jack and his efforts, I called a true 30 starboard too.

The captain conned his submarine to the normal approach course while Chief Ware and his electricians poured in the juice, bringing *Wahoo* to standard speed. We would close handily if she did not zig away, and that did not seem likely if she intended to hug the coastline northward. To be sure, the captain stopped our screws so Buckley could grab a sound bearing of the enemy. It did not check with TDC; her bearing had drawn to the left, and the following periscope observation showed why. With a 60-degree zig, she now presented a 30 port angle, halving the firing range. With a simple turn, the captain was assured of a better position than even hoped for.

I had now seen the details and called them after the scope was lowered. She was another mast-funnel-mast ship similar to, but longer than, the *Tottori Maru:* There were king posts with long booms just forward and aft of her long superstructure. She could best be classed as a passenger freighter. Pharmacist Kohl received the information from Lindhe's former perch, and then dropped below to the books. In minutes he reported the probable ship's masthead height and her length. That was all I needed for accurate ranges and a stadimeter check on the angles after I had called them; the name of the selected ship could wait.

Our approach to the firing point moved swiftly, in part because the enemy ship was cruising at 11 knots, and because of our compensating speed. Again, the captain selected a 120 track. That meant *Wahoo*'s torpedoes would strike from 30 degrees abaft her beam, and I made a mental note for the future to accept any broad track and hit before another zig. Two more observations checked with Chan and Richie; then word came up from Kohl that the ship was a 7,210 tonner. Morton ordered three torpedoes spaced along the length of the ship—to stern, bow, and amidships. With any error at all, two of them would hit.

We slowed for the firing, and I mentally sighed with relief when Buckley's bearing checked with the TDC: she had not zigged. Morton confidently said those welcome words, "Any time, Dick."

"Bearing—Mark," read by Krause, "Set," by Richie, and my "Fire" had the three torpedoes on their way as directed within 23 seconds. Chan was calling the seconds till our torpedoes should hit, a total of 104. We had been too accurate: the first torpedo of the spread missed astern, the second was ahead (unless they were duds), but the third hit exactly as aimed. The torpex crack, whack, and wallop gave the freighter an almost instant down angle that increased with the passing seconds. With the captain's nod, I passed the scope to Richie, who described the sinking for the battle telephone talkers. It did not take long, for she dived to Davy Jones's locker 4½ minutes after the detonation. There were about 30 survivors amongst the flotsam, one of whom had already made a raft out of the wreckage and climbed clear of the sea. Others would do likewise, and being in full view from the point, would undoubtedly be rescued. A patrol could be on its way, and Simonetti brought our head to 225 degrees, the ordered course of southwest.

To go with breakfast, we had ONI-208J flagged to the page of our target. There could be no mistake; we had sunk another ship of the *Seiwa Maru* class.

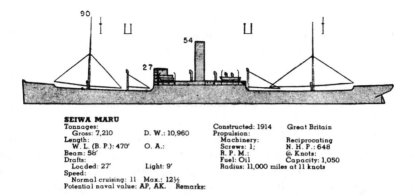

SEIWA MARU
Tonnages:
   Gross: 7,210   D. W.: 10,960
Length:
   W. L. (B. P.): 470'   O. A.:
Beam: 58'
Drafts:
   Loaded: 27'   Light: 9'
Speed:
   Normal cruising: 11   Max.: 12½
Potential naval value: AP, AK.   Remarks:

Constructed: 1914   Great Britain
Propulsion:
   Machinery: Reciprocating
   Screws: 1;   N. H. P.: 648
   R. P. M.:   @ Knots:
   Fuel: Oil   Capacity: 1,050
   Radius: 11,000 miles at 11 knots

The 3-knot southerly current would take *Wahoo* dangerously close to the Daisei group, but the westerly component of our own 4-knot speed would keep us well clear while leaving the attack scene at close to 7 knots. At the captain's request, I had Krause bring the area chart to the wardroom after breakfast. There he planned the rest of the day and night to follow. First, we would continue with the current, slowing after an hour to conserve our battery. Then, after dark, *Wahoo* would head across the sea again to the Shantung Promontory. Thus we might convince the enemy that there were at least two submarines patrolling in this area. He would then have to guess where a submarine might strike next, or spread his antisubmarine forces unacceptably thin.

With breakfast and the grand strategy decisions finished, the captain reached for the cribbage board. The first two hands were relaxing, and then Morton dealt again. I picked up my cards to find four fives. That's not too rare, counting the two discards as extra chances, but it was the makings of a twenty-eight cribbage hand, needing only the cutting of any face card or a ten. We had a quorum watching as I cut a jack for the captain, allowing him to peg two, while my twenty-eight hand ran out the rubber game. Captain Morton exploded, "Why, I'll never play another game with you," and tore the remaining cards into bits, pitching them through the pantry window.

"Oh well," he continued, again in his calm, friendly manner, "it's time for another ship anyway. I'm going to the conning tower." Pushing back his chair, he had only half risen when the Bells of St. Mary's rang out for the second time on this fifth day of spring. The clock read 0930.

The commander had a ship, still partially hull-down, with an estimated angle of 5 starboard. The periscope stadimeter range read 13,000 yards or 6½ miles. This checked closely with our distance to the horizon tables, so she would indeed close to a firing position in a half hour. The ship came on zigging mildly or steering poorly. With my periodic stadimeter ranges, both Chan and Richie had her clocked at 10 knots. This should be a precise firing.

Captain Morton had made ready forward and after tubes, and now waited on the enemy's projected track, pulling off to the east when the range closed to 4,000 yards. The enemy would thus present a starboard track when she passed us to seaward, with little likelihood that she would zig in our direction towards shoal water.

Her angle had opened rapidly, keeping Krause and me busy with water-lapping looks across a flat sea. Now visible was her typical mast-funnel-mast and midships superstructure. Our confidence grew with quiet "Checks" from Richie. The angle was 45, and then 60, changing rapidly for the range was short; Hunter read 800 as the scope lowered. Perhaps this time the captain would shoot early.

"Any time, Dick." We were clicking.

Richie called the TDC's generated bearing; Hunter twisted the tube so the scope came up already on the freighter. It had taken no more than 3 seconds and was better than a synchro mechanism, for ours had anticipation. The "Bearing–Mark," "Set," and "Fire" were repeated for the captain three times, and his palm on the plunger sent torpedoes that should hit under her stack, mainmast, and foremast at 10-second intervals.

We had felt and heard the sounds of firing but welcomed Buckley's report of all hot, straight and normal. A few men were physically urging them on with a left jab or right cross; this must certainly be true in the after torpedo room, for this was their only firing since the first unsuccessful attack of this patrol.

Chan was counting down for the 52-second torpedo run, but his final seconds were smothered by two devastating detonations under the ship's bridge and mainmast. Our camera bugs were already manning the search scope when she slid under the sea, timed by Chan at 3 minutes and 10 seconds after the torpedoing. A sweep-around showed two junks closing the scene, and Morton immediately ordered preparations for a battle surface. Shifting stations, with many hands coming to and through the control room and then breaking out ammunition, took extra time.

The battle surface itself was fast, but so were the junks, which we found fleeing towards the nearest shoals. A quick plot showed that their engines would win the race to the 10-fathom curve on our chart, so reversing course headed *Wahoo* to the scene of the sinking.

There had been long-standing instructions to retrieve a copy of the *Japanese Merchant Marine Code,* and as we approached two overturned lifeboats there were indeed books afloat amidst the other flotsam. The skies and horizon were clear, the seas flat calm, and we had not sighted a single plane in the area, so I was not surprised when the captain called for life rings, lines, and *Wahoo*'s best swimmers. A good third of the crew responded, but Chief Lane wisely allowed only a dozen topside including the line handlers.

The scene that followed surely was unique in modern submarine warfare, and rather resembling swimming call. Morton had but to point, and one or two hands would dive in to retrieve the object. I bent my efforts in getting the swimmers back aboard, getting the upper hand but not before we had a pile of flotsam to strike below. In the pile were books, one of which might indeed be the code, but souvenirs for shipmates predominated, with three notable exceptions: two great house flags of the steamship's line and a large life preserver with the ship's name in both Japanese and English block letters spelling *Nitu Maru.*

There were several survivors who showed their desire not to be rescued by ducking under the overturned boats, so we cleared the area at full speed, to the southwest for deception, and then slowing, commenced a surface patrol en route again to the Shantung Promontory.

6

Simonetti's entry in the Quartermaster's Notebook showed 1138 as the time we had left the scene of the last sinking. Now, an hour later, including our dogleg route, the dividers showed *Wahoo* 15 miles from the action. Whenever possible, surface runs would be our evasion until we reached deep seas. When the enemy found two more ships overdue, they might well mount a respectable antisubmarine effort. This might already be underway, spurred by the previous losses, so both high-periscope and regular lookouts were searching.

In all of the patrol reports I had read, no submarine had put four ships on the bottom while still having half her torpedoes remaining. If we had no further torpedo failures, this could become the leading patrol of the war even if the *Tottori Maru* did not sink. Our crew knew this, and certainly in a wartime submarine, enemy ships on the bottom was one of the keys to a happy ship. Even between the torpedo rooms— which had the same batting average—the bickering had stopped, at least for the moment.

While the captain was about the ship congratulating his crew, our PCO and I relaxed with a game of cribbage. It extended to three, the commander winning the rubber, and then he went over my figuring of the odds against holding a twenty-eight hand. In this, only the four specific cards, the fives, are required, and to go with them any face card or ten. There being sixteen of those versus the one specific card required for the twenty-nine hand, I had just divided Pappy's figure by 16 giving 1 in 15,625. And the commander agreed that it should be close enough for submarine use. I made a duplicate of the odds and called Manalesay, who took the sheet aft to be typed and to go with the signed hand that was on display in the control room. Even the noncrib-

214

bage players would see those figures, and coupled with the previous hand, might join the ranks of those who heeded omens.

Movies are never started until the captain arrives or has indicated that he will not attend. Morton seldom did, but this night, by way of celebrating the patrol's halfway mark (and perhaps to keep his word about cribbage), he surprised the messenger and went forward. In surface ships, where there is room, the officers and crew always stand when the captain arrives and until he is seated. In submarines, this isn't practical, but those attending recognize him by holding their conversations and nodding. This night, for the first time in nearly 9 years of sea duty, I heard the captain greeted by a spontaneous cheer and glad hand.

Patrolling off the promontory brought no ships, but did allow all hands to return to normal after the actions off Chopekki Point. And there was a more important development: One of our main motors had developed noises that could be the warning signal of major trouble. During one of our short dives, Chief Pruett and his electricians quickly traced the noise to a loose carbon brush and repaired it on the spot. It did not seem like much, but had it fallen off we could have been without that motor for the remainder of the patrol.

Wahoo was in the enviable position of having a skipper who had traveled this area in peacetime, so on March 22 our surface patrol continued towards the Laotiehshan Promontory that juts out just to the west of Port Arthur into the broad entrance to the Gulf of Pohai. In that vicinity, we should find shipping to or from Chinwangtao, which lies at the gulf's western extremity. Our progress was hindered by two power sampans that turned out to be trawlers. They were not worth torpedoes brought 5,000 miles for a bigger job, and we avoided them.

Increasing numbers of sampans and junks posed a problem this night. Often too small to show on our radar or to be seen at any distance against the dark background of the sea, we'd find them close aboard and sometimes underfoot. So far, our OOD's had missed them all. Lookouts down on deck would seem to be the answer, but not when diving was so imminent. It became just that when a small ship came into sight presenting a sharp angle on the bow. The time was 0043 on March 23. We dived for an approach, only to lose our target in the haze and spend 2 hours in getting back to the surface without damaging our shears or radar.

After the watch had changed, just before 0400, we barely missed a rowboat and hand who was frantically rowing across our bow from starboard to port. The fisherman may owe his life to John Campbell's instant, "Right full rudder!" Back on course again, we enjoyed a few minutes without sampans in sight, when Seaman Gerlacher, manning the SJ, reported a possible pip that had faded. Continuing to examine across the original bearing disclosed a pip that was unmistakably taller than the normal grassy line across the screen. Jack, as operations officer, called the relative bearing, and there she lay about two points on our starboard bow. We stopped, the radar range was closing, and Captain Morton took the conn.

Reversing course, we would run ahead of the ship for tracking, and then dive for a periscope firing at dawn. Once more, we threaded our way through the maze of fishing boats and again very nearly ran down the same rowboat, rowing frantically across our bow. What thoughts of monster demons must have been whirling in that fisherman's head?

Richie and Chan quickly had the ship on a course that would clear the channel; she was smarter than we had been. We followed suit, crossing to her port bow where we should be completely clear of sampans. Again, the Bells of St. Mary's held reveille, but truly no crewman would object to such an awakening. Minutes later, two blasts took us down as we continued to pull off her track. A convenient zig or change of course helped open the range, and the captain turned for a bow shot. This would save our remaining after torpedoes for a later attack when a stern shot might be required.

My angles would not be as good as those Chan and Richie could read from the chart and TDC. Hunter and I gave bearings only, and I remarked, "Her silhouette looks broad." Richie announced, "Range 1,000–88 port track," and the captain directed, "One torpedo any time, Dick."

"Mark," "Set," and "Fire!" Morton hit the plunger, sending a torpedo with its new warhead to hit under her stack. It was 0443, and the run would take 65 seconds. Buckley called the bearings of the torpedo's propellers as Hunter read my bearings on her stack. The bearings were drawing together nicely. Both scopes were on the freighter when the warhead detonated under her stack, the explosion raising an enormous black cloud above her. She had been a collier, and now down by the stern, was sinking rapidly. We surfaced at 0457 and closed her position, but she had sunk while we were going up.

The first hint of dawn was showing to the east, and we raced for the area chosen for the day's submerged patrol off the Laotiehshan Promontory. The place selected was northwest of the point, really in the Gulf of Pohai, and still 10 miles distant. In the increasing light, we found that weaving our way through the field of sampans was less difficult. Not one of them showed any activity, so we went unnoticed, but the same might not have been true if the promontory had lookouts, so we dived short of our selected area and moved on in submerged.

7 _____

Richie, with his torpedo work done, had manned the search scope during the torpedo run and through the detonation. So the two of us now sat down with ONI-208J and rather quickly arrived at the class of the collier as the *Katyosan Maru* of 2,427 tons.

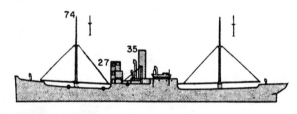

KASAGISAN MARU
KASUGASAN MARU, KATURAGISAN MARU, KATYOSAN MARU

Tonnages:		Constructed:	
Gross: 2,427	D. W.: 3,881–4	1924–25	Japan

Length:		Propulsion:	
W. L. (B. P.): 285'	O. A.:	Machinery:	Reciprocating
		Screws: 1	N. H. P.: 181
Beam: 42'		R. P. M.: 85	@ Knots: 10
Drafts:		Fuel: Coal	Capacity: 341 tons
Loaded: 20'	Light: 10'	Radius: 4,800 miles at 10 knots.	

Speed:
  Normal cruising: 10   Max.: 12½
Potential naval value: AK, AP
Remarks:

We were relaxing after breakfast when George reported smoke to the southeast. I went to the conning tower to investigate. The ship seemed to be milling around, and could be another of the captain's pet *Smoky Marus,* for the bearing of her smoke changed little. Not too unexpectedly, the distant crack and rumble of a depth charge seemed to come from that general direction. Stepping to the chart, it became clear that the

Maru was not far from where we had dived. The time of the depth charge was 1003, and it brought the captain to the conning tower. He immediately had a plan: Instead of remaining here, we could spend the day en route towards Chinwangtao. He sketched on our chart the lay of the piers at the harbor to show how we could blast the ships that were moored there. To this point, I had willingly gone along with all of his proposals—except that down-the-throater and there we had no option. But this was stretching it a bit too far; we were finding ships for our torpedoes right here, so why accept the extra hazard?

As a wartime expedient to save paper, the Gulf of Pohai had been included on our chart and separated only by a faint, blue line. And unless the smaller second legend was noted, there was no reason to suspect that the soundings in the Gulf of Pohai were in *feet,* not fathoms.

"Oh no!" said Morton on discovering the applicable legend, and then laughed at himself for not having read it first. This also applied to our present position, but for the moment I didn't bring that up.

Four depth charges over a half-hour period was the sum total of the antisubmarine effort. They were all out in the channel, probably because no submarine would seek shallow water for evasion. Factually, it was all so shallow that the little loss of depth would not have made much difference.

There was, however, the problem of our long periscopes, which had to extend too high above the surface, unless we continued to run uncomfortably close to the bottom. But *Wahoo* had a still-untried experimental installation to use in this situation. The section of our attack periscope well extending through the control room had upper and lower flanges. Fitted with nuts above and cap screws below, they could be removed, allowing the section to telescope into the pump-room extension below. Our sanctuary was just the place for a trial, and Captain Morton directed that the well be rigged. Lowering the sleeve required only a few minutes, and observations from the control room continued. Raising the sleeve, however, required three hands, leaving no room for another to twist on the nuts. "Moose" Hunter took over, wrapping his arms about the sleeve as the others ducked clear; in a single motion he raised the sleeve, fitting the flange over the studs. McGill twirled on the first few nuts, and the reinstallation from there on was quite routine. Welding two pads on the overhead and eyebolts on the tube to receive lowering and hoisting lines would take care of any future rigging. But the loss of watertight integrity between the conning tower and the control room remained an overriding fault, and I would doubt that our captain would use the arrangement again.

In late afternoon, we ventured from our sanctuary, and keeping well clear of the promontory, surfaced at dark. Again, we had to run the gauntlet of sampan alley to put *Wahoo* on course 065 for Round Island light, which served as a beacon for shipping to Port Arthur and Dairen. The light had been extinguished, confirming an afternoon conclusion that the enemy would reroute the shipping. Our next task was to find out where.

Captain Morton selected a position east of the light for our submerged patrol this Wednesday, March 24, and we dived at 0505 before there could be a chance of our being sighted. It was well we did, for just over an hour later George sighted a floatplane, searching. We moved cautiously, using just one scope, and with time-honored fast sweeps in low power to initiate any search after the periscope's lowering. It might seem a step backwards from our rather bold tactics, but we did not expect to attack this day, just to establish a route and remain undetected.

Our submerged course was again 065 and should cross the probable routes from the east. It came close at lunchtime with smoke ahead, which provided a drill for our tracking party. At our best sustained speed on a normal approach course, we maintained a nearly constant bearing, but on Chan's plot, the firing position would clearly be inside the harbor of Dairen. Nonetheless, Morton continued to close the ship until we had plotted her track on our chart, the whole giving us one shipping route.

Our surfacing was normal for a close-to-shore patrol, giving Krause and me barely enough time for stars on a fading horizon. Our plotted position was soon confirmed by SJ ranges on the Gaichosan Retto, also shown as the Blonde Islands on our chart. The seas were calm, so Richie as OOD gave permission to dump the weighted sacks of trash and garbage through the mess-room hatch. Morton would not attend the movies, so perhaps he would break his abstinence and seek revenge on the cribbage board. But if so, an immediate resumption was preempted by the phone buzzing in its recessed box to his left: Seaman Ater had a ship leaving the Gaichosan Retto.

By the time we reached the conning tower, the pip on the screen was just breaking clear of the group; we had a ship heading our way, and the bells sounded for the seventh attack of this patrol. The troops would gladly exchange the excitement of an attack for a rerun movie, and had apparently raced to their battle stations with us.

The conning tower clock read 1927 (the year of Lindbergh's flight) when I went to the bridge to man the TBT. The blurb of her shape was already in sight, and I called down the always-accurate visual bearings, commenting on the visibility. *Wahoo* lay nearly on the enemy's track, so turned immediately for a stern shot—to do so later would present our broadside silhouette at a range where we might be sighted. I shifted to the after TBT, and the captain kept our stern pointed at the enemy, now identified as a large tanker, and advised me of the expected firing range of 1,700 yards. She was coming on fast as I called 80 starboard, and received the welcome words, "Any time, Dick."

Like clockwork the "Mark," "Set," and "Fire" sent torpedoes to hit under her stack, amidships, and forward. Also like clockwork (magnetic–vacuum tube clockwork), the first torpedo detonated 18 seconds after firing—in our face instead of in the enemy's. The second torpedo followed suit, blowing up 18 seconds after it had been fired, the two of them raising a wall of water that looked like Niagara Falls rising from the sea. Our third torpedo undoubtedly turned a somersault in passing through the cavern in the sea. The captain fired a fourth torpedo directed by the TDC. It should have been nearly as accurate, but by the time it reached the enemy's track she had undoubtedly zigged.

Ours was not a profane ship, but if Admiral Farragut could say, "Damn the torpedoes" (really mines), so could we, and I would not be surprised if all hands did not orally or at least mentally say, "Damn the magnetic exploders." These premature detonations could truly be dangerous, and just how dangerous we found out as soon as the spume had cleared: There was the tanker beyond torpedo range, and quite suddenly the whacks of shells hitting the sea in our vicinity, and their swish-swish-swish as they ricocheted through the air, became more than disturbing. The enemy was using their truly flashless powder, and to have a shell's detonation as the first indication one is even on its way is a bit unnerving. When one burst just forward of our bow, throwing hunks over our shears, Captain Morton found it so too, and his two blasts took us down to think this one over.

Below, the whacks seemed louder, but these we could take. At the chart, the captain was stepping off the time it would take the tanker to reach Dairen at her speed of 12 knots. We could be there, waiting, but not if we dallied here submerged. The whacks of the shells were diminishing as the tanker proceeded on her way, and the captain ordered all preparations for surfacing. It was the commander's turn as OOD to go topside first. The three blasts sounded. As directed, McGill gave safety and the ballast tanks an extra long blow, almost like a battle surface. The commander whirled the handle opening the hatch, but kept the lanyard in hand, holding the hatch only part way open, and called, "They're still shooting at us!" Hunter, who was close behind the commander, looked to the captain for instructions, and in the dim, red light saw his skipper raise his fist with his thumb up. Either a long pent-up urge or immediate action in carrying out commands in the Navy took charge, perhaps both, for his quick goose sent our PCO flying to the bridge. The time was 2014.

The commander kept the conn, four engines fired, and by the time our turbos had raised her to cruising trim, *Wahoo* was racing at flank speed on a circuitous route to gain a position ahead of the enemy. With an extra knot from Chiefs Pruett and Keeter, our overload experts, we reached a position ahead of the enemy and still 4 miles from Dairen.

The captain pulled the plug at 2054, for we had the tanker silhouetted in the late-rising moon, and then maneuvered off the tanker's track. She was heading directly for the harbor, undoubtedly feeling safe. Our lads had not left their battle stations, so the Bells of St. Mary's for the eighth time on this patrol were just a formality. The tanker came on nicely, her angle opening as it should, and now angles as well as bearings flowed to TDC and plot. When Richie called 1200 to go with my 90 starboard, the captain gave his "Any time" at 2122.

Our constant bearings sent torpedoes amidships, aft, and forward. Chan was counting, and my heart sank when time ran out for the first torpedo, lower for the second, but the last clipped her under the stack. It is the only spot that will always sink a tanker, and she went down by the stern, sinking in 4½ minutes. Twelve minutes later, *Wahoo* was on the surface clearing the area, and the movies had started in the forward torpedo room. Pharmacist Kohl had brought the merchant marine book to the wardroom, already flagged to the tanker section. It took only a few minutes to identify the class of our tanker as the *Syoyo Maru* of 7,499 tons.

SYOTO MARU

Tonnages:
  Gross: 7,499   D. W.: 11,531
Length:
  W. L. (B. P.): 431'   O. A.:
Beam: 58'
Drafts:
  Loaded: 28'   Light: 8' 6"
Speed:
  Normal cruising: 11   Max.: 12½

Constructed:
  1928   Japan
Propulsion:
  Machinery: Reciprocating
  Screws: 1   H. P.:
  R. P. M.:   @ Knots:
  Fuel: Oil   Capacity: 1,920 tons
  Radius: 17,000 miles at 11 knots.

Potential naval value: AO.
Remarks: Oil-carrying capacity: 75,500 barrels (42 gallons). 13 watertight bulkheads, 9 to upper deck. Guns: Mounts reported and probably armed with 5" guns on forecastle and poop.

8 _____

Our course was 150 heading for another likely spot to the east of Round Island that had been selected by the tic-tac-toe method. I had expected that Captain Morton would discuss the premature detonations, the four extra torpedoes that had been required (totaling one-sixth of our load), and the unnecessary exposure to shelling. But the ship had been sunk; all of that was past, and his words concerned the coming days and how we might best use our remaining torpedoes. First came the speed error that had caused a near miss on the tanker. Since Chan and Richie, on plot and TDC, had agreed on 10 knots, there had to be a speed error in our Pit log or in its transmission to the TDC and conning tower indicator. But we should have recognized that a tanker, having been fired on while making 12 knots, would hardly slow down. The captain took the responsibility, but it truly lay with all of us. The solution, after the mechanical error was corrected, lay in having TDC and plot announce their speed and course determinations during the approach, followed by a "Check with TDC," or plot. Then at least one of us would note such an error.

The arrival of the duty chief's messenger changed the subject as he reported that the SJ training gear had jammed and that the auxiliarymen were working on it. That would mean Chief McGill and Lemert or Chisholm. The captain liked the report (not the breakdown), for it was complete and showed action already taken. "They're upstaging us," he commented, and taking the hint, Richie and Chan went after the Pit log troubles. SJ jamming was not unexpected, since lubrication had failed to relieve its erratic rotation. The training gear was, after all, just a bit more than a jury rig, whose most dependable part was the never-failing General Electric washing machine motor.

To fully use all of the talent embarked in *Wahoo,* and perhaps to make amends for Hunter's impulsive action, Captain Morton had asked the commander to share the nighttime command responsibilities. And so, when Krause called me for a round of stars on the rising moon's horizon, I found the commander on the bridge with his first wartime contact. He was in complete charge of the situation, and surely this would be true in whatever submarine he would soon command. The initial contact was a faint light that had drawn to the left, giving every appearance of a port running light. The commander had ordered the normal approach course, and now the faint outline of a ship could be seen by the lookouts, who were above a light surface haze.

Quietly, the fire control party was called. With the commander's agreement, I informed the captain of the ship that the commander was conning *Wahoo* to a position ahead for a dawn submerged attack. He thanked me, and I assured him that he would be called in ample time before we dived. He seemed to welcome the chance for more shut-eye, which was certainly understandable after our successive attacks.

We missed the SJ, but everything else was in our favor: sufficient moon for nighttime tracking, time to gain the best possible position, and a target that was zigging only mildly—all of these promised success for a submerged, crack-of-dawn attack. Calling accurate angles in partial moonlight is difficult and has to be based primarily on the length of the ship seen rather than on details. Nonetheless, tracking was soon able to establish her base course of 345 heading for Port Arthur at 9 knots. Except for mild variations—some of them zigs and others probably poor steering—she maintained course and speed. It was now 0330, with *Wahoo* maintaining a position 10,000 yards ahead of the enemy and 1,000 yards to the east of her projected track. I called the captain personally, but left it up to the commander to provide him with the details. About 10 minutes later, he took the conn, thanking the commander, and two blasts took us under the sea at 0355.

Roger had leveled her off nicely, reporting, "Satisfied with the trim," and the Bells of St. Mary's held reveille again. Now in the first gray of dawn, with her angle opening, I could call respectable angles with details as well. She was a smaller plumb-bow, mast-funnel-mast freighter with a short superstructure amidships; Kohl at the lower hatch made notes. If she continued on, the firing range would be about 1,300 yards, which was fine, but if she zigged towards, the range could be halved. Then the captain might fire a single torpedo to really make them count. So I was not surprised when he had only two tubes readied.

But that was the captain's business, and I now concentrated on mine, calling, "Port 30," when I could see a half ship's length, then "45," and finally, "Port 90," when the square face of her bridge came in line. Hunter read the accompanying 1,300 and 85 degrees; the angles had to be good. "Shoot when you're ready, Gridley" came from Morton by way of variation, but there was no change in the firing procedure. "Constant bearing–Mark!" "Set," from Richie. Her mainmast was about to touch the wire. "Fire!" and the captain hit the plunger.

Fifteen seconds later the second torpedo went to her foremast. The run would take 52 seconds and Chan's count had already passed 15 when we heard Buckley's, "Both hot, straight and normal." Hot and straight they may have been, but not normal, for the first torpedo detonated 48 seconds into the run, throwing a monstrous geyser into the sky. The second torpedo continued unperturbed and so did the enemy ship. I watched the torpedo's wake leading the freighter properly. On time, the second crack of detonation hit our hull and a cheer filled the conning tower.

"She's still going, Captain," I had to report, and received his, "She can't be." I stepped aside and for a moment he took the scope. He asked if I had seen any guns on her, and when I replied, "Not a one," Morton ordered, "Make all preparations for battle surface!"

We had just had a trial run in shifting from battle-stations-torpedo to battle-stations-gun and today it paid off with all preparations completed in under 10 minutes. With gun captain Carr, pointer Smith, and trainer Wach in the conning tower, and the ammunition train with canned rounds at the mess-room hatch, *Wahoo* made a fast battle surface. Four times the normal high-pressure air brought her decks well clear of the sea; the gun was cast loose and loaded and the first round was fired at 0448, just 12 minutes after the last torpedo had been fired.

The very first round hit in the after deck house of the fleeing ship, a good shot from about 2 miles, and Richie, who would have spotted the splashes to a hit, was able to call, "No change." Shortly, a shell exploding in the freighter's stern knocked out her steering, and her bow fell off to port. Morton quickly closed the ship, as Carr concentrated the fire on her waterline abreast the engine spaces. An incessant fire, now from a point-blank range of 100 yards or so, poured round after round into her vitals, until her lower side looked like a colander.

"What's that, an escort?" said Morton, after swinging his 7 × 50s to the thin mast our lookouts had reported. I thought of the "antiquated coal-burning corvette'' and knew that the captain had the same apprehension. Here, we'd have no secure depth; our freighter had been stopped, holed, was listing, on fire, and sinking. Prudence called for distance, but based in part on hope, my answer came out, ''I don't think so.'' Then I added, ''If you'll order check-fire, I'll be able to tell for sure through the scope.'' Captain Morton did one better, ordering, ''Cease fire,'' and the commander, who had dropped below during our speculation, beat me to the scope, reporting that she was a small, engine-aft tanker or freighter. Apparently, she had been closing to find the reason for the smoke, and *Wahoo* made that easy by heading to intercept.

The following minutes gave the gun crews a chance to rest, to kick the empty ammunition cans over the side, and for the 20-millimeters to cool down. The large, 4-inch brass cases were valuable as a critical material (as well as for the manufacture of souvenirs, no doubt) and were quickly struck below—none too soon, for the deck gun action resumed immediately.

The captain had turned *Wahoo,* putting the tanker on our quarter. Keeping her there, Carr would still be able to reach her with the 4-inch; and with speed, as necessary, we could keep the enemy from closing to machine gun range. We underestimated her a bit, for her machine guns were about 40 millimeters and ranged uncomfortably close until we put her dead astern to open the range. Obviously, we had not given sufficient thought to her possible speed, which we now plotted at 14 knots. That was sufficient to overtake us whenever we turned enough for our deck gun (forward) to bear. She was tough and kept on boring in while *Wahoo* went through successive maneuvers in opening the range and turns to shoot. Carr and company were able to fire about fifteen rounds on each maneuver, concentrating on her engine spaces aft; Richie, with battleship gunnery experience, spotted successive shell splashes to hit. After our fourth or fifth maneuver, 4-inch shells finally disabled the tanker's engines. Morton conned *Wahoo* to a safe position on the enemy's beam, and from there our deck gun silenced her machine guns and set her afire. At no time during the action had Commander Morton endangered a single member of his crew. The freighter sank at 0614, and the captain followed through by ordering full power to clear the area before the first enemy plane could arrive.

9

The two lines of our wake stretched back to the scene of the last action, which was still marked by a fading column of smoke. The commander, manning the attack scope, had seen the tanker sink there at 0625, and he was now scanning the horizon for an expected patrol. Topside, our lookouts were concentrating on the skies for an almost sure plane. Our track on the chart led to O To, our original destination. That vicinity would still offer good hunting if the ships *Wahoo* had just sunk were unable to report our presence. A tall, dancing pip on the SD radar answered that question at 0640, and two blasts took us down for the day. The jig was up for the northern area and we changed course to south. This would throw off any search based on our having been sighted heading for O To; and not to be overlooked, *Wahoo*'s bow was heading for the barn.

Now, for the first time, Kohl was able to present the findings of his party and the crew. There could be no dispute; the ships were of the *Sinsei* and *Hadachi Maru* classes with gross tonnage of 2,556 and 1,000, respectively. And for any later verification, our camera bugs had had a field day throughout the surface actions.

Simonetti had also come forward bringing the Quartermaster's Notebook showing tallies of ninety and then eighty rounds of 4-inch. For the 20-millimeters, the entry simply read, ''lots of pans.'' These could be counted later. Obviously pleased, and proud of his crew, our captain went aft to congratulate them. For sure, this had been their day.

Seabirds provided our only contacts during the morning, which suited most of us who welcomed a few hours of normal cruising, but at noontime a call for the tracking party came over the 1MC. George, on the search scope, had a large passenger freighter at about 16,000 yards, according to our height of eye tables. She was presenting a broad, but not impossi-

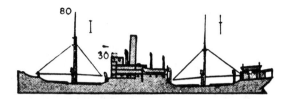

HOZAN MARU
HOZYO MARU, KOSIN MARU, SINSEI MARU #5, SINSEI MARU #17, SINYO MARU #3, SYOKO MARU, TOGO MARU, BOYACA, FUIERE CONSOLINE

Tonnages:			Constructed:	
Gross: 1,863–2,556	D. W.: 3,000–4,460		1919–20	America
Length:			Propulsion:	
W. L. (B. P.): 251'	O. A.:		Machinery:	Reciprocating
Beam: 44'			Screws: 1	N. H. P.: 315
Drafts:			R. P. M.:	@ Knots:
Loaded: 24'	Light: 8' 6''		Fuel: Coal and oil	Capacity: 422 tons of coal
Speed:			Radius:	4,800 miles at 10 knots
Normal cruising: 10	Max.: 1			

Potential naval value: AK.
Remarks: U. S. S. B. Lake type. BOYACA, former Panamanian, believed captured by Japanese. FUIERE CONSOLINE, former Italian, believed captured by Japanese.

ble, angle and *Wahoo* was off at high speed to intercept. No further observations were made until the generated range on the TDC read 8,000, since they would have slowed our approach. Morton killed our speed quickly by backing for a minute. Krause raised the scope and I called starboard 40 as my assistant read 7,500. We could reach a firing position, and again the steersman rang up full speed.

"If she keeps coming, we'll go to battle stations," advised Morton, for after all, getting two tubes ready could be done in a minute. At an expected range of 5,000, we looked again, and I sadly reported that the ship had reversed course and was making smoke in her departure. We could surmise that she had just received a submarine warning and would never know that she had missed being torpedoed by less than 30 minutes.

An hour after the freighter had reversed course, our volunteer on the search scope reported a plane and pushed the button to starboard, lowering the scope. Jack swung the slim search scope to the bearing and reported the plane on various courses, searching. We kept her in sight until she departed, probably low on fuel, but she was replaced by a new-looking echo-ranging destroyer with a 15-degree port angle on the bow. With two torpedoes of dubious value and a sick battery, *Wahoo* went on the defensive for the first time on this patrol.

Fortunately, perhaps, we were in one of the deeper parts of the Yellow Sea, 30 fathoms, so we eased down to 150 feet, 30 feet off the bottom, and slithered away from the echo-ranging destroyer. During the following 3 hours the intensity of the echo ranging became gradually weaker, and was punctuated by a single depth charge before fading out altogether. We were in no rush, so waited until dark before surfacing, and then cleared the area at three-engine speed.

A day of cruising in murky weather, without drills or contacts, provided rest for all of us, and also brought us to the East China Sea, at least according to our chart. Without stars, Krause and I were relying on dead-reckoning and estimated positions modified by soundings, and also a working SJ to warn us of land. With the captain's agreement, our tracks were laid down on the safe side, well clear of land. So on March 27, when the fog cleared disclosing our SJ contact as a trawler, we believed that our position was 40 miles west of Saishu To.

The time was 1022, and the trawler had an antenna array far in excess of the need of any fisherman. She was probably sending out a contact report on *Wahoo,* or would as soon as she spotted us. The captain meant to prevent this, and the Bells of St. Mary's chimed again for battle-stations-gun. Our 4-inch, with its remaining eleven rounds, would immobilize the trawler, and then the three 20-millimeters would wreck her upper works. Finally, George and his *Wahoo* Commandos, waiting in the wings, would complete the destruction by setting her afire, and incidentally dispose of those Molotov cocktails once and for all.

Seldom do such plans proceed as directed, but this one did, up to a point. Carr's professionals laid their shells into her hull, stopping her after the fifth or sixth round, and then, using the "meatball" of the Japanese flag painted on her deckhouse as their point of aim, fired a 4-inch shell right through its middle. "Show-offs," said Morton, obviously tickled with their proficiency. We watched the remaining shells strike at or just below her waterline, the latter sending small geysers up her side. The trawler was a rugged ship and seemed to absorb all of the hits with little more than a shake, and not even that for the deckhouse shot. Further, she showed no signs of fire, sinking, or of even settling, so perhaps the majority of our shells had plowed into her holds filled with fish.

The roar of the 20-millimeter gun was more impressive, and so was the wreckage, but that was because it was topside and plainly visible.

The gun experienced jams, but the crew was able to dunk the barrel into the cooling tubes that filled with saltwater when we were submerged, so there were no explosions. By the second barrel exchange, the water had boiled away; the crews had completed their task, and to prevent a possible explosion and injury, the captain called, "Cease fire!"

The commandos formed a cocktail train manned by Kirk, Berg, Muller, Seal, and Carter, with Chief Lane in charge. It led to O'Brien and Ens. George Misch, who would heave the Molotovs from our bow. If we had had another half hour at Midway, they could have practiced heaving quart whiskey bottles filled with water; for there had been lots of empties near the workmen's barracks. So today they found that you cannot throw a 2-pound bottle like a football. Captain Morton took care of that by putting our bow so close that the job would be easier than pitching horseshoes. The following bottles smashed against her deckhouse, each bursting into a roaring sheet of flame, but dying out as soon as the fuel had been consumed. The cocktail train moved forward so that each commando could pitch his bottle and then fall in at the start of the line with another in hand. Regardless of the number of bottles or where they landed, the soggy trawler would not catch fire. The flame and smoke did give our cameras another field day, and more important, all of the Molotov cocktails had been expended.

The captain backed *Wahoo* clear, and to our surprise, a half dozen or so crewmen came up from the far side of the trawler where they had weathered the attack by hanging onto her port rail or ducking into the trawler's small boats. In unison, they thumbed their noses at us as *Wahoo* withdrew. With such pluckiness, they would probably get their ship back to port, and I would not be surprised if they had shut down their engine so that, believing it wrecked, we would shift our fire.

10

Our course was 120, a route that would take *Wahoo* to the south of Danjo Gunto. If the overcast continued and thus permitted surface running, we should make a radar landfall on the island by late in the afternoon, still Saturday, March 27. From there, we would patrol the shipping lanes between Shimonoseki to the north and Formosa about 500 miles to the south.

On March 28, two motor sampans absorbed all but our emergency 20mm ammunition as we patrolled from Danjo Gunto to the southeast. Our track was exactly 145, and not entirely by chance would pass close to Kusakaki Shima and from there through the Colonet Strait. By Monday, the twenty-ninth, still without a suitable target, Morton was becoming impatient, and even more so as he examined the chart that Krause had brought to the wardroom that evening. Circling a shoal at the entrance to Kagoshima Wan, the large bay at the southern tip of Kyushu, he pointed out that shipping had only two routes to the large city of the same name that lay at the bay's upper reaches. Further, a submarine would have but a short run to reach the 100-fathom curve after an attack.

In almost every venture, I had been wholeheartedly in support, but with only two torpedoes, a sick battery, and the currents that I had pointed out upon our entrance to the East China Sea, I had to recommend saving that spot for another patrol. Morton thanked me for my frank opinion, saying, ''We'll put that on the shelf, at least for a day or so,'' and we had the first rubber of cribbage in very nearly 2 weeks. By winning, the captain seemed to regain his usual patience, and we searched ahead, having left Kusakaki Shima astern. Deteriorating weather could preclude dawn stars, so I requested an 0230 call for a night star fix, and flopped on my bunk. In a twinkling, or so it seemed, I felt the customary shake of my shoulder, and Krause saying, "Lieutenant Commander, you're needed on the bridge. We have a ship and your promotion just came in on the Fox." I believe there is a saying that good things come in pairs, and for sure I could not have wished for more, especially the chance to get these last two torpedoes on their way.

The enemy ship, still an indistinct, black shape, lay well back on our starboard quarter. Radar and our after starboard lookout had reported her at the same time, which might pose a problem for Chief Lane in dividing the crew's pool. We had forgotten all about taking stars, as I was marking TBT bearings for Krause below. This was just another advantage of our system, for my manning the scope would be the only fire control change upon diving. At the moment, the fire control party had manned their stations and the captain was with me on the cigarette deck.

Any change of bearing was unnoticeable to us on the bridge, but not so to plot and TDC, who also had accurate SJ ranges. She was overtaking on a course of approximately 080 that would cross our track, and had probably been sent on a southern route from Shanghai to avoid the submarines to the north. So our captain had been right in attacking the trawler and snuffing out her radio transmissions. He now conned *Wahoo* to the enemy ship's track and ordered the same course.

We were not hurried, as we had been with the tanker off Dairen, because morning twilight, which Krause had entered in the captain's Night Orders Book, did not commence until 0345. Stopping and killing our way temporarily, we checked her speed with the decreasing radar ranges only. There was no change; she was making 8½ knots, and since first tracked, had not zigged. In ample time before twilight, the captain conned *Wahoo* off the enemy's track, and the Bells of St. Mary's bonged surely for the last time on our fourth patrol.

There was still only the faintest sign of light in the east when two blasts sent us under the sea a thousand yards off the target's track. From there, Morton conned our submarine to a normal course, putting the bow perpendicular to the target's track, which we closed at 4 knots. The sky was now gray and I could call her general shape with stack amidships. She was another freighter of medium size, and as the angle opened, disclosing a longer-than-usual superstructure, I changed her classification to a passenger freighter. The periscope bearings and TDCs checked.

The initial angle at 30 degrees received a "Close," from Richie, but then as the angle broadened, I took another quick look. I had seen this ship before, or one constructed along the same lines, and I had to inquire whether or not our submarine tender *Holland* had escaped from the Philippines, for this ship even had her clipper bow. The answer would make no difference; if in Japanese hands we would sink her anyway, so the mixed reply did not affect our approach. The word, however, did provide Kohl with all of the information his party would need.

The ship came on, apparently feeling secure in her southern routing, and at 0415 Captain Morton gave his, "Any time, Dick." In no more than a minute, the constant bearing had been marked and set. Her mainmast was about to touch the wire in my stationary periscope.

"Fire," and Morton hit the plunger. The shudder, the zing, and then the momentary pressure on our ears were all normal. Our very last torpedo headed for her foremast, and Buckley announced a welcome, "Both hot, straight and normal." Chan commenced counting the seconds to go for the 900-yard torpedo run, and I was able to report that both torpedo wakes were leading the freighter properly when they had faded in the still-dim light.

One at a time, each torpedo had been pulled from its tube; the after bodies had been checked for dryness, and every other test, short of those that have to be done in the shop, had been performed. And one more—before reloading, fresh, sharp eyes had been painted on the warheads. I also had noted Deaton, now a TM1c and in charge of the after room, and his gang helping forward. Surely such a cooperative effort for our ship and their captain would pay off, and only duds or prematures could prevent it.

A violent crack of detonation hit our sub as the total explosion literally tore the after half of the freighter asunder and stopped the forward part in its tracks with a sharp up angle. Everyone in the conning tower was congratulating one another with a well-meant handshake, and this included Morton and me.

Sometimes a sinking ship makes tremendous breaking-up noises, perhaps when compartments or bulkheads collapse; the total sound could be like a bridge or other steel structure being slowly scrunched by a monstrous bulldozer. Such was the case with this ship, the noises becoming frighteningly loud. In plenty of time, we noted that in our exuberance, neither the captain nor I had changed our course from directly at the sinking ship. After ordering right full rudder, to allay any fears, especially amongst our new hands, Morton said to Jack, who was next to the 1MC, "Tell the crew that the noise you hear is the enemy ship breaking up." Somewhat excited, as all of us were, Jack complied by announcing throughout our submarine, "The noise you hear is the ship breaking up," and by leaving out the word "enemy," he scared at least some of our new shipmates half to death.

Jack joined us in a good laugh. The freighter had sunk, and the captain asked the course for the barn. That was easy, "One four five, Sir," I replied.

"Why, that's what we've been steering!"

"Yes, but I had not extended the line as far as the Colonet Strait," I advised, and received his customary nod and smile of approval, for we had been thinking alike—the shortest route to our base. Still at battle stations, he ordered, "Take her up, Dick." After another healthy blow by McGill, *Wahoo* hit the surface running. The screeching turbos raised us to a cruising trim; four main engines took over the load from our batteries, and our submarine was streaking for the strait just 13 minutes after firing her last torpedoes.

Now secured from battle stations, Rowls put down an early breakfast. It was not a change in the menu, just any quickly prepared items that the troops tossed up from the freezer. In anticipation, a box of fry cuts had been thawed, and the odor of their frying brought the freezer-searching to a halt. Perhaps with some priority, Krause wangled two steak sandwiches. They took precedence over piloting, for already the mountains marking the strait were in sight, and we had only to bisect them for the next hour.

The Colonet Strait proved to be more than just a passage through the Ryukyus; it was a north-south thoroughfare as well. During the passage, there were small craft in all sectors and a small freighter as well. They seemed to pay no attention to us, and *Wahoo* returned the favor, passing out of the operating area at 0740 and slowing a knot to 300 turns. On the wardroom table was ONI-208J opened to the *Kimishima Maru*. Though the drawing didn't show the clipper bow of the accompanying photograph, we would accept her just the same.

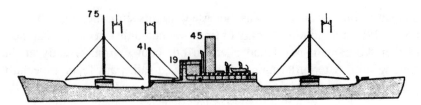

KIMISIMA MARU

Tonnages:
  Gross: 5,193   D. W.: 7,572
Length:
  W. L. (B. P.): 400′   O. A.:
Beam: 54′
Drafts:
  Loaded: 24′   Light: 9′
Speed:
  Normal cruising: 12½ Max.: 15
Potential naval value: AP, AK.
Remarks:

Constructed:
  1938   Japan
Propulsion:
  Machinery: Steam turbines
  Screws: 1   N. H. P.: 500
  R. P. M.:   @ Knots:
  Fuel: Coal   Capacity: 1,800
               tons
  Radius: 15,000 miles at 12½ knots

11

Our course was 092 heading for Sofu Gan, the pinnacle that had served as a radar and TDC target for us 3 weeks ago. Now it would serve as a final departure point on leaving the Empire, and it lay sufficiently far south to keep us clear of air search. Of course that advantage would not come until another day, and within the hour an SD contact at 12 miles drove us down. *Wahoo* now had one priority, to get to our base safely and quickly, so we searched with both scopes for the better part of an hour before getting up and on our way.

Three engines were now on propulsion, since the fourth would add little in the increasing seas and could better be used in charging our weak battery for an unforeseen emergency. *Wahoo* still retained her affinity for ships, and SJ had a tall, dancing pip just before the movies, still Monday, March 29. There were no friendly submarines to whom we could pass the contact, and with obvious reluctance, the captain directed Richie to continue on course.

With uninterrupted cruising, the captain was able to get on with his project of sewing on new rating badges, watch marks, and chevrons for his troops. He had performed minor mending to skivvies and such, but few had expected that those great hands could sew with the speed and dexterity of an accomplished seamstress. A few of us were not surprised, for he had shown us his intricate needlework, which I believe would have taken ribbons at any state fair.

With two daytimes and a full night of high-speed running, we had left the pinnacle of Sofu Gan behind, but not our affinity for ships. Running in the trough of increasing seas, *Wahoo* was rolling a bit, but not slowed appreciably, when dancing pips showed above the considerable sea return that made the normal grassy line of the scope look more like a hayfield. Spotting the momentary pips was good performance by

Torpedoman's Mate Tyler, and he was congratulated by Morton, who had found them difficult to discern in the high grass. The sighting was timely too, for their bearing, from our port beam to 5 degrees forward, had drawn aft only a degree or so. The original range of 9,000 now read 7,000 on the lighted scale operated by the small-range crank. We could be on a collision course with a convoy. Reluctant to turn back, a fourth engine went on the line and tracking manned their stations.

The great black shapes of the individual ships were soon visible through my binoculars, now set into the "V" of the after TBT. The convoy was spread out, not in the usual column, perhaps to ease the problem of station keeping in such seas. Or were they warships? Sparking at our antenna insulators told me that a contact report was being transmitted, and the arcing light due to the salt spray did not make me feel more comfortable at this lonely billet.

To gain time in getting clear of the approaching ships, *Wahoo* had been conned to put them on our port quarter. Now I could feel and hear our bow bashing into the seas, some of them racing down our deck past the conning tower. And great rollers from aft were obviously testing our steersman as we yawed in the following seas. But our submarine could ride out any sea, and if our new course did not pull us clear, we could always dive.

We very nearly did just that, for a great roller came up into my 7 × 50's field; I jerked them clear of the TBT to see a monster rising above our stern. Turning forward, I shouted, "Close the hatch! Climb the shears!" I just had time to wrap my arms and legs around the TBT before the sea rolled over my head. It could have been only seconds, but it seemed as though we had dived, before the sea receded from the bridge. Racing forward, I found that George, our OOD, had made it to the lookout's platform, and the conning tower hatch was being warily opened with lanyard in hand. The only light was from the emergency lanterns, whose batteries are always on charge, for the captain had ordered the great battery-disconnect switches thrown to stop the electrical fires in the maneuvering room.

The captain had gone aft, leaving word for me to take over. There was not much to take, for *Wahoo* was wallowing in the trough of the sea without any power whatsoever, except our sound-powered telephones. I called for Krause to bring the battery-operated Aldis lamp to the bridge. If a ship of the convoy was going to ram us, we would give the vertical flare-up signal of a fisherman. With that ready, we received the word phoned to the conning tower, though much of it had already been surmised: Orders to close the main induction had not been given to control in time, so a water slug of a few tons had gotten by the great mushroom valve. The forward and after engine rooms had swung the readily accessible lever, closing their hull valve; so the full force had hit the smaller maneuvering room valve, with its shorter handle. The force had been so great that the electricians could not close it and the room was half flooded. Deaton had opened his after torpedo room door, thus taking the sea above the door's lower coaming into the torpedo room. Then, with the after engine room watch, they had dragged the electricians clear of the smoke-filled room. It was probably in the nick of time, and both electricians were revived.

Krause had kept his binoculars on the convoy, and happily reported a zig to their right. Even a zigging back would still take it clear of our position. We thanked the Lord for this favor; there were troubles enough for any submarine over 3,000 miles from her nearest base, with the possible prospect of becoming a sitting target for enemy planes in the morning.

With the captain present and Chief Pruett in charge, jumpers were quickly rigged from one battery to the trim pump controller, and pumping the maneuvering room commenced. While this was going on, Morton had Chief Keeter and his hands start one engine to take a suction and clear the smoke. Within a quarter hour, the maneuvering room bilge was dry and the electricians began clearing up the grounds in the control cubicle and replacing burned parts with our available spares. The main induction had by now been cleared of water and the torpedo room pumped. By 2040 we went ahead with turns for standard speed on port shaft with No. 2 main engine on propulsion. It was truly a remarkable performance by dedicated petty officers who knew their job.

The electricians continued to work throughout the night, and before dawn *Wahoo* had No. 1 engine driving the starboard shaft as well. Hopefully, the two engines would take us clear of Japan's north-south flyway, but that was asking too much. The electricians were checking the watch's ability to shift to battery propulsion, when a low-flying plane came out of the deep overcast and summarily drove us down. Everything worked and in less than an hour *Wahoo* was up and on her way. In another 2 hours, repairs for No. 4 main engine were completed. It took its share of the load and stayed on the line as *Wahoo* rolled for the barn.

Captain Morton had been prudent about sending our departure report, waiting till clear of the Empire. When he asked Jayson for a pad of lined paper, we wondered what he would include in this one. He wrote straight ahead, with little crossing out or change, and then passed the pad to me and the others in the wardroom. I read:

ONE SURFACE RUNNER ONE DUD FOUR PREMATURES ONE TANKER SUNK ONE FREIGHTER HOLED AND BELIEVED SUNK FIVE FREIGHTERS SUNK BY TORPEDOES TWO FREIGHTERS TWO SAMPANS SUNK BY GUNFIRE AND LARGE TRAWLER WRECKED WILL REQUIRE FOLLOWING CONTROL CUBICLE PARTS BEFORE NEXT PATROL

Usually, a boat doesn't air its laundry in a departure message, but ours was not a usual skipper and certainly he had the prestige to put our torpedo performance on the line for all to read. I believed that Admiral Lockwood would thank him for doing so, since it provided immediate ammunition to support the admiral's efforts to deactivate the magnetic feature of the exploder. Also, in specifying our needed parts, the captain was not only putting our failures on the line, but also giving the Base time to procure them, perhaps from Mare Island.

Roger had the parts listed and gave the sheet to Jack. It included:

3 Generator rheostat clutch switches
1 Generator trip switch
2 Generator rheostat field contactors
100 feet of wiring

Without these parts, just as now, we would not be able to use the fourth engine or to run any of them above an 80/90 combination because the required parts of the field rheostats had burned up.

NPM, the high-power naval radio station on Oahu, did not come in this night, so attempts to transmit our departure report were put off. On Thursday, April Fool's Day, Carter received a "Roger" after the first transmission. A long, low sailboat, possibly from Marcus Island, proved to be our last contact as we headed across the expanse of the Pacific. The captain decided to have me navigate back to port again; this was no imposition, for the patrol report had been kept current during most of the patrol and navigating without pressure had become a pleasure.

Considering our torpedo failures and the patrol results, in which half again the number of ships were sunk when compared to any other patrol of the war, we rather expected another upkeep at Pearl. This was fortified by the necessary discussions concerning our failing batteries. So many of the crew were making plans accordingly, especially the young lads who had met pretty dolls after our first and third patrols.

ComSubPac's congratulatory message, composed for reading by all boats, contained the meat of our captain's dispatch, and noted that this was Lieutenant Commander Morton's second consecutive outstanding patrol. Sadly for our younger hands, the message closed by assigning *Wahoo* to Midway Island for refit and rehabilitation, and I wondered who on the staff had inserted that last word.

We enjoyed two Mondays, April 5, on crossing the international date line, and at 1000 on the sixth, *Wahoo* turned north towards the slot through the reef. The seas seemed angry to port and starboard as they broke on the reef, but Hunter kept our yaw within its natural bounds, and threaded the slot like a needle. Inside, the lagoon was like a lake, and Morton conned his submarine to the pier, which was manned by hands, the band, and well-wishers. Not to be outdone, *Wahoo* put on a show of her own: flying from our raised periscope was a Morton-sewn Indian headdress battle flag carrying a train of sixteen red-centered white feathers, one for each ship *Wahoo* had sunk; and the two great *Nitu Maru* house flags streamed to port and starboard from a two-swab-handle yardarm that the troops had affixed atop the SD mast. On deck, a full section, in machine-washed dungarees, again stood proud of *Wahoo,* of her captain, and rightfully, of themselves. We had been met with more gold and photographers at Pearl, but that was surpassed by the warmth of our welcome here.

FIFTH PATROL
The Kurils and Honshu

1

Midway had mustered its best from the Marine Corps and the Base, including a band that quickly switched to Dixieland as soon as the senior officers had gone below. It was obvious that *Wahoo*'s fame and catchy name had preceded her, and those great house flags streaming straight out told everyone that she had been at it again. Just wait until they learned the results of our last patrol!

The typed tabulations from our patrol report were on the wardroom table. These seven pages told the story at a glance and helped move the senior officers along so that the wardroom could be cleared for payday. We had been advised that here on Midway, contractors' civilian workmen gambled as a pastime, and attempts to stop it had proved futile. They would be waiting like leeches for our crew to come ashore, so we would adopt the procedure of other boats. Each hand drew all of his monies as he entered the wardroom, but surrendered all but a ten spot to Jack and Pappy, who put it in an envelope bearing the individual's name for storage in the communications' safe. The lads could learn the easy way by losing only ten dollars, and if they wanted to try again, Jack and Pappy would disburse daily.

After payday, the Base repair officer and his assistant sat down with us in the wardroom. The repair requests were minimal, except for the cubicle, and for that, most of the spare parts and wire listed in the captain's message had already come in by air. The remainder would probably come from Mare Island in plenty of time, but if not, the Base would provide substitutes or build them. Their confidence was convincing, and we adjourned after finishing our coffee, with the understanding that this refit would be conducted in conjunction with ship's force and the relief crew as Captain Morton desired.

Our crew had evaporated; the relief crew was aboard, but accommodations ashore for officers would have to wait until another boat had departed. This was no great hardship, for what we wanted was the feel of land beneath our feet and the chance to really stretch our legs. Chan joined me for a hike around the island on sand that proved firm close to the shore. The hundreds of seabirds, most species quite unfamiliar to us, took our minds from patrol. The exercise in absolutely clean air, scrubbed by rainstorms across the Pacific, soon made us hungry and we headed for the Gooneyville.

Originally, it had been the Pan American Hotel and had served as a stopover for passengers in the China Clipper days. The Gooneyville was no Royal Hawaiian, where seating for meals was immediate, but we were not rushed and rather enjoyed lounging in the lobby and greeting friends. The meal was good, but lacked the dishes we craved: fresh salads, lightly cooked green vegetables, and yellow ones boiled only until tender. It was too early to make a judgment, but for the moment I doubted that an advance base only 3 day's run towards the enemy was justified, especially since there were always rooms at the Royal.

After a more satisfying supper and relaxing on board—without stars to shoot or watches to stand—we headed again for the Gooneyville, this time to locate a corner room that had been set aside as an informal meeting place or wardroom. A background noise of simultaneous conversations served as a beacon that led directly to the outside entrance. Inside were a half dozen or more tables, most of them with poker cloths, and all with ample chairs. Against the far wall were two refrigerators, filled with bottled beer. The wardroom of each departing boat would settle the outstanding bill, which seemed to be a convenient and impartial way to pay.

We split up to seek friends, and I spotted Fritz Harlfinger. He had participated in the terrible Aleutian campaign as exec of *S-35*, and then as exec of *Whale* in the Marianas, followed by an inshore patrol off Honshu. We were swapping stories and patrol information when he stopped, and with his thumb over his left shoulder, called my attention to a conversation at an adjacent table where our PCO was belittling most everything that *Wahoo* had accomplished on patrol and including some disparaging remarks about me.

What a series of circumstances and coincidences had followed the commander: losing the original command of *Wahoo* to an officer 3 years his junior, through the intervention of an admiral; being ordered to the same submarine for his PCO run, now commanded by an officer 4 years his junior; and finally, seeing an officer who had been 8 years his junior in *Argonaut* when he himself had been her executive officer, now manning the scope or TBT and firing *Wahoo*'s torpedoes. Though aware of the foregoing, I had seen no resentment, and the commander had seemed to be doing well.

Now, turning my head, I saw Captain Morton, also within earshot, flipping the pages of *Life* about one each second, and just short of tearing them out. He beckoned and I joined him near the door. "Let's get out of here before we get into a fight," he advised, and we headed for the dock in silence. On sighting *Wahoo,* we stopped, and I could read the captain's thoughts, "Say what you want to about me, but don't lambaste my ship and crew!"

"Let's go back and square this away," he said, and we did an about-face to head for the Gooneyville. Probably in anticipation, someone had cleared the corner room; the lights were out and nobody was about. Having been up a good part of the night before our landfall, I headed for *Wahoo* and my bunk aboard. Seeming still a bit riled, Morton headed for the nearest game to take out his anger on a pair of dice.

The Base had all of the shops of a submarine tender, excepting optical and a foundry. The one affecting me was the gyro facility, for ours had been transmitting its heading to the repeaters erratically during the last few days of our return voyage. This had kept Krause and me up most of the night, punching out more stars to insure an accurate landfall. I found our gyro set up in gimbals that could be electrically oriented as if on a moving ship. The trouble lay in the rollers, which transmit the gyro's orientation and which have gold plating to insure the electrical contact. This plating had worn through in places. The shop would replate and polish them, and then give the gyro a complete test before installing it aboard.

Completely satisfied, and with an improved opinion of Midway, I set out for a turn through the small island with Jack. On my first visit in 1935, a residence and the lonely cable station were the only structures. I was then serving in the cruiser *Chester,* with Commander Air Force Pacific (ComAirPac) embarked, which had anchored off the reef. The cable on across the Pacific had now been closed, of course, but new buildings ranging from shops and warehouses to Quonset hut residences were spread out over the island. The lagoon had now been dredged, the coral forming another island where only a sand spit had lain. Called Eastern Island, it had become a U.S. Naval Air Station and a part of

Midway. Nowhere did we see any remaining evidence of the damage sustained during the Battle of Midway.

Wahoo's crew already had a spontaneous softball game underway, while others watched or perhaps participated when the mood struck. Over the bank, where the sand and grassy soil led down to the beach and provided a lee from the ever-present wind, other groups lolled in the sun, some reading, others content in doing nothing.

Early April offered only borderline swimming. Fishing was another matter, and though the present seas confined it to the lagoon, a motor sailer with about twenty hands was anchored with lines over the side and a few boat rods in sight. In the bilges were two cases of beer obtained by Pappy for this organized party. It would not be counted against the individual's daily ration of beer chits, like movie stubs. And I could see a lot more organized recreation in the days to come!

On the third day our officers moved to the hotel. It was not that the accommodations were better, it was the change that really counted. There was something to be said for space to move around in without taking turns, and a window that gave a pleasant view by day and admitted a cool breeze by night instead of shipboard forced ventilation. I modified my first thoughts about Gooneyville.

The captain had enjoyed his corner room for only one night when dispatch orders called him back to Pearl. It was obvious that Admiral Lockwood wanted Morton's first-hand accounts for other boats, so he would get to the Royal after all. Because of his absence, I was in command, and this included the repairs. It became our goal to have all of this completed before the captain returned.

The late afternoons and evenings at the corner room had indeed developed into a patrol school. Like an informal seminar, we exchanged ideas derived from actual patrol, sometimes by relating a whole experience—even Krause's torpedo, and I contributed my well-considered views concerning harbor penetration and down-the-throat shots; and I learned much, especially from Fritz.

I was feeling pretty good about all of this while lying awake in bed listening to the mating calls of the boatswain birds when suddenly someone shouted in the corridor, "Emergency, all boats get underway!"

No one would pull a prank such as this, and by the second call I had my khaki on and was racing out the entrance. It was after midnight, and hands were running for the dock. Some had further word: an enemy task force had been reported some 300 miles from Midway, and that meant bombers could be here by dawn. Surprise emergency drills were not held west of Pearl Harbor, so this was an emergency in fact.

I know it sounds impossible, but our crew literally picked up a welding machine and set it on the dock. *Wahoo* was ready first and backed clear. The range lights came in view, and with rudder angles to Simonetti, I conned *Wahoo* until the lights lined up and on that line through the slot in the reef into the angry seas. Buckley guarded the usual 4155 KCS, Carter the SJ. The other boats joined us, and then came the first message:

THE DRILL HAS BEEN SUCCESSFULLY COMPLETED

Our Pearl Harbor Commission, which had been meeting off and on since the attack, had forgotten the rules that they themselves had established.

On a normal coastline, even in mild storms, breaking rollers lose their momentum on the slowly shelving beaches. Quite the opposite is the case at Midway, where they increase in size on the steep coral incline and frequently carry over the reef into the lagoon. So *Wahoo* would have heavy seas astern during the last hundred yards or so before threading the slot through the reef, and could expect a yaw of 10 to 15 degrees on either side of the range line. Normally, the steersman uses only enough rudder to keep the yaw equal on each side of the compass course; then during the last minute the ship steadies and passes through the slot. We would have to do this without a compass!

After two practice runs on the range, with Krause at hand to advise me, Simonetti as steersman followed precisely my directed rudder angles and a sequence of "rudder amidships" between them. This try looked good; the seas were crashing on the jagged reefs to port and starboard, but our bow was not yawing much beyond the channel. We were a bit to the right of the range and in seconds there would be no turning back. I glanced towards Krause, who had been looking down at the coral heads to starboard. He nodded, and about 10 seconds later the yaw disappeared and *Wahoo* slid through the slot into the lagoon. I truly believe that all, from lookouts to the OOD, breathed out in unison with me.

A week later our gyro was returned. Captain Morton had returned as well, with an advance copy of our next operation order and our new PCO, Lt. Comdr. John Moore. He was a year junior to the captain, and by reputation would be a grand shipmate. Also Ens. Eugene Fiedler, with a background in radar repair, reported for duty—to Chan's delight. Eugene would go on the watch list immediately to replace Jack Griggs, who had been transferred to replace a sick officer in *Seal*. Presumably, Jack would return to *Wahoo* in another month or so. The other changes affecting our boat were sixteen new hands; the designation of Chief Carr as chief of the boat to replace Pappy, who had orders to the Submarine School; MacAlman relieving Kohl; the captain's leave program for CPOs; and Hunter relieved by Kemp.

As we had planned, all of the repairs had been completed before Captain Morton had returned; all of the changes to our Watch Quarter and Station Bill had been made; and except for final fresh produce, *Wahoo* was loaded for patrol, including charts. This had left time for 2 days underway training and finally, a personnel inspection.

With seasoned hands to instruct, the training went well, and even the seas cooperated upon our return through the reef. For the first time since Pearl, hands broke out their whites, and having been properly rolled, they came out ready for inspection. We were assembled on the dock, as sharp a ship's company as could be found anywhere, when Captain Morton returned with the senior officer on the island, the commander of the Naval Air Station. Instead of receiving the Navy Cross, for his actions in command of *Wahoo* on her third patrol, from Admiral Nimitz back at Pearl, he had elected receiving it with his crew assembled, and did the same for me by bringing my Silver Star Medal. No ship's company could have been more proud than were we of our skipper.

With the ceremony over, the troops had until midafternoon to write letters, and for quite a few, to buy money orders with their winnings from the big games to enclose in them. At 1430, I was able to report, "All hands are aboard and *Wahoo* is ready for patrol, Captain."

2

It was 1500, Sunday, April 25, 1943, and only our bow and stern lines held *Wahoo* to the pier when our acting division commander went ashore. Hands from our friendly Base snaked the brow to the dock and took in the remaining lines as they were let go. Then, with the DivCom, they stood at attention as the rumbling diesels moved our submarine clear and then on out to the range line. To the well-wishers on the pier, the whole maneuver must have seemed quite simple, and it was, but only because the outboard submarine had taken her bow line to the pier and had then taken a strain with her capstan to give us a generous "V" for clearing the dock and the boats.

Our bow sliced through the slot in the reef; the coral heads, a moment ago menacing, faded into the deep, and *Wahoo* was on her fifth patrol. Below, our new hands under closest supervision were participating in rigging for dive. Above, a plane from the air station was escorting us, but only until we were over the horizon. Our course was due west, but when the escort had disappeared, we would come to the course for latitude 49°30' north and longitude 155° east. This position was specified in our secret operation order, which also directed a speed of 13 knots. Both the position and speed were a most unusual specification in a submarine operation order.

But *Wahoo* was part of a submarine task force including *Steelhead, Pickerel* on patrol, and *Scorpion,* which had been waylaid while on her way back to her base. The four boats would apparently form a moving scouting line, with tactics directed from Pearl. The object of the search was a reported possible small enemy force headed for the Aleutians. Should our search prove this to be true, we presumed that necessary forces would be dispatched to intercept them. The loading of extra foul-weather gear at night and our ruse of an initial course west

251

was probably not necessary as it pertained to this operation, but a workman who was about to return to the States could have noted the loading in daylight and a submarine departing to the northwest. These small items, perhaps added to others, could tip off our breaking of a Japanese code. No extra effort was involved on our part, and this covered a remaining possibility.

Our course was 314, and just to be sure of maintaining the required overall speed, another diesel engine went on the line. *Wahoo* crossed the international date line, skipping Monday, so it was Tuesday, April 27, when we made our first dive of the patrol. Roger was an old hand at accurately figuring the required compensation for our loading, and immediately requested one-third speed. In another minute, he had reported, ''Satisfied with the trim,'' and three blasts had us back on the surface. There would be ample time for training our new planesmen, but weather might not cooperate with a different pending test: to try out our new powder.

I presume that the Bureau of Ordnance had heard from all quarters about the enemy's flashless powder, for they had gotten off their horse and produced some. In our magazine was a half load, and we would first try it out on the crests of the swells. This would give the gun pointer (elevation) just as much training as would a real target, and the gun trainer can always stay on a target anyway. With some anticipation, we awaited the first blast. I would have to admit that, in daylight anyway, there was little visible flash; however, the new powder's smoke had us coughing on the bridge. The smoke had blown clear of the gun crew, but with a following wind, I could visualize all of them standing around half doubled up and hacking away to clear their throats while wiping their eyes. When using this, we would have the wind as well as the conning tower to contend with. If ships have enclosed gun mounts and director fire from high above the bridge, this powder could be a night asset indeed, but we were glad that half of our shells were loaded as before. We had heard that the British and Nazis had flashless powder comparable to that of the Japanese, so maybe when the war in Europe was over, there would be some for our boats.

Increasing lazy swells and a dropping barometer on April 28 foretold a storm ahead. We fortified our dawn star fix with sun lines, the last at midafternoon before *Wahoo* entered the fog bank that had been visible ahead for an hour. Just as anyone could have predicted from the information in *Knight's Seamanship*, *Wahoo* entered a stormy area on the following afternoon. The winds somewhat dispersed the fog, so our lookouts could provide us with adequate security, but the task of spotting the enemy rested solely on Eugene and his SJ watch.

With the seas moderating and *Wahoo* a few miles ahead, at least according to our DR position, we made a belated trim dive. She went down beautifully in less than 40 seconds—again Roger's compensation was right on—and we surfaced normally to the point of rigging in our bow planes. The shear pin in the rigging gear had carried away, just as it is supposed to do before the great gear teeth are damaged. Some were overly concerned by the bashing of our planes into the sea, but having made the greater part of a long patrol in *Argonaut* with her bow plane rigging motor burned up and her great planes pounding the seas without harm, I was able to allay any fears. After all, we could still dive, even in less time, and use the planes submerged. As it turned out, this was not necessary, for Chief McGill and company, with safety lines snapped to our single center lifeline, went into the superstructure and replaced the pin. Again, our auxiliarymen could fix most anything.

The delay of lying to in the swells had put *Wahoo* back on schedule, and the evening Fox carried a message with the call signs of all four boats. Eugene already knew how to run the electric coding machine, so he installed the correct wheels, and the decoded tape came out of the machine as if the radio shack were a telegraph office. The message only advised that we were astride the most likely position for intercepting the enemy. We had expected more instructions, such as conducting a retiring search (a broad zigzag ahead of the enemy to increase the frontage as he overtakes), but none was forthcoming. Neither were there any contact reports from the other boats, who would now be carrying out the remaining provisions of their operation orders: *Scorpion* returning to base, while the others proceeded to areas off Hokkaido and Honshu for their patrolling. Sailing on to patrol the Kuril island chain, we would next patrol Honshu.

Our search continued in the fog, for a ship was always possible, and Eugene's SJ was hot. On the first of May, fleeting pips showed above its grass. They would be the reflection from shorebirds, almost a sure sign that land lay ahead. We tried fathometer sounding again, hoping for the submerged mountain ridge shown on our chart, but nothing yet. Sunday, May 2, greeted us with hail and snow, just as a reminder that *Wahoo* was invading the Arctic. I thought of the post–WW I S-boats patrolling from Dutch Harbor to Paramushiru, the northernmost island

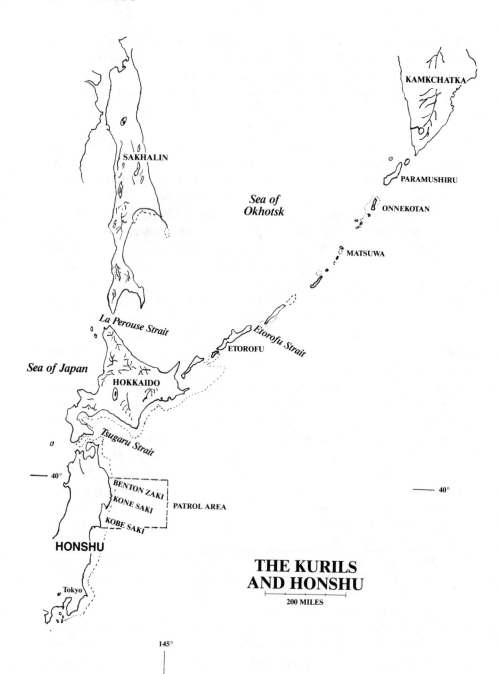

KAMKCHATKA

PARAMUSHIRU

SAKHALIN

ONNEKOTAN

Sea of
Okhotsk

MATSUWA

La Perouse Strait

Etorofu Strait

ETOROFU

Sea of Japan

HOKKAIDO

Tsugaru Strait

40°

BENTON ZAKI

KONE SAKI   PATROL AREA

KOBE SAKI

40°

HONSHU

Tokyo

**THE KURILS
AND HONSHU**

200 MILES

145°

of the Kurils. Lacking adequate heat, with bridges that swamped, and crews smashing off the ice that coated their upper works, it's a wonder that the S-boat crews didn't all get pneumonia. In contrast, *Wahoo* was as snug as ever, and even the damp foul-weather clothing was drying in a special, heated locker for those relieving the watch. None of us had reason to feel other than good about our lot.

We had not had a star or sun line since entering the first fog bank, so Krause and I experienced a touch of what the Norsemen must have felt when making a landfall on Greenland or our continent. A shout from topside brought us to the bridge, Krause pausing to enter 1423 in the Quartermaster's Notebook. Almost dead ahead, way up in the foggy sky and barely visible, was a snow-capped mountain peak. "I hope it's Onekotan," whispered Krause. I gave him my assurance, but was glad to see the shoulders of the mountain, as we closed, appearing the same as the sketch at the top of our chart. For sure, Midway had done a perfect job in repairing our gyro.

Captain Morton closed the island until we had good radar contact that would show intervening ships, and then commenced a slow surface patrol along the islands to the southwest. *Wahoo* would thus start any approach with a full can, or at least as much juice as ours would hold. Astern, just to the north of Onekotan, lay Paramushiru with its naval and air base. That was S-boat territory, but naval and supply shipping to and from the Empire should pass close to our track. Johnny Moore was in the conning tower, and as operations officer was keeping *Wahoo*'s position cut in along the track laid down on the chart.

Feeling like relaxing on completion of the transit, I dropped down to control to find Chief Andy Lenox holding forth: Andy had experienced no trouble in getting a flight from the States to Hickam Field, but from there had ridden in one of three B-24s on a training mission. According to the chief, they had needed more training in navigating, for they had missed Midway altogether and had not found it until they were nearly out of gas. Always with animated accounts, Chief Lenox finished by patting the duty chief's desk.

3

In the wardroom, the captain was waiting with the cribbage board. Over a leisurely game he outlined his plans for the Kurils. Complying with an oral request from Intelligence, we would reconnoiter Matsuwa, an island about 100 miles ahead that had suspected facilities. This would take care of May 3, leaving 3 more days before *Wahoo* could enter her true area off the east coast of Honshu. That was not much time for the 600-mile-long Kurils, and precluded patrolling on their western side, or even picking a likely spot between two islands where we might intercept enemy shipping moving to the west or east of the chain. It was an example of the trouble that can accompany detailed staff operational planning instead of leaving maximum flexibility to the submarine captain. We discussed this, and it led to the captain's decision to move on to Honshu at the earliest hour allowed by the operation order; but first we would dive off Matsuwa.

Like all of the Kurils, Matsuwa was a mountain peak, really two peaks we would judge, with the southern one forming a shoulder sloping up from sea level. I gasped a bit when the upper works and bow of a ship came into the scope as we cleared the offshore island of Banj To, but they were canted and she was a wreck, perhaps from a storm or quite possibly beached following a torpedo hit. This ship provided an exercise for our new pharmacist's mate, MacAlman, with his party, and possibly an identification for an attack by one of our submarines. (Lindhe had made chief and had received orders instead of returning from leave.)

Of more immediate interest was the air facility on Matsuwa. Built on the low tableland, it appeared well developed with four fairly large hangars; dispersal stowages in back; and a large landing field apparently equipped with floodlights, administration buildings, radio station, and barracks. Altogether, the installation appeared comparable to Midway's Eastern Island. After taking several pictures and plotting the positions on our chart, we cleared the immediate area. The sky and sea remained clear during the following hour, so we surfaced to continue our patrol southwest.

Though U.S. knowledge of the Kurils was probably meager, we had missed the opportunity to study the Japanese monograph at Pearl. Perhaps someone from the staff had made a study and concluded that it was not worth forwarding with our operation order, but even negative information can be valuable to a submarine. So at 0420 on May 4 we dived to conduct a reconnaissance of Moyoro Wan on the northeast tip of Etorofu Island. According to the *Sailing Directions,* the bay held a sulphur works. If it also held a ship, *Wahoo* could torpedo it, and if there were no activity, Carr and company might do considerable damage to the works.

Dawn came almost immediately, disclosing a not-too-distant fog bank in the Sea of Okhotsk but clear of the small bay's mouth. On approaching closer, I found any structures in the bay obscured by fog— white fog; no, it was jammed with ice. Swinging back to the original fog bank, it also was too white, and the current had brought the floes much closer, in a somewhat menacing arc. Johnny Moore, in anticipation, had a line to the southeast already drawn on our chart, and the captain ordered course 145 to take his submarine clear. Leaving Johnny in the conning tower to get experience in command, we went to the wardroom for coffee. The phone buzzed, and Johnny had a small ship or patrol.

Back in the conning tower, I took the scope, and with difficulty found a patrol intermittently visible in the surface mist. Her angle was about 30 starboard as Johnny had advised on our reaching the conning tower. The captain took a look, agreeing, and together we estimated her range to be about 6,000 yards, or 3 sea miles. She already lay on our quarter and would pass about 3,000 yards astern, so no evasive maneuvers were required. But just to be on the safe side, the Bells of St. Mary's chimed through our ship. Watching continuously, we caught the following zig. It was just 5 minutes into the evasion and we had her course exactly, for she now presented a zero angle on the bow.

This aspect on any patrol never failed to raise the heartbeat a bit, at least with me, but the captain was already conning *Wahoo* off the track. The enemy's bow, now becoming distinct, could be that of a small freighter. I asked Captain Morton to take a look, and he too could not decide. I was familiar with inversion layers that bring a ship's image above the horizon, but could this be the opposite in holding the image down?

Richie's TDC showed the generated range at 3,200 yards, and with the ship coming out of the mist, I was able to call a 15 starboard, and more—she was a ship worthy of our torpedoes. Orders went to both torpedo rooms, ready lights came on, and the captain ordered, "Outer doors open aft."

On the next observation, my heart jumped and I called, "She's got planes on deck!" and then gave the angle 30 starboard. This time I did not have to invite Morton to take a look; I just stepped aside so as not to be mowed down.

The enemy ship had changed from a small patrol to an unmistakable auxiliary plane tender or transport, an XAV in Pharmacist MacAlman's book. The details of how we happened to be in this position, including the floe that she was avoiding by coming from the west side of the islands, were unimportant, but our location was. The ship should pass within 1,500 yards, and the captain would be able to choose his favorite track where maximum target maneuvers would avail her nothing.

I called the angle at 45, broad on her bow, and again at 90 when *Wahoo* was abeam. QM1c Wendell Kemp, Hunter's competent relief, had called the bearings and read the stadimeter. We heard Richie's, "It all checks, 1250 from the track, speed 11 knots." The seconds seemed to drag and then came Morton's firm, "Any time, Dick."

Kemp followed my hands in raising the scope and then twisted the tube to the bearings that Richie was calling. I brought the wire to the ship's great goal-post mast forward.

"Constant bearing—Mark." Kemp read the bearing. "Set," came from Richie. Her big stack amidships was about to touch the wire.

"Fire!" and Morton whacked the plunger.

The second and third torpedoes were fired to hit under her after and forward goal-posts. We heard the zing, felt the shudder, and then the poppet valve pressure for all three; now Buckley called, "All hot, straight and normal." Chan commenced calling the seconds to go for the 1,350-yard torpedo run.

No two attacks are the same, but our fire control system could accommodate any of them. At 10 seconds to go, Kemp followed my hands up with the scope. The crack of the detonation reached us instantly, beating the visual result by a fraction of a second. A great explosion between her stack and bridge rolled the ship to port, but she kept on going. Our next torpedo, which should hit in her engine spaces, would take care of that. The firing interval was 11 seconds, and we waited, and waited—the torpedo was a dud and our third torpedo missed forward.

Four unexpected detonations drove us deep, perhaps unnecessarily so, but with the sight of planes had come the thought of bombs. We talked this over for about 2 minutes and were back at periscope depth. The XAV was reversing course and firing her gun away from us. We tracked the ship with stadimeter ranges and periscope bearings. Though listing about 5 degrees, she was still making 11 knots and heading back towards the western side of the Kurils. Had our failing battery permitted, *Wahoo* would have followed, but gaining a position for a later attack all in daylight on an alerted ship that could outgun us was a bit too much even for *Wahoo*.

In the wardroom, we looked over MacAlman's book. What we had seen and he had recorded identified the ship as of the *Kamikawa* class capable of 21 knots, so surely she must have sustained considerable damage or she would not be retiring at such a low speed.

After continuing eastward to clear the floes, we surfaced and headed southwest to investigate Hitukappu Wan on the short south coast of Etorofu. Again, floes prevented entering the bay, so we continued normal patrolling of the Kurils through May 6. A damaged ship, which should have been sunk, was all we had to show from these islands.

The intervening days held one memorable event, at least for Krause and me. We had missed the almost-daily flying fish in the temperate zones, so noting fish on deck after the next morning's trim dive, Eugene had sent for Manalesay, who proudly brought two handfuls of squid to the ship's office. When I inquired if he knew how to cook them, he replied, "Yes, Sir," and scurried aft, presumably to prepare one batch for us and the other handful for himself and Jayson. We had anticipated something crisp and fried, but they were boiled and had a peculiar, sour taste. After two of them, I inquired. "Oh, you have to boil this kind in vinegar to take out the poison," Manalesay explained. We could hardly wait until he had stepped forward so we could give the remainder the deep-six.

4

Our operation order had specified dawn of May 7 as the time *Wahoo* could enter our new area on the northeast coast of Honshu. That would not leave time to close the coast and so would mean a wasted day. Surmising that the northern part would have been vacated (friendly submariners cooperate), we continued past Hokkaido during the night and across the hundred-mile bay that led to Honshu. This let us cross the imaginary boundary and, closing the coast at full speed, to dive at dawn (0420) 12 miles from the coast off Benten Zaki. Within the hour, Richie and Kemp had two freighters and their *Chidori*-type escort in sight but far out of attack range. A third lonely freighter passed, but with our half battery, high speed with its quadruple battery drain would have left little capacity for attack and next to none for evasion.

The crew took this more lightly than did we, probably because of their confidence in the captain and his demonstrated ability to find ships. He did not let them down, for 2 hours later George and Simonetti had two ships coming up the coast. They did not bother with messengers or phone and at 1049 called us all with the general alarm, the Bells of St. Mary's. The leading ship was a midsized freighter; the other, about half her size, was painted slate gray and sported gun mounts. She was apparently escorting as well as carrying cargo. My angles and Kemp's bearings and stadimeter ranges flowed to TDC and plot. Quickly, Chan and Richie agreed on an enemy course of 350; it couldn't have been much to the left without the ships going aground. The speed checked at 9 knots, which frankly could be applied for any midsized coastal freighter.

Their solution was timely, for I had called 90 starboard and Captain Morton had given his nod.

"Constant bearing–Mark!" "Set." "Fire!"

The captain hit the plunger before I had completed the firing order, or so it seemed, and the first torpedo was speeding to hit below the leading ship's mainmast, the second to her foremast. We then shifted to the escort ship, firing a spread of four. During this firing, our first torpedo, a torpexer, broke the back of the larger freighter, but the escort threaded our spread and we rigged for depth charge.

A burst of speed during the surface confusion, followed by silent running at ever-increasing depth, cleared the initial depth charges. Those to follow seemed less severe, though should a person laugh at any of them it would surely be a sign that he was going off his rocker. Back at periscope depth before lunch, we cautiously watched the enemy planes and distant antisubmarine vessels giving the fish a bad time as we cleared the area by heading south.

MacAlman brought ONI-208J to the wardroom, his party having written down the bits of information they had overheard. It had been insufficient to do more than flag the book. This proved to be all that was necessary, for by then I had acquired firsthand training in remembering ship's details. We quickly narrowed the choice to a *Yuki Maru* class freighter of 5,704 tons.

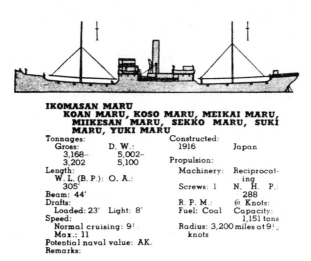

IKOMASAN MARU
KOAN MARU, KOSO MARU, MEIKAI MARU,
MIIKESAN MARU, SEKKO MARU, SUKI
MARU, YUKI MARU

Tonnages:		Constructed:	
Gross:	D. W.:	1916	Japan
3,168–	5,002–		
3,202	5,100	Propulsion:	
Length:		Machinery:	Reciprocat-
W. L. (B. P.): O. A.:			ing
305'		Screws: 1	N. H. P.:
Beam: 44'			288
Drafts:		R. P. M.:	(a Knots:
Loaded: 23' Light: 8'		Fuel: Coal	Capacity:
Speed:			1,151 tons
Normal cruising: 9¹		Radius: 3,200 miles at 9¹	
Max.: 11		knots	
Potential naval value: AK.			
Remarks:			

The day had not been lost, even though hits in the escort would have simplified things. Like their predecessors, our new hands would get their submarine combat pins or bronze stars to fit in the holes if they already had the pin. Then too, everyone in our ship's company was up to date in their indoctrinal depth charges. Frankly, it seemed to me that the troops enjoyed the hits, while in the wardroom we mused over the misses; that is, until someone broke out the cribbage board.

Captain Morton came across the narrow passageway late in the afternoon and sat down on my bunk. I started to get up from the desk, but he motioned me down. There's really not room for standing anyway.

"Dick," he said, "I've been thinking about this morning, our diving 12 miles out. When the two of us get involved it's like a committee decision. We are each tempered by our thought of what the other is considering, and we don't come down with the quick aggressive decision either of us would make if alone. After thinking it over, I realize that you had wanted to make a dash for the coast. Now as navigator, you have to be up there anyway, so starting in the morning, I want you to take *Wahoo* in and plunk her down, and then call me when you've got a ship."

The captain had rather concisely reflected my own thoughts, and had added a solution that called only for my, "Aye Aye, Sir." I followed him to the wardroom, sitting down to a four-handed game before surfacing.

All was clear, and a round of stars fixed our position so I could lay down the route that the captain had desired for the night—to Kobe Saki farther down the coast. The following hours were normal for our submarines on patrol—good meals on time, the movies, the battery charge on the finishing rate with the smoking lamp out, the hot rolls and bread coming from the ovens—and all because one-third of the crew was alert and competent on watch.

Krause and I were customarily up and about before dawn, so my added responsibility was not an extra chore, but rather a challenge that should have been the navigator's task. After skirting a fishing fleet, I conned *Wahoo* towards Kobe Saki while searching with 7 × 50s until the gray light of dawn was sufficient for our search periscope, and dived when a mile and a half off the promontory. For sure, nothing would pass inshore of *Wahoo* on this May 8. The test came promptly at 0512, when Johnny Moore spotted a small ship coming up the coast. The bells held reveille and we had a tracking exercise as the ship turned into every cove, while remaining no more than 1,500 yards from the beach. As she drew near, we could see that she was too small for a torpedo, so our cooks put down early breakfast instead.

I liked the way our new procedure had worked: the captain arriving apparently refreshed, sizing up the situation, and then returning to his cabin or the wardroom. There would be more targets, undoubtedly well-escorted ones, for it seemed that *Whale* had heated up this area for us. Under Morton, *Wahoo* had been a fast-moving boat and had left the antisubmarine forces far behind or guessing. Many of our newer hands had probably volunteered for *Wahoo* because Morton filled the criteria for the best wartime skipper—one who would lead his crew into battle and swiftly get them out. But now this had been made more difficult by a high ratio of escorts, our failing battery, and a very confining final area.

It was early afternoon, 1432 to be exact, when the next ships hove in sight coming down the coast. Three in number and zigzagging, they were soon identified as a large auxiliary and two freighter-type escorts, and the bells bonged for the second time this day. Buckley was able to call their zigs by the momentary change in cadence of the screw sounds, and these were followed by new angles on the bow of the auxiliary. Between looks, I kept the captain apprised of the escort disposition and MacAlman of the ship details as I could recall them. Richie and Chan had no trouble in arriving at a similar speed solution of 10 knots, and Chan, who was plotting the actual positions down the coast, could provide the skipper with the enemy's changing base courses, and more. From the enemy's track on the chart, it was evident that he was staying about 1,500 yards from the beach, and *Wahoo* could remain at least a like distance farther to seaward and still be assured of an attack.

Her opening angle kept pace with that shown on the target dial of the TDC. We had an excellent solution, and at my call of "Port 90" came Captain Morton's, "Any time, Dick." The time was 1503, and using our exact procedure, torpedoes went to her midships, the mainmast, and foremast. She was a dead duck.

The first torpedo detonated at 52 seconds, approximately halfway to the large auxiliary. The second torpedo, running down nearly the same track as the first, was evidently deflected by the premature and failed to explode. The third torpedo hit the point of aim and threw a column of water about 10 feet into the air as the air flask apparently ruptured. Both Buckley and Carter's report of the thud of the dud had coincided with the water plume, and *Wahoo,* already turning to north, followed a quarter helix down to test depth while rigging for depth charge.

One or both of the escorts would now be running down the last torpedo wake. The remnants of the first two wakes would intercept it at a narrow angle marking the firing point. The torpedo run of 1,500 yards was favorable; it would take the escort at least 5 minutes to reach that point, and by then our speed up to 10 knots would have us a good four ship lengths away. Propellers could not cavitate (form bubbles that collapse, making propeller noise) when so deep, so Buckley was able to give good bearings, while confirming that there was just one escort heading our way. Chan plotted the bearing, their trend indicating that the escort would pass astern of *Wahoo*. The first of a series of depth charges commenced detonating at 1510, and it was the captain's initial burst of speed that had placed them well astern. Though shakers, they did not seem too bad, but that was in part due to Buckley's ears that had told us they would miss. Within the hour, we made the long climb to periscope depth. All was clear, and upon surfacing in evening twilight, Morton ordered the course for Kone Saki.

5

After such a day, some relaxation in the wardroom seemed in order, but I arrived in the midst of a torpedo argument between Jack and George. Both turned to me, not to settle the dispute, but for information. They could hardly believe that nearly all peacetime fish had run hot, straight and normal in *Argonaut,* and had had the same controls as those we had been firing. Two things had happened, however. The Geneva Convention had outlawed firing at merchantmen, and since warships would be our targets, authorities thought we needed a torpedo that would detonate *under* a battleship, for their blisters and armor plate would protect their sides, or so they thought. So influence features, which were supposed to be activated by a ship's magnetic signature, were added to our simple inertia exploders, secretly as far as the operating forces were aware. There were two results: the new, heavier exploder made our torpedoes run about 10 feet deeper than the running depth set on the torpedo; many then ran too deeply for their exploders to be triggered by a ship. Also, ships proved to have irregular magnetic signatures that would trigger the exploder before it reached the ship, or more frequently, not at all. In this last instance, the inertia feature of the magnetic exploder should have detonated the warhead, but it also had proven unreliable.

All of this had led to the firing of large salvos when a single, reliable torpedo and exploder would have sufficed. Such salvos had exhausted our supply of prewar Naval Torpedo Station handcrafted torpedoes. They were now assembled from parts made by dozens of subcontractors, many of whom were probably unaware of the vital function of their products.

For the last two patrols, *Wahoo* had carried this combination of unpredictable exploders and unreliable torpedoes, and as we all knew, our captain had obtained results by hammering away with what we had.

Krause and I had punched out a round of stars on the night horizon, correcting the dead reckoning position and slightly modifying the course for tomorrow's position off Kone Saki up the coast. Before dawn I would close it, just as we had Kobe Zaki. Although Krause had made SM1c, he would hold the same billets until his expected transfer. That way, Kemp, who would be staying in *Wahoo,* could continue heading the quartermasters watch list and be the periscope assistant as the captain had desired.

My assistant called me early for our landfall, having as usual put in his own call ahead of mine. It was 0230 on Tuesday, May 9, according to the wardroom clock and the calendar over the sideboard, and still waking-up, I took my coffee to the conning tower. Torpedoman's Mate McSpadden, from *Argonaut,* had Kone Saki as a dancing pip on the SJ. The Japanese Current could account for our early arrival, but the radar contact at 18,000 yards was in part responsible for my early call.

Fifteen minutes later, McSpadden had two more and somewhat smaller pips at slightly lesser range. Johnny Moore arrived in the conning tower, and I concluded that many of his calls were matching mine. We stopped and killed *Wahoo*'s headway to check on the movement of the new pips. They were closing, and we had headed for the coast to stay ahead of them when Captain Morton answered his call to the bridge.

Tracking had arrived; the captain took the conn and, asking for the time of morning twilight, he closed the enemy to identify the ships. We had a large tanker and freighter, without escort, attempting the night run between bays. Tracking now had them on an average course of 210, the slant of the coastline, and steaming at ten knots. With *Wahoo*'s full power available, since the battery charge had been completed, Morton could choose any position for the attack. The best would be their position at dawn, and *Wahoo* headed for the "X" Chan had marked on the chart.

The enemy came on hugging the coast. At 0330 we held reveille so the crew could have coffee too before battle stations. Fifteen minutes later, the Bells of St. Mary's made battle stations formal, and we dived to radar depth still 5 miles ahead of the enemy. Tracking continued with radar bearings and ranges. At 3 miles, in the first light of dawn, I could make out the ships through the search scope, their angles opening. The captain had conned his submarine to a position 1,000 yards off the enemy's track, and had then turned to bring our bow tubes to bear.

The forward torpedo room reported tubes ready, outer doors open, and running depth set on 18 feet. After a last radar range, we moved on down to 60 feet. When the angle had opened to 90, the captain gave his customary, "Any time, Dick," and, not varying our procedure, three torpedoes went to the tanker, leading, and three more to the large freighter.

As the fifth torpedo was firing, the first hit the tanker amidships, sighted by Johnny Moore on the other scope. The fourth, a torpexer, hit the freighter under the bridge, and the fifth hit her aft. Both ships had broken in two, the tanker going down in flames and the freighter following to Davy Jones's locker minutes later. We cleared the area to the east.

We heard distant depth charges throughout the day, and one echo-ranging antisubmarine vessel passed close to *Wahoo* on one occasion. Our bathythermograph, which had shown a 2-degree temperature gradient as we passed 170 feet, gave us extra confidence at our 300-foot cruising depth; and acey-deucey, cribbage, or a good book replaced the Plan of the Day. In the wardroom, however, Johnny Moore and I, as the ones who had seen the two ships in daylight, had another task. We had little trouble in arriving at a *Huzisan Maru* class tanker of 9,527 tons and a *Hawaii Maru* class freighter of 9,467 tons; then we turned to cribbage.

Distant explosions and echo ranging were still heard on sound, and the detonations sometimes through our hull when we surfaced into a

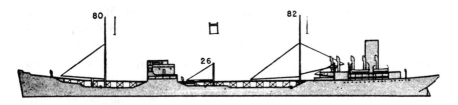

HUZISAN MARU

Tonnages:		Constructed:	
Gross: 9,527	D. W.: 13,586	1931	Japan

Length:		Propulsion:	
W. L. (B. P.): 493'	O. A.: 512'	Machinery:	Diesel
		Screws: 1	N. H. P.: 1,857
Beam: 65'		R. P. M.: 110	@ Knots: 15
		Fuel: Oil	Capacity: 1,120
Drafts:			tons (bunkers)
Loaded: 28'	Light: 10'	Radius: 16,000 miles at 15 knots.

Speed:
Normal cruising: 15   Max.: 19

Potential naval value: AO, AV.

Remarks: Oil-carrying capacity: 93,000 barrels (42 gallons).   Guns: Provisions for mounts on forecastle and poop and probably mounting 5" guns.

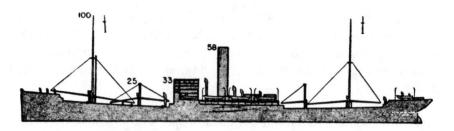

AFRICA MARU

ARABIA MARU, MANILA MARU, HAWAII MARU

Tonnages:		Constructed·	
Gross: 9.467–80	D. W.: 11,100–400	1915–20	Japan
Length:		Propulsion:	
W. L. (B. P.): 475'	O. A.:	Machinery:	Reciprocating
		Screws: 2	N. H. P.: 995
Beam: 61'		R. P. M.:	Knots:
Drafts:		Fuel: Coal and	Capacity: Coal,
Loaded: 27' 7"	Light: 11'	Oil	1,300 tons; oil,
Speed:			2,000 tons
Normal cruising: 14	Max.: 16	Radius: 8,000 miles at 14 knots	

Potential naval value: AP, AK, AH. MANILA MARU and ARABIA
MARU declared hospital ships.

Remarks:

black night. It rather appeared that the coast would be heated up for
the next few days, and with only half a battery, submarine seamanship
called for a four-sided area, one in which we could evade in any direction.
Morton picked the position where *Pickerel* had reported the small group
of fast enemy ships, the contact that had set this whole game of musical
chairs in motion, and at 2020 we headed for it.

Two engines were on charge, two on propulsion. It seemed good
to be cruising, and the enemy might indeed send shipping offshore in
view of torpedoes, even the frightening prematures, along the coast.
Even if we found no ships, the change would provide all hands some
needed rest. This included the captain, for though he apparently thrived
on action, not for a minute did he neglect his command responsibility,
which in itself had become too much for our first captain.

Wahoo patrolled the Tokyo-Paramushiru route for 2 days, with only
a trawler providing interest to the crew. Legitimately fishing and carrying
normal antennas, we avoided her. Also of interest, especially to me,
was the Fox schedule on May 10. It contained my orders to report to
Mare Island for fitting out and command of the new submarine *Tang*.
The advantage of serving in a small force was evident, for in the assignment, the detail office had obviously picked a boat close to my family.

Refreshed, we returned to the coast, diving close in to Kone Saki at the first gray of morning twilight on May 12. Starting our own musical chairs, John Campbell would relieve Roger as engineering officer and had taken her down this day. He had dived *Wahoo* many times, so there was nothing unusual, except that in the quiet after leveling off, fairly loud explosions resounded through our hull. Numerous sampans and a glassy sea made periscope searches difficult. We maneuvered clear as best we could without using extra watts, more mindful of wrecking a scope than of being detected. Whether or not we had been sighted, a light bomber commenced searching our general vicinity at 0630, and several fairly loud explosions rumbled through our hull during breakfast. They set the theme of our conversation: searching for us, or just clearing the area for daylight shipping well inshore? The wardroom was about evenly divided, with my heading the latter group.

At 0730 the phone in the recess to the captain's left buzzed; we could hear George Misch's voice and feel *Wahoo* taking a down angle. "That's good, George, rig for depth charge," was the captain's reply, and rising, he cut us in, "We have a bomber heading for our scope!" Nothing dropped, or if so, the bomb or depth charge was a dud. More likely, our scope had lain on the bomber's circling path, but George's action was right in any case.

We remained at deep submergence heading east. It appeared that the Japanese were bringing in their first team, so why attack under those conditions with a partially crippled submarine when we could attack at night and then hightail it on the surface? This was the captain's decision, but I was sure all of us agreed. Numerous bombs or depth charges continued to rumble, like distant thunderstorms, but faded in the early afternoon, leaving us wondering what had caused such an assault on the sea.

We now searched with both scopes, coming up to expose 17 feet periodically. As before, the hands for the second scope were all volunteers, including some engineers breaking their vow not to see daylight until our return from patrol. Their motive was probably twofold—a pool for the sighting, and like all of us, the desire for two more targets.

The first sighting came at 1725, that is, if far-distant smoke to the northeast could be developed into a ship. Another bearing showed that the ship below the smoke was heading southward, and *Wahoo* commenced an approach at standard speed to close the enemy before sunset. Within the hour, the masts and then the upper works of two freighters came over the horizon. Steaming in column, they offered an early opportunity for identification, and perhaps the last, so the captain called MacAlman with his book to the conning tower to see for himself. It took only two looks and using the coded system to settle on the *Myoken Maru* and *Anyo Maru* classes of 4,021 and 9,257 tons, respectively. Tracking had manned their stations automatically and had the enemy's speed at 10 knots, zigging on a base course south. They had already passed any submerged attack position, but we had all the information we needed for a night surface and submerged action in partial moonlight.

Almost routinely, we had our evening meal submerged, and were on the surface for only a half hour before we again had the smoke in sight. Three engines drove *Wahoo* along an arc past the enemy, where we dived. The Bells of St. Mary's sounded to make battle stations official, and we waited for the ships to come into the moon streak that always comes to the eye or scope. Constant bearings sent torpedoes to the mainmast and stack of the *Anyo Maru,* the trailing ship, and then two more, aimed similarly, raced for the *Myoken Maru.* The time of firing was 2245.

We heard the zing, felt the shudder and the poppet pressure for all four torpedoes. Buckley called, "All hot, straight and normal," and Chan counted the seconds for the 1,200-yard torpedo run, but only the first torpedo to the *Anyo*'s mainmast detonated.

I reported the *Anyo Maru* still going. Morton waited until the range had opened to about 5,000 yards and then three blasts sent *Wahoo* up for an end-around and a night surface attack. The screeching turbos raised our hull; the weighted sacks of trash went over the side; and all engines, including the auxiliary, went on propulsion or charge. Our best lookouts sighted the smoke within the quarter hour, and *Wahoo* raced through a now black night towards an attack position on the *Anyo*'s starboard beam. Fortunately, the *Myoken Maru* was far ahead and could not interfere. At 0107, in position just forward of *Anyo*'s beam, the captain twisted left for a straight bow shot, and gave his, "Any time, Dick." Her stack touched the wire, and "Fire!" Johnny Moore, below in the conning tower, hit the plunger. The sounds of firing were normal, but no phosphorescent wake was visible.

That was our last bow torpedo, and Morton was now twisting *Wahoo* with starboard ahead full and port back emergency for a stern shot. The *Anyo* continued on, apparently unaware that she had been fired on.

At 0111, our last torpedo, with all the normal signs, raced towards her midships. It hit between stack and bridge with an explosion audible on our bridge, but lacking the "whack" of a true detonation. Sparks were seen about the deck above the hit as *Anyo Maru* turned away, seemingly under control. At this time, *Myoken Maru* laid down accurate gunfire and forced us to dive.

Six minutes had passed when three blasts took *Wahoo* up again. *Anyo* was lagging a mile behind the *Myoken,* having slowed to 6 knots. Feeling that she would drop back farther, we switched to battle stations gun. In minutes we were ready with ammunition on deck and Carr awaiting the captain's, "Commence fire!" But the *Myoken* opened up first, and Morton ordered the gun crew below, commenting, "That whole lousy *Maru*'s not worth one of my crew." Helpless to stop the cripple, at 0225 *Wahoo* cleared the area to the east.

6

The initial course of east ordered by the captain was by chance within 3 degrees of the first leg of the great circle course specified in our operation order. I changed the course to 87 and then informed my captain before sitting down to a three-handed game with him and Johnny. Then turning in, I was asleep when Carter reported a receipt for our departure message at 0336. By habit I was about to get up when I remembered that Roger and Kemp would take over navigation starting with morning stars. I was still the exec and just as responsible for our ship's safety as before, but this extra time would permit working on the patrol report. There was another reason for the change: the captain was behind in sewing, and this included a project behind a drawn curtain.

Our operation order had directed best speed commensurate with remaining fuel for our return, not anticipating a short Morton patrol. The batteries were charged—the auxiliary could keep them topped off—and a fourth engine went on propulsion. There would be no reason for stopping at Midway, so our next report would be from the 1,000-mile circle from Pearl.

Again, without specific instructions, hands were holding field day in their compartments, except for a half dozen or so who were taking turns in rearranging the cold room. For this, they had appropriated the gun crew's hot-shell-man's gloves, and though a bit clumsy, they would prevent any frosted fingers. Missing, as far as I could tell, was the odor our freezer space had acquired on the last patrol. Many boats had mentioned this in their patrol reports, some having installed charcoal filters and fans, and one having replaced the insulation. The senior doctor and supply officer at Midway, lured by a cup or so of submarine coffee, had found our problem: it had come from several boxes of semiputrefied meats, which apparently had been partially thawed a few times before coming to *Wahoo,* and which they had found amongst the boxes we had turned in on arrival. Perhaps we should have found them, but after a month or so of submarine odors, we probably would not have noticed anything unusual about these boxes. The relief crew had used a concoction similar to Lysol when cleaning the spaces, and now *Wahoo* must have had the best-smelling freezer room in the force.

On the evening of May 16, our Quartermaster Kemp brought the chart to the wardroom, as had become customary. The track showed the rhumb line, a straight course, that had been specified for this portion of our return voyage. It ran several miles to the north of Kure Reef and a little north of Midway. Roger apparently did not consider this too close, and not wanting to butt in, I took other action, first stepping off the distance from the reef to our track, 10 miles, and noting that *Wahoo* could reach the reef right after daylight. I then put in a call for myself and Krause for 0345. It was no imposition, since by habit we were still waking up about that time anyway.

Roger and Kemp had taken their stars and were below, working them out. Krause manned the lookout platform while I remained on the bridge. The twilight sky changed to emerald, a sign of shoals below. Krause waved his arm from our port bow to our starboard beam; I looked down to see coral heads and shouted, "All back emergency!" After slowing, we backed along our still-visible track to deep seas, and from there ran to the north for about 5 miles before resuming our original course. When traveling 3,000 miles, clearing a reef or island by 25 miles instead of 10 might add 5 minutes to the voyage. And a star fix must consider all the lines that are plotted, even though a majority pass through a point. I had not known this to be the error in the last fix, but taken altogether, it would be a lesson that Roger would never forget. It was also a lesson for me to speak up when a possible danger to our ship was involved.

We enjoyed two Mondays, each May 17, on crossing the international date line, and made our last sighting, a friendly convoy heading for Midway, on the eighteenth. Sterling was already typing the stencils for duplicating the patrol report by the division staff. Krause was completing the track chart tracing, and all that remained was the rendezvous with our friendly *Litchfield* at dawn of May 21.

Roger had gone all out with sun lines and star fixes, and our four-piper lay on the horizon dead ahead at dawn. To our passing view, Pearl Harbor had changed only by the row of great cables and supports that were righting the battleship *Oklahoma*. Rounding ten-ten dock brought *Wahoo*'s reception party into view, complete with dignitaries and the band.

Our patrol, with three ships down and two damaged, had not been auspicious, but compared to the other boats' departure reports, had been the best. Apparently, they had experienced similar troubles. In any case, the crowd had turned out for *Wahoo* as she came alongside Pier 1, and I wondered if members of the band were thinking of the time they had found sanctuary beyond the escape training tank.

The flurry and initial greetings over, Admiral Lockwood and the division commander accompanied our skipper below. They soon emerged from the after torpedo room hatch and, greeting members of the crew on deck, proceeded on to headquarters. Neither paymaster nor busses for the Royal were waiting, which told that the final decision concerning *Wahoo* was still pending or we would have been informed already. Not affected were the patrol report and track chart, and delivering it gave Krause and Sterling a quick excuse to leave for the Base. Others could have left, but seemed to prefer staying on board or about the pier with fingers crossed. We did not have long to wait before the captain came hustling back, and those topside knew the answer by his generous smile. We would start unloading extra ammunition and stores immediately, but would not be loading any torpedoes. On the next day there would be an awards ceremony, followed by payday, with scheduled departure for the States on the following morning.

From the Dark Ages through the privateers of '76 and into the First World War, plunder and then ships as war prizes had served as incentive to the participants. The capable leaders or ship captains received the lion's share of the booty or the prize court's final monetary awards, for they were the ones who had brought back the loot or captured the ships. Now war prizes were forbidden in our Navy, and medals had replaced other incentives. The submarine force command had adopted a very conservative awards policy that had been approved by the Commander-in-Chief Pacific Fleet. It required so much time in recommendations and reviews that too often the prospective recipient's submarine had by then been lost, and posthumous awards hardly serve as an incentive to anyone. So a new policy had been approved in 1943 that seemed somewhat mechanical but in practice was quite just, for our personnel losses were already the highest.

While reviewing the patrol report, the division commander could call witnesses if necessary, and if a captain had sunk one ship, the DivCom could recommend the Secretary of the Navy's Letter of Commendation with medal (the Commendation medal). For two ships, the recommendation could be a Silver Star medal, and for three or more ships, the Navy Cross. The captain so cited could then recommend lesser awards for his officers and crew.

As at Midway, the whites had unrolled, ready for a seagoing crew's inspection, and each rating badge, chevron, and watch mark was neatly sewn in place. Fleet Admiral Nimitz arrived promptly at 1000 to present awards for the fourth patrol. He may have greeted a crew in "starchier" whites, but never one more proud or with more stars in their submarine combat pins, worn above the ribbon of their Presidential Unit Citation. After walking the length of the formation and back while acknowledging every man with a nod, the admiral presented the second Navy Cross to our captain, a gold star to be affixed to the ribbon of the Navy Cross that Morton was wearing. The congratulatory handshake was accompanied by a spontaneous, muted, heartfelt cheer. It was their tribute to the captain, just as the admiral's acknowledgment had been to them. Without fanfare, I proudly received a second Silver Star medal.

Oil King Lemert and John Campbell were busy taking on diesel fuel for our continuing voyage. John was already in the process of taking over as engineering officer from Roger and heeded the latter's advice to allow a good safety factor. The final item in our preparations was a packet of eight new movie films, and lest we might be letting down our guard, Captain Morton penned taut instructions that applied to everyone, but especially to the OODs and duty chiefs. Though our operation order specified 1230 the following day as *Wahoo*'s departure time, all hands were aboard and departments ready for sea the night before.

Monday's dawn would have been the best time to depart, but the morning did provide the crew an opportunity to purchase last-minute gifts from the Base ship's service store, whose stock had little to do with ships and carried much that would not be found easily in the States. And for the few who had neglected to do so, it gave a last chance to get their seabags or a replacement from the chief master at arms, for all personal gear would have to be removed from the ship within an hour or so after reaching Mare Island.

Just as if we were departing on patrol, Admiral Lockwood and our DivCom came to see us off. Only our bow and stern lines still held our submarine to the pier when the rumble of the diesels called attention to the wardroom clock. Morton saw the admiral ashore; the brow was snaked to the pier by hands from the Base; and at the captain's nod, I ordered the lines cast off, a prolonged blast, and then backed *Wahoo* from the slip. Twisting, and then ahead two-thirds, I conned her out of the harbor and to the waiting PC escort. It was a gesture from the captain, who had become my closest friend, to let me handle his ship this last time.

Wahoo was already exceeding by a knot the speed of 14 knots speci-fied in our operation order, but only until we were well out of sight. After that, the speed that our PC could maintain in the moderately heavy seas would be the limit. All of this was due to the details of our op-order, which seemed to have been written more for a train keeping an exact schedule than for a ship that could run into slowing storms at sea. Exact points, Charlie, Dog, Easy, Fox, and George, would keep us clear of other shipping, except *Spearfish* and *Searaven,* whom we might meet; and at the 1,000-mile circle from San Francisco we were required to report our daily position, the last such report to be the rendez-vous point with an escort. The crimp came in a commitment that the captain had somehow made to Mare Island to be there at high noon on Saturday, May 29, just 5 days hence. There was only one solution—to establish a dawn rendezvous point that would insure our arrival in San Francisco Bay by 0900. From there, the 2-hour run to Mare Island would leave an hour for dressing ship and contingencies. So as soon as the PC turned back, we could bend on the turns for point Charlie to get and improve our position as we passed each point.

Krause brought down the chart, which showed our complete track on to the rendezvous 30 miles from the Golden Gate Bridge. Captain Morton seemed much relieved after seeing that *Wahoo* really could make the appointment. He first suggested a point 20 miles instead of 30 for our rendezvous, but decided to leave the positions as they were and arrive at the point an hour early. Taking action, he picked up the phone and directed that the PC be dismissed with a "Well-done" and that all four engines go on propulsion.

On my usual turn through the ship to see that we were secured for sea, I heard the main motor reduction gears, beyond the maneuvering room bulkhead, whining at close to high C. Passing through the door, I noted the propeller shaft tachometers indicating 315 turns, 15 below full power. We continued on, dropping to three engines when the seas were knocking down our speed anyway. As we left each alphabet point behind, *Wahoo* gained more and more time.

We had passed to the operational control of Commander Western Sea Frontier, reporting our successive points as required. The command had a copy of our operation order, and we awaited the reply with more than ordinary interest. It came the following evening and simply stated that USS *Lawrence* would meet *Wahoo* at the designated rendezvous.

The crew loved this homeward-bound passage as if the speed was all for them, and in truth it was. Our hot SJ had *Lawrence* before morning twilight, she too allowing an extra hour. Instead of a challenge, her first searchlight message read:

FROM COMWESSEAFRON CONGRATULATIONS AND WELCOME TO THE STATES

A front had blown the customary summer fog away, and we followed *Lawrence* into a sunrise beyond the Golden Gate Bridge. I thought again that this had to be man's most beautiful steel structure.

Leaving sparkling San Francisco astern, we proceeded to the bight north of Tiburon to be free of any shipping and clear of the stronger tides. There, the OOD would maintain our approximate position during breakfast and while the crew dressed ship in submarine style. Our special yardarm atop the SD mast carried the *Nitu Maru*'s great house flags to port and starboard. The halyard below each flag carried one small Japanese rising-sun ensign and then nine civilian flags that represented the two warships and the eighteen other ships that *Wahoo* had sunk. Above them all went the captain's latest project, to which he had sewn a sleeve to fit snugly over the top of the attack periscope.

There was still time for final clampdowns, and for sneaking the last weighted sacks of trash and garbage over the side, before continuing between the Brothers and up San Pablo Bay. About a mile short of the Carquinez Bridge across the Sacramento River, we turned left, and keeping red buoys to starboard, entered the Napa River. The flags and Old Glory streamed beautifully in the north wind, and above them all awaited the captain's project, to be unfurled when abreast our mooring.

Mare Island's waterfront was packed like football bleachers—man for man or ton for ton, no ship could have had a greater reception. *Wahoo* headed slightly towards the waterfront so the wind and current moved her very slowly to her mooring. While still in the stream for all to see, Morton gave a nod and Simonetti pulled the line that broke an enormous pennant free. In minutes we were alongside, brows came over fore and aft, and I stepped ashore to embrace my beautiful family. Close at hand was Admiral Friedell, the Navy Yard commandant, who had been my first Sub Force commander. With her lorgnette, his wife was examining the pennant, asking, "What does it say, Admiral, what does it say?"

"Madame," he replied, "that reads, 'Shoot the Sons of Bitches!'"

_____Part Seven

THE SIXTH AND SEVENTH PATROLS
PATROLS
The Sea of Japan

Sixth Patrol

1

While en route to Mare Island, Sterling had made out leave papers for all hands who would be continuing to patrol in *Wahoo*. The crew was allowed to choose the first or second 3-week-leave period, ironing out any differences amongst themselves prior to Sterling's dating the papers. With money drawn at Pearl, the first leave section evaporated in minutes; the captain and Mrs. Morton went on to a luncheon; and we drove to our home across from Hamilton Field, 22 miles away.

At the arrival conference on the following morning, the Navy Yard readily agreed to our outstanding repairs and to the routine overhaul of our main engines. Included also would be an upgrade of *Wahoo*'s equipment so she would depart nearly on a par with new construction. Back aboard, the captain asked me to take good care of *Wahoo,* and when he left his ship, to send every last man that I could spare on leave.

Within the hour, I had *Wahoo* underway, and with the assistance of tugs, we put her in drydock. This was necessary for pulling our port shaft, which had a persistent squeal at evasion speeds; and the dockside cranes would be right there at hand for removing and installing battery cells. There would be no more wardroom or mess room coffee, for already the tin knockers were dismantling the forward- and after-battery living spaces. And if that weren't enough, our battery emergency disconnect switches had been thrown. *Wahoo* was cold iron, and would soon have two square openings through her pressure hull above the battery wells for removing the individual battery cells.

All of the foregoing and the Navy Yard's cooperative attitude at the conference provided an idea of how to carry out the captain's request concerning leave. It worked—the Navy Yard readily agreed to take over the watches for welding, usually a ship's job, and for below-decks security. That left only the deck watch and supervisors for our engines. We had them in Chiefs Lenox and Keeter, plus hands going to new boats here.

I could not recall telling anyone of a new leave plan, so some hand must have overheard Morton's final words to me at the gangway. In any case, all of our equipage had been moved to the provided storerooms within a couple of days and we had extra men waiting around. Andy Lenox took care of that by passing the word to get their leave papers and bring them by for signing. We had been provided an office close at hand where the line formed immediately, and in short order the second leave party had disappeared.

Soon the first battery cells were being lifted through the holes in *Wahoo*'s hull and lowered into special shipping crates atop railroad flat-cars. We could only watch and admire the accuracy of the operators. Not so another change, the removal of our conning tower's after door. This vertical oblong door, fitted into the circular convex bulkhead, had distorted on some boats during depth charge with leaks and near rupture. Not essential to our operations, it was being removed. I watched the shipfitters find the bulkhead's center and then inscribe a circle that included the door and frame. This would then be burned out and another dish of the same curvature would be welded in its place. To my objection, I was assured that the result would be just as strong as a new bulkhead. The constructor who arrived was less convincing, and conceded when I pointed out that my captain and his crew wouldn't believe it. So *Wahoo* received a brand-new bulkhead and not a patched one.

These were the items, mostly small ones, that we were following. All was going well when a letter from SubAd, Submarine Administration Mare Island, ordered *Wahoo* to supply six mess cooks. Other hands with priority orders going to new construction boats had already been sent on their way, and we were down to a total of twelve, with only one of them even eating at the barracks. Since the letter was by direction and signed by a warrant officer, I called on him at SubAd, explaining the situation. He seemed satisfied and I returned to the office.

Before opening the door, I could hear the phone ringing. Commander Submarine Administration (ComSubAd), Capt. J. B. Griggs, our Jack's father, wanted to see me immediately.

"What's this I hear about your sending everyone on leave?" he demanded.

"Sir, not everyone, just those we didn't need after the Navy Yard had agreed to take over security below decks and all fire watches. *Wahoo* is cold iron, in drydock, and we have a continuous deck watch and duty officer,'' I replied.

"Why, if that drydock flooded you wouldn't have a leg to stand on,'' the captain retorted.

"Nothing is going to happen, Sir,'' was my assurance, while thinking that in such a flooding there would now be fewer hands drowned.

"There better not be,'' was his final word, and I was not invited for coffee.

Most of the married officers' and petty officers' families had remained in the general area after *Wahoo*'s commissioning, so there was much going on besides the shipyard work. The most important involved Chan Jackson, for his pretty Wave, Iona, was waiting and they were married at Mare Island's historic chapel. Following the late-afternoon ceremony, they came by our home for a reception, and were greeted by fellow officers who had raced ahead. Rationing did not permit a sumptuous meal, but crisp salads, fresh from the garden, exactly hit the spot as far as the submariners were concerned. They continued raiding the garden to build more until Chan and Iona had gone on to San Francisco.

Official temporary additional duty orders for Chief Andy Lenox came from ComSubAd. He was to go to Hollywood as a technical advisor for the production of the movie *Destination Tokyo*. This put a crimp in our watch list, but that was soon squared away by hands returning from leave. This was well, for there had been no dallying by the Navy Yard.

All scheduled work had essentially been completed when the captain returned refreshed, jolly, and finding his ship right where he had left her. Within a few days, the remainder of the crew reported, except for Chief Andy Lenox. This had come about through an appeal by the film company direct to the Navy Department, and Lenox's orders were extended until the completion of the film. So the captain's plan to keep key personnel had retained only one of the three, Chief Keeter. Also, eighteen of the crew who had made *Wahoo*'s fifth patrol had gone to new boats, but their replacements were already reporting aboard. And Jack Griggs had returned from his patrol in *Seal*. The turnover in personnel per patrol had probably been no more than many other boats, but *Wahoo* had completed her last three in record time. As expected, Morton made no complaints.

Following a final lunch in *Wahoo*, I again walked along the waterfront, this time towards my own submarine still on the ways. Under my arm was a beautiful, oblong, silver cigarette box, engraved from the officers and crew. I turned and waved, but saw them through misty eyes.

Note from the Author

To continue the authentic writing of *Wahoo*'s true story, I have relied on the account of Rev. Chandler Jackson and Capt. J. B. Griggs for the period until her departure on patrol. For the sixth patrol, the secret operation order for *Wahoo* and her companion submarine, *Plunger*, are at hand, together with their patrol reports, *Wahoo*'s containing a page for each torpedo and a day-by-day diary, plus the comments of the reviewing seniors. An additional source is Forest Sterling's excellent book, *Wake of the Wahoo*, and a personal account by Captain Griggs.

2

Morton's influence at Mare Island was phenomenal. During the few days before underway trials, the shipyard changed *Wahoo*'s topside configuration to nearly that of a *Tang* class. Gone was the bulky bridge cowl forward. Aft, the conning tower fairwater had been trimmed down to the height of the bridge deck. Now, when her conning tower was hull-down to another ship, her bridge from any angle would look like the deckhouse of a trawler. Below, she sported an auxiliary gyro compass in the control room, and forward, in the torpedo room, a new sound-listening device, the JP. Its listening elements were at either end of a crossbar atop a vertical shaft extending through the torpedo room's over-head, and provided amplified listening in the sonic range even if the boat were on the bottom. Radar training exactly like sound's finished the list.

Roger had become *Wahoo*'s executive officer, a jump of 5 years in only 1, but what a year it had been. In general administration—especially with a good yeoman, Sterling, and Carr as chief of the boat—*Wahoo* would practically run herself, thus permitting Roger's required concentration on training the new crew members. Cooperation was not lacking, for the next patrol loomed just 3 weeks ahead. A 10-day underway training and post repair trial showed *Wahoo* in all respects ready; Capt. John B. Griggs presented awards on July 20, and Wednesday, the following day, *Wahoo* departed for Pearl, with Ensign Campbell her engineer.

The course of 285 degrees led to point A, but instead of following the alphabet, a great circle course would be laid down from there to point B and thence to the rendezvous. Along the track, a submarine need only remain within a rectangle moving at the prescribed speed, thus permitting dives, drills, and other variations en route. Calm summer seas were welcomed by the new hands, and also by the captain and Roger, because they would permit higher speed and consequent time for drills within the moving rectangle. At the moment, *Wahoo* was providing target services to both sea and air escorts, a new twist in making their task more meaningful. To add realism, the plane simulated an attack from 4 miles, with *Wahoo* diving barely in time, and receiving their ''Well done'' upon release.

No wartime passage is routine, but in near-yachting weather, with Rennels's baked goods rousing the oncoming midwatch, this came close, until Roger developed signs of appendicitis. The dawn rendezvous with *Litchfield* had already been scheduled when Pharmacist MacAlman put the exec on the binnacle list. So Chan's first turn as navigator would be the most exacting. He more than welcomed it, for in the dispatches brought aboard before sailing were his orders to a new boat, and by his seniority, as executive officer. With the thought of rejoining his bride, he quickly forgave Jack for not having read the messages before sailing.

Roger was transferred to the hospital immediately after mooring on July 29. An additional fumigation had proven necessary, and although done by a professional agency, Chief Carr became ill during the subsequent ventilation, and he too was hustled off to the hospital. Fortunately, Chief Boatswain's Mate Lane, who had made *Wahoo*'s third and fourth patrols, returned as chief of the boat. From ComSubPac's staff, while awaiting his exec's billet, Lt. Comdr. Verne L. Skjonsby, in the class of '34, reported as *Wahoo*'s executive officer. Sandy haired, medium tall, and with Nordic features, he had stood near the top of his Naval Academy class, and had completed postgraduate studies in ordnance including torpedoes.

Captain Morton scheduled a 3-day underway training period to include ship's drills and torpedo firing to familiarize Verne with *Wahoo*'s method. On the last three firings, the torpedoes had run hot, straight and normal; *Litchfield* observed all of them passing under her keel, and in turn each torpedo surfaced properly at the end of its run when its low-pressure flask valve operated, blowing the water from the yellow exercise head. This had been the expected normal peacetime performance, and its overall result was noticeable throughout the ship's company. Immediately upon mooring, Morton visited Roger and Chief Carr, who were recovering from potentially critical situations. Richie, with Johnson and McSpadden, had completed witnessing the final adjustments to *Wahoo*'s last torpedoes at the Base shop, and they would be loaded within the hour. Other loading for patrol was on schedule for a 1300 departure on the following day, Monday, August 2.

3

Before lunch Verne had reported all hands aboard and *Wahoo* ready for patrol, receiving the captain's, "Very good." An hour later, two diesels had already fired when Morton welcomed Admiral Lockwood aboard for the traditional cup of submarine coffee. This time, there was an additional reason, for armed with Morton's firsthand report on erratic magnetic exploder performance, Lockwood might obtain the concurrence of ComSubSoWesPac in the elimination of this feature. *Wahoo*'s present torpedoes, as suspected, had only an inertia feature. Morton saw the admiral to the pier, and Verne backed *Wahoo* clear. As had become customary in the boats, the new hands were at quarters, facing our devastated ships till clear of the harbor, while below, the boat was rigged for dive.

The track Kemp had laid down on the chart passed through the Kauai Channel and thence north of the Hawaiian chain to Midway, as stipulated in the operation order, but then added a dogleg to the usual spot south of the channel. To a query, he told his new navigator why; they would get along well.

Wahoo moored at Midway's fuel dock routinely. While Ensign Campbell and Oil King Lemert were topping off, Morton talked with Lt. Comdr. Raymond "Benny" Bass, skipper of the *Plunger* and an Olympic champion gymnast who had retained his competitive spirit. Not before known, *Plunger, Permit,* and *Lapon* had made a 4-day feasibility probe into the Sea of Japan during July, sinking three ships (and quite possibly insuring some A.S. vessels for boats to follow, and they were to be *Wahoo* and *Plunger*). By the secret operation order, *Wahoo* was to precede, so she would sail after fueling. It had been agreed that *Wahoo* would patrol north of Tsugaru Strait, and *Plunger,* departing the next day, to the south. For a rendezvous in an emergency or for

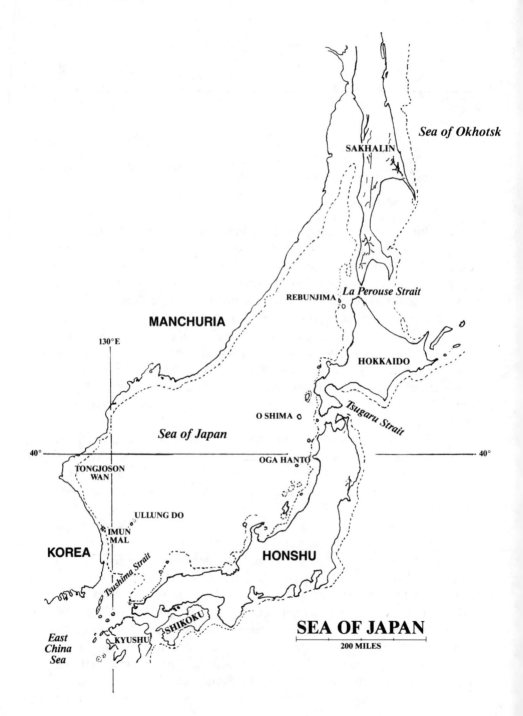

Sea of Okhotsk

SAKHALIN

REBUNJIMA   *La Perouse Strait*

MANCHURIA

130°E

HOKKAIDO

Tsugaru Strait

O SHIMA

Sea of Japan

40°   OGA HANTO   40°

TONGJOSON
WAN

ULLUNG DO

IMUN
MAL

KOREA   *Tsushima Strait*   HONSHU

*East
China
Sea*   KYUSHU   SHIKOKU

SEA OF JAPAN

200 MILES

another urgent reason, a point 10 miles west of O Shima had been selected.

Wahoo left the coral heads astern on passing through the slot in the reef, and upon clearing the island, steadied on course 315 degrees, the first leg of the great circle route to the Etorofu Strait through the Kurils, as prescribed in the operation order. Any other boat would be advised of the transit and routed clear. Fair winds and following seas increased the daily run until one more engine would cut a day from the transit, and *Wahoo* went to three-engine speed. Besides the 8 hours of watches, morning and afternoon drills filled a taut routine, but now, with both the exec and captain satisfied, a rope-yarn Sunday was followed by normal patrol cruising.

Verne and Kemp's stars had shown the strait only a day's run ahead; seabirds added confirmation, and at 2147 on August 12, the SJ picked up land. The exact time was important, for some hand had won the pool. There would be no sighting, for dense fog surrounded *Wahoo* shortly after the radar report. Three hours later, she entered the Sea of Okhotsk without sighting land, and the navigator had been initiated.

Verne had laid down the recommended route to La Perouse Strait, showing *Wahoo*'s dawn position at two-, three-, and four-engine speeds. As he had expected, with fuel to spare, Morton had chosen the last. From there, a short daylight dash and then submerged running at the new batteries' sustainable speed would reach the desired position on the chart. It would insure a night passage through the strait.

A small SJ pip reported by the AOOD, Lt. (jg) Eugene Fiedler, could not be seen from the bridge, but Kemp's periscope sighting of an *Otori* patrol on the following day warned of what might lie ahead. The passage was routine, but left 150 miles to clear Russian shipping.

4

The new hands did not have long to wait, for immediately after the movie came a call for the tracking party. It was just smoke over the eastern moonlit horizon, but *Wahoo* was off with a bone in her teeth. The smoke, now three rather widely separated columns, was drawing to the right, and Morton accepted Verne's recommendation of course 145, ordering two more engines on the line. The smoke soon became three freighters—two of medium size and one small. Tracking had their course as 205, steaming at 7 knots. Jack's plot agreed, and the Bells of St. Mary's chimed in earnest for the first time on *Wahoo*'s sixth patrol.

The captain decided to sink the trailing, medium-sized ship first, since it might be attacked without the other two knowing what had taken place. Verne's angles in the bright moonlight checked with Richie's on the TDC. The leading ships were now crossing about 1,000 yards ahead; the target would be closer. With the rest of the night for more attacks, Morton decided on one torpedo under her stack. He announced, "Any time, Verne." The exec swung the scope to the freighter's bow, calling, "Constant bearing—Mark." Kemp announced the bearing; "Set," came from Richie. A few seconds passed before the stack touched the steady wire at 0035, bringing Verne's, "Fire!" Morton's whacking the plunger was simultaneous. The slight shudder, a healthy zing of the torpedo's props, and the momentary poppet pressure all gave assurance, but the proof came with Buckley's, "Hot, straight and normal." Jack had picked up the count at 20 on the 35-second torpedo run for 900 yards, calling 25, 30, and then the last seconds, but there was no detonation.

In tactics, Morton never dallied, so 20 minutes later, three blasts sent *Wahoo* up and after the still-unalerted enemy. Passing beyond the sighting range would require over an hour, but all of that changed when a larger, northbound ship headed for *Wahoo*. For sure, she had not lost her affinity for ships, and with four in sight, the captain pulled the plug to attack the new arrival. She came by at 1,150 yards, and following Morton's precise procedure, Verne's constant bearing sent a single torpedo, set to run at 6-foot depth, to her midships. Again, all signs indicated a perfect run, this time with Carter's, "Hot, straight and normal." He was right, Verne reporting a water plume amidships as Jack's count reached 41 seconds. The major cylindrical section of the torpedo, the air flask, with air at close to 3,000 pounds per square inch, had ruptured on impact, but again, the warhead had not detonated. Quartermaster Simonetti had logged the time of firing as 0222, but for a ship that had not sunk, it could be of little interest.

Shortly after firing, the captain ordered, "Secure from battle stations," for at this pace, the crew would be up all night, and with further watches pending. After time for setting the regular watch, the order, "Make all preparations for surfacing," came over the 1MC, and the following three blasts set off an end-around on the ship that had just been attacked.

After helping with the torpedo reloads, groups in relays raided the crew's mess to find that Rennels and Chief Phillips, as they had come to call him, had hot coffee and soup awaiting, with the makings for sandwiches laid out. Some tried their bunks for awhile, but with section tracking and the exec at work in the conning tower, and knowing their captain was about, a few at a time, and then all, returned to stand easy at their battle stations.

The end-around proved also to be a race against the morning twilight, which Kemp had figured for 0415. The quartermaster had been right on, and Morton's two blasts took *Wahoo* down for the third attack. The bells' peal had been unnecessary, for stations were already manned. From a position on the freighter's bow, Morton conned his submarine for a sharp track, but one where the ship would still present more than half her length. The combined relative motion brought on the firing point quickly, and from a range of 750 yards, Verne's, "Fire!" sent one torpedo to her foremast, and repeating, another fish to her mainmast. Both torpedoes had a running depth of 6 feet. At least one had to hit, and perhaps the smaller angle of impact would activate the exploder mechanism, but there were no detonations or other explosions.

Immediately after firing, with full speed and rudder, Morton swung ship to point *Wahoo*'s bow directly up the freighter's broad stern. The torpedo run would be about 1,500 yards. No fire control was involved, just Verne's, "Fire!" when the wire in his scope—held steady on zero degrees by Kemp—bisected the target's stern. It zinged, and was tracked by Buckley blending with the freighter's screws. It could have salvaged a bit from a frustrating night, but it too failed.

There had been two detonations, logged by Simonetti at 0423 and 0427. The times did not jibe with possible hits by *Wahoo*. More likely, they were depth charges dumped as a deterrent by one of the freighters who had diagnosed the thump of a *Wahoo* torpedo. Such would not deter Morton, but daylight and the likely arrival of antisubmarine forces put *Wahoo* on the defensive, seeking deeper seas, while hands not on their regular watch sought their bunks.

5

Echo ranging commenced at 0930, and was followed by the arrival of an *Otori* torpedo boat, which carries a sizable number of depth charges. A second echo ranging commenced, but these did not interfere with the tasks at hand. Now with sufficient space in the forward torpedo room, and an assured steady platform, Richie and Jack, with Torpedo-man's Mates, First Class Johnson, Deaton, and McSpadden, were about to swing a torpedo to check its vertical and horizontal rudder throws and with this its gyro steering and the depth mechanism. Verne went forward to witness. The gyro was spun as upon firing by compressed air from the flask, and then the turbines similarly, but without the alcohol fuel. Suspended by a chain fall and the spliced-wire handling strap, the torpedo was swung in azimuth and then elevated and depressed. The whole mechanism operated perfectly, just as it had in the Base shop. There was one more check, not involving material. Had Buckley or Carter reported hot, straight and normal for all five torpedoes? Their answers were the same; they might have missed one, but certainly would not have missed an erratic fish. The problem, as suspected, was narrowing down to exploders, for duds are not heard through the hull, and seldom by the sound operator unless a ruptured air flask is involved. Incorrectly, they're called misses.

Quartermaster Kemp had run the tracks of the ships to the south; they made a pattern indicating that they were using the Tsugaru Strait. This would not affect *Wahoo*, but it most certainly could *Plunger*, who now would be patrolling to the south of that passage. Her torpedoes, from *Sperry*, would still have erratic magnetic exploders, though most would work. But she could be without ships. The captain looked it over, thanked Kemp, and then said simply, "We'll take care of that."

By noon, both patrols had withdrawn, but with evening twilight,

295

the *Otoris* returned, obviously knowing that it was time for the submarine to surface. *Wahoo* slithered away, and after an hour, came up into a clear night and under a rising full moon. There would be no further shipping in this general area during the following days, so the captain asked for the course to the Hokkaido-Korea shipping route, where unalerted traffic should be found. Verne picked 170 from the chart and received Morton's, "Make it so."

A single engine was driving *Wahoo* quietly along the selected route. Two more were on a charge that would take twice as long as it did on the fifth patrol, but correspondingly, there would be twice the submerged endurance on the following day, Tuesday, August 17. Diving after Verne and Kemp had taken their round of stars, first sound and then high periscopes found no ships. But the day provided an opportunity to run back through the TDC the data that Quartermaster, Third Class Terrell had recorded. The first four fish, all with fresh eyes, should have hit at or within a very few yards of their point of aim. But this was another day, and there were nineteen torpedoes left.

Verne, who excelled in math, was finding that there was an art in playing cribbage that verged on just plain luck. Phillips, officially *Wahoo*'s chief steward, had steaks thawed and ready for frying, so Morton obliged with three blasts. The diesels would now gobble up the smoke from fast frying; a main course of steak and potatoes would always satisfy the troops, and the same could be said of the wardroom. Verne's stars had fixed *Wahoo*'s position, and during the dark before moonrise, she headed for Hokkaido's coast, searching.

It was going on midnight when the first ship hove in sight. She was a freighter heading south and zigging so radically that gaining a position for an assured attack was proving difficult if not impossible. After midnight came a patrol, and more distant, another freighter. Diving, *Wahoo* avoided the patrol and then surfaced to find the new ship offering a better opportunity than the original freighter, so the captain shifted targets and pulled the plug for a moonlight periscope attack. The bells bonged, and a half hour later, on Verne's, "Fire," Morton hit the plunger, sending a single torpedo to hit the freighter in her port quarter. Perhaps the glancing blow, which other submarines had tried, would make this exploder work, but the fish—not the ship—went to Davy Jones's locker.

The time of firing had been 0226, and 20 minutes later, *Wahoo* commenced a 2-hour surface run away from the coast for another day submerged. In the wardroom, not dejected but grim, Captain Morton announced his plan for the following days. During daytime, officers not on watch would witness and assist in pulling and checking torpedoes for the following night's firing. This would include rudder throws and depth mechanism. *Wahoo* would continue to close the coast during darkness, and attack submerged after moonrise.

At 2224, still on August 17, Morton fired a single torpedo, with a depth setting of 4 feet and engine in low power, at a freighter 1,100 yards distant. The firing was controlled by the TDC instead of by his favorite constant bearing. Again there was no explosion, and Morton announced the procedure for the next firing: Torpedo gyros would be set on zero manually, checked visually, and then the setting spindles would be withdrawn. The Mark-8 manual angle solver, an improved version of the prewar banjo, would be used to figure the lead angle. Though lacking the flexibility of the TDC, for a single lead angle it was just as accurate, maybe more so. It was the method Morton had been brought up with in submarines, so he would fire.

The one highlight of an otherwise frustrating patrol had been the quality and quantity of all meals. The immediate frequency of shipping had apparently convinced Phillips that this would be a short patrol. So he had been following the approved menu rather broadly, having pulled out most of the stops. Rennels was not far behind with the baked goods, and as had become customary in *Wahoo,* his bread came out of the ovens before the midwatch. Would that some of the torpedoes might run as smoothly.

Battle stations at midnight for attack number seven could not have been more timely. Tracking had been following a northbound freighter for three-quarters of an hour in moonlight, reaching a good solution as two blasts were sending *Wahoo* down. Tracking's data was precise: speed 8½ knots, torpedo run 850 yards, track 90 port, torpedo gyro angle already set at 000. The lead angle for the low-power shot was 16. The captain kept the freighter's bow in the scope, Kemp holding it at 16. The stack touched the wire; Morton barked, ''Fire!'' and the submarine, like a gun barrel, sent the torpedo straight ahead on the course to intercept. During the torpedo run, a southbound freighter passed the target close aboard, but even with two targets there was no detonation.

Surfacing, *Wahoo* chased the southbound ship, but on closing the dark shore, she became difficult to see, so tracking was directed to work on a northbound freighter well to seaward. During this surface chase, two more small ships were passed up, but a likely position was reached by 0300. Diving for a submerged approach, an attack position was reached in 11 minutes. From 1,100 yards a torpedo sped to hit broad on her port bow, and as feared, another warhead or torpedo failed.

As if to get the shooting over with, a second torpedo sped to strike her port beam. It broached 23 seconds into the run and detonated about 3 minutes later.

6

Ten torpedoes in nine attacks fired at six ships on an average track of 89, from an average range of 1,070, with no proper detonations had been enough. If a submarine is going to encounter one ship for each torpedo, and *Wahoo* had nearly doubled that, the maximum torpedo spread is obtained by firing one torpedo to the middle of each ship. This Captain Morton had done, and further had required all possible on-board torpedo checks. Adding to this, the firing by different methods left only the firing of more torpedoes to find that they would not work. Better by far would be the return of the remaining fourteen for examination and investigation. Only if the faults were thus found could this patrol become meaningful.

Following a run to the west, away from the Tsugaru Strait, Buckley keyed the captain's encoded message to ComSubPac and *Plunger*. It briefed the torpedo performance and Morton's intention of bringing the remaining fourteen home. A receipt from NPM was immediate, and so was Morton's order, "All ahead full," as *Wahoo* headed for La Perouse Strait. The dash, lasting 2 hours, would clear the area of the radio transmission, and then Verne's recommended two-engine speed would reach Soya Misaki late the following afternoon, August 19. The promontory would be the departure point for running the gauntlet during the dark of the night.

The evening Fox brought ComSubPac's orders to return to Pearl, but completely illogical was the accompanying instruction to leave ten torpedoes at Midway. That instruction had been noted before as a way of keeping Midway supplied, so had the staff blundered in tacking it on the admiral's message? For sure, *Wahoo* was not going to inquire and give the enemy another radio direction finder position so he could station patrols to greet her, and Morton said simply, "Let them work it out."

Dawn again demonstrated *Wahoo*'s affinity for ships when a fine freighter came over the horizon on an intercepting course. Working torpedoes or not, two blasts initiated an approach until the captain called Pharmacist MacAlman to the conning tower so he could see the ship's Russian flag. Another engine made up the lost time; Soya Misaki was passed submerged; and though challenged by light, a surface passage to the Sea of Okhotsk was completed before dawn. From there, a dogleg to the south avoided patrols along the direct route, and another zero-visibility passage through Etorofu Strait was completed without incident.

The return route quickly intercepted two large motor sampans. At least the troops' weapons should work. They did, destroying the sampans and taking six prisoners. At midnight, 5 days later, *Wahoo* took a large dogleg to the south, completely avoiding Kure Reef, and enjoyed two Tuesdays before mooring alongside *Sperry* at 1107 on August 25.

After the semiformal greetings, Captain Morton accompanied *Sperry*'s skipper to the latter's spacious cabin to brief him concerning the torpedo performance. On receiving assurance that the torpedoes with their warheads would be segregated for possible shipment to Pearl, and that every possible inspection and test would be performed, Morton provided a list of the torpedo and attached warhead serial numbers, given to him by Richie, so there would be no mistakes.

Appearing somewhat relaxed on returning aboard, and noting that the 1730 sailing was more than 6 hours away, the captain ordered 2 hours ashore for each watch section. He would have preferred to follow suit, but luncheon with the deputy ComSubPac would this time be the dubious reward accompanying command.

With only the national ensign flying from her main, *Wahoo* moored at Sub Base Pearl at 1035 on Friday, August 29, 1943.

Seventh Patrol

1

After the usual greeting, coffee, and walk through the boat, Morton accompanied the senior officers to headquarters. The paymaster, with satchel in hand, moved into the wardroom as soon as it was vacant, so payday followed without wasting a minute. Sizing up the probable outcome of the captain's conference, Verne sent two watch sections on their way to the Royal. His judgment was good, for soon a messenger brought the same instruction from the captain, who was going on to lunch.

There was little Morton could relate that hadn't been covered in the very complete patrol report. Besides the usual narrative and required sections, a separate page had been included for each attack. These pages were so detailed that there could be no doubt, on the part of any knowledgeable reader, as to exactly what had taken place. Further, the reviewing senior could not help recognizing that these small- to medium-sized freighters steaming at 7 to 8 knots posed a much simpler problem than did the shorter target for the single torpedo fired during qualification in submarines. The report had been kept current during the short patrol, and Sterling had been kept busy typing until 1 day before mooring, when the captain signed the forwarding letter. So with the time of arrival entered, he and Kemp were off immediately to deliver the report and track chart to the DivCom's office, and from there, on to the Royal.

The captain returned at midafternoon to tell Verne and those who needed to know of *Wahoo*'s next, or really continuing operation—cruising 3,430 miles to the Sea of Japan, sailing a week from Thursday, September 9. He would seek the southern half, although *Plunger* had reported sinking three ships in the northeast. The operation order would be secret, since it would involve *Sawfish* as well and the new, still-classified, Mark-18 electric torpedoes. *Wahoo* would be carrying a full load, while *Sawfish*'s load would be twelve Mark-14s and twelve Mark-18s. So starting the next day, all torpedomen would attend special instruction in these torpedoes.

Chief Carr, all well from his ordeal, had reported back aboard, relieving Chief Lane. Verne arranged for a car and driver to retrieve the torpedomen each morning and take them back to the Royal after school. Carr, with the easy job, merely removed their names from the watch list. Richie and George would also attend, and soon found the ready-made transportation better than fending for themselves.

After their last days at the Royal, *Wahoo* would be losing eight men, mostly to new construction, but already their replacements were reporting aboard with two to spare. Similarly, Jack Griggs had orders to a new boat, and was good-naturedly boasting that it was taking two lieutenants and a lieutenant junior grade to replace him. They were Bill Burgan, a classmate of Richie's; Hiram Greene; and Donald Brown. All were experienced, especially Bill and Hiram, so *Wahoo* would again have a breadth of submarine experience in each watch section.

The angle-solver section of *Wahoo*'s TDC had cams that compensated for the original curving path of a torpedo fired with an angle. On a 90-degree Mark-14 shot, the curve ranges about 270 yards ahead, requiring a fairly accurate range determination to insure a hit. Similarly fired, a Mark-18 torpedo curve would range only about 50 yards ahead, so required only a rough range determination. In fact, the angle shot could probably be fired just as if it were a straight shot, but a cam especially designed for the Mark-18 was being installed by the Base. The other preparations were battery-charging panels and ventilation ducts. Everything was being completed handily. But all of this was overshadowed by a single feature of the Mark-18 torpedo itself: it left no wake, so a ship would not even know she had been attacked if the torpedo had missed, and if the fish hit, there would be no telltale wake pointing towards the submarine.

The division, squadron, and acting force commanders were orally attributing *Wahoo*'s attack failures to Morton's not using torpedo spreads. They were unable to realize that since there were more ships than torpedoes, he had applied the broadest possible spread by firing one or more torpedoes at each of the targets. The op-order required a commanding officers' (CO) conference, which was scheduled at the Royal. It would also provide Morton an overdue visit with his crew, and at least a day away from headquarters. On the way, he gave a copy of the patrol report to the Sub Base commander, who not only had a willing ear, but told of a confidential dispatch from *Tinosa* at Truk, who had stopped the *Tonan Maru,* one of the enemy's two largest tankers, but on trying to sink her from abeam, had had eight consecutive duds. She was bringing the one remaining torpedo back for investigation. ''So it looks like you've got some support, both firing from ninety tracks.'' And Morton told him about the ten more in *Sperry,* with their serial numbers in the report.

A swim at the second reef was shortened by the arrival of Comdr. Eugene Sands, skipper of the *Sawfish* and a classmate of Morton's. Tall, sandy haired, and pleasant, he more than welcomed the copy of *Wahoo*'s patrol report brought for him, though he was warned that much could have changed. To avoid a traffic bypass, like *Plunger*'s, they would share the whole sea, guard 4155 KCS, and keep the rendezvous 10 miles west of 0 Shima.

The watch sections returning to the boat told of meeting former marine and heavyweight boxing champion Gene Tunney, who was now a Navy commander. In subsequent reports, the novelty changed to apprehension when the crew learned that Commander Tunney had been appointed by President Roosevelt to conduct a study of the physical fitness of naval personnel on the shore establishments. Like the Pearl Harbor Commission, he had found the Royal to his liking. Soon, he had let it be known that he could condone the first night's revelry by crews returning from patrol, but on subsequent days there should be an early reveille and calisthenics before breakfast, and midmorning roadwork. For the afternoons, he had relented, proposing organized softball and volleyball tournaments between the boats. On returning to *Wahoo,* Yeoman Sterling had summed it up with two words, ''Oh brother''; but all of this would be left behind, for the exec had already reported, ''All hands aboard and departments ready for patrol.''

Captain Morton returned from his departure visit at headquarters accompanied by the acting force commander, Capt. John H. Brown, and Commander Tunney. While they were below for coffee, a mess steward came aboard with a B-4 bag. *Wahoo*'s catchy name had again hit pay dirt—the luggage telling that Commander Tunney would be super-cargo as far as Midway.

2

The prolonged blast from *Wahoo*'s whistle brought those topside on nearby boats or on the piers to an immediate attention. So they remained until the submarine's propellers headed her out the channel, for there were few who did not have a friend on other boats. Amongst the section at quarters were the new officers and hands, except for Bill Burgan, who was standing his first watch aboard. Also on the bridge was the commander, for Captain Morton, having been apprised at headquarters of Tunney's pending recommendations, had agreed to show him some of the other side of a submariner's life.

No crewman could ever consider the passage through the harbor as routine; he just had learned to give the wrecks to port and starboard a fleeting glance. Following Lt. Hiram Greene's orders of "About face," to those at quarters, Commander Tunney faced each ship or wreck with them and did not attempt to hide the handkerchief he had pulled from his hip pocket.

Turning right upon clearing the swept channel, Verne directed the course for the PC escort to the south of Barbers Point and advised the captain, who had gone below with the commander. Carr reported, "Ship rigged for dive," and a half hour later, he relayed the information to the captain that *Wahoo* was approaching the PC. Suggesting the control room as the best spot to observe the dive, Morton left the commander and went up the ladder to the conning tower. Two blasts and down she went. Any dive appears to be somewhat of a slam-bang procedure, especially to the uninitiated, but with the troops' cooperation, this one would have shaken many a seasoned submariner.

In the conning tower for indoctrinal depth charging, Morton explained keeping both scopes up for the PC to see so the depth charges wouldn't be dropped too close. He had told no one aboard, except Verne, that he had suggested a shorter distance for this demonstration. All four were tooth shakers, and with a straight face, the captain explained that we had to do this lest new hands fly off the handle when receiving charges that were close, and that the effect increased inversely with the cube of the distance.

Thus started 2 days of drills for the crew and indoctrination for the commander. At first shocked to see men in their bunks during the middle of the day, after nearly being mowed down by hands manning battle stations and at other drills, he had found sanctuaries and eventually his own top bunk in the captain's cabin. And by the time *Wahoo* turned north on Sunday, September 12, to thread the slot through the reef, the commander had become a friend and shipmate of the whole ship's company.

Other than topping off, a chance for new hands to get about the island, and for anyone to drop a ten spot or so, two important things took place at Midway: Morton visited the *Sperry*'s captain to learn of any findings concerning *Wahoo*'s ten torpedoes, and *Wahoo* received the latest mail flown from Pearl by PBY. In it was the list for Advanced Yeoman's School, which included Forest J. Sterling. With this school on his record, he could count on making yeoman first class, and he would have to complete it before making chief. Abandoning all else, Sterling headed for the *Sperry* and found Y2c William T. White. The two of them found their respective skippers in conference, and waiting until just the right time, White's transfer to *Wahoo* and Sterling's to school were approved by their captains.

Fueling was completed by noon; Verne made his report; and at 1300 Sterling, taking in the last line from the submarine that had embraced his war effort during the past year, watched until her tops disappeared below the horizon.

The endorsements to *Wahoo*'s patrol report were similar to the oral comments. Distributed shortly after her departure, they would surely be considered by many as a whitewash for the torpedoes at the expense of the leading skipper with the highest percentage of hits. Doubts came with *Tinosa*'s revelation, and the truth on *Plunger*'s success with *Sperry*'s unaltered warheads. There could be no doubt: the much-maligned magnetic exploder had sunk practically all ships to date; the Base had removed it, and *Wahoo* had been sent to the Sea of Japan with a complete load of duds.

Fleet Admiral Nimitz, himself a submariner, immediately concurred with the plan to test two warheads against the cliffs of Kahoolawe, an uninhabited island used for target purposes. The warheads, attached to proven exercise torpedoes, were fired where they could be recovered. Neither of them detonated, and upon recovery, the exploder mechanism had been so mangled by the impact that the reasons for their failure could not be determined. The very fact of the crumbling was a clue, however.

At the Navy Yard, an exploder without booster was fitted into a dummy warhead attached to a dummy torpedo used to test tubes. Able to vary the impact speed by dropping the torpedo from various heights into a drydock, the mystery began to unfold: the exploder had a firing pin that traveled at right angle to the motion of the torpedo. Made of steel, the pin's inertia, when the torpedo hit, had made it hang up against the wall of its guide. The pin thus hit with insufficient speed to fire the detonator.

Fortunately, the remedy was right at hand in the Sub Base machine shop, by the manufacture of light-alloy firing pins with reduced inertia as replacements. With the original pins, the exploder could work when dropped on its side, so boats carrying them were advised to fire on sharp tracks. (They should have been ordered to return.)

Note from the Author

Through the sixth patrol, this history is fully documented and eyewitnessed. The seventh patrol was written without an American eyewitness. So, from Sterling's view of *Wahoo*'s shears disappearing below the horizon until the next eyewitness, the writing concerning *Wahoo* will be italicized. Following is a detailed explanation that shows how this writing was possible.

For the seventh patrol, the secret operation orders for *Wahoo* and her companion submarine, *Sawfish*, were used, including the latter's very complete patrol report. *Wahoo*'s patrol routes were derived through plotting from the meticulous "Report of the Japanese Imperial Navy," which shows the date, name, ship type, tonnage, and position of each ship *Wahoo* sank. For her near disaster, I have my Mark-18 circular run from forward, which became deadly aft, with identical results verified by postwar circular running Mark-18 test firings; the fact that no other casualty fits all the criteria; and my submarine knowledge acquired on eleven war patrols, and twenty years with the boats.

In the continuing narrative, I have relied on my thorough knowledge of Morton, gained as his co-approach officer during three patrols, to judge the tactics he would have used in approach, attack, evasion, and other crucial situations. And for *Wahoo*'s final encounter, I have the detailed Japanese report of the prolonged action. So to every extent possible, this is authentic history, with only some variations in tactics, which would have brought about the same known results.

3

Wahoo *continued west, retracing the dogleg that had cleared Kure Reef on the return voyage. Conveniently, the fine No. 4 pencil track leading to the great circle course still remained on the chart, but at this intersection, the captain ordered a deviation from the route repeated in the operation order. Too many submarines had followed this shortest track, which from the start had been a natural for an enemy submarine patrol. Quick calculations by Verne showed that a track 50 miles to the north would add less than 40 miles to the voyage. Morton replied with his customary, "Make it so."*

Bill Burgan had taken over plot, Don Brown was manning the angle solver, and Hiram Greene was Wahoo's *new battle stations diving officer. Morning emergency drills soon satisfied Verne and the captain, but an afternoon torpedo fire control problem became routine. It was not boring, however, for* Wahoo *had a wealth of recorded time versus bearing exercises. Even the actual periscope procedure was involved as Verne and Kemp provided the recorded bearings on time, while giving an occasional approximate range.*

Increasing seas called for another engine, while the accompanying rain and overcast permitted another surface passage through Etorofu Strait and on to the diving point for La Perouse. The night transit was unchallenged. Had the Otoris *been assigned to escorting, now that* Plunger *had sunk three, for a total of six ships, along the direct trade routes?* Wahoo *would find out as she headed for Rebun Jima and a submerged daylight patrol towards the Tsugaru Strait. No tops came over the spotty horizon, nor SJ pips on high searches, but* Wahoo's *new diving officers were learning how to handle her at various depths. After 2 days of this, Verne set course 195 for the point 10 miles west of O Shima as the captain had ordered. Two blasts took her down in morning twilight, heading east, searching.*

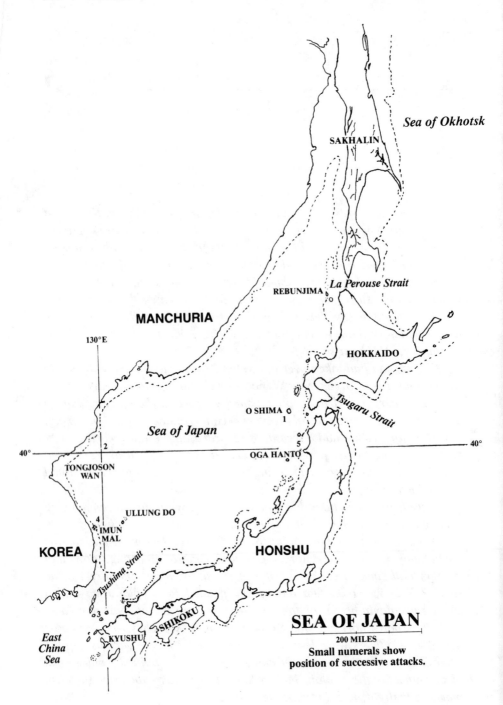

Sea of Okhotsk

SAKHALIN

La Perouse Strait

REBUNJIMA

MANCHURIA

130°E

HOKKAIDO

O SHIMA
1

Tsugaru Strait

Sea of Japan

2

5

OGA HANTO

40°   40°

TONGJOSON
WAN

ULLUNG DO

4

IMUN
MAL

KOREA

HONSHU

Tsushima Strait

3

SHIKOKU

*East
China
Sea*

KYUSHU

SEA OF JAPAN

200 MILES

**Small numerals show
position of successive attacks.**

The sea through the periscope seemed unusually calm this September 25, and served as a reminder that tried and proven periscope procedure would always have its place. The captain joined in the periscope search towards the tiny islands of O Shima and Ko Shima, lying about 15 and 5 miles, respectively, off the 10-fathom line at the entrance to Tsugaru Strait. Ships had proceeded on their way in this vicinity during the sixth patrol, so more should pass between the islands at any time.

Bill Burgan and George Misch had inherited George Grider's lucky forenoon and evening watches. Customarily, these would continue throughout a patrol. That way, the captain, by glancing at his cabin clock, would know which two men were on watch. The team, for they exchanged the dive for OOD a couple of times each watch, had established a reputation similar to that of Grider's. In part, this was due to their particular watch, but early on George Misch had learned to concentrate on the scope (until it seems as if your eyeballs are out on the horizon) and Bill had followed suit. So, with nothing sighted before the eight-to-twelve, it was almost presumed that Bill and George would luck out again.

Careful sweeps followed by 17-foot searches up the coast, beyond O Shima, and towards the strait disclosed only sampans and an occasional trawler. After a trick at diving, Don Brown took the conn and promptly had mast tops nearly in line. Having just come over the horizon, the ship below them had to be heading towards nearby O Shima, and the Bells of St. Mary's rang out in earnest for the first time on Wahoo's *seventh patrol.*

One after another, by rooms, battle stations were reported manned. Terrel, now a quartermaster, third class and conning tower talker, kept track on his fingers and signaled stations manned before Chief Carr's report. The upper works were now in sight, and Verne called the configuration following his initial angle. He had a mast-funnel-mast freighter, and with the island limiting her course, an almost-assured firing position inside of a thousand yards. Buckley called a propeller beat of seventy-two turns, the count that had shown a speed of $7\frac{1}{2}$ knots before. Richie had her speed at 8 knots; it was close enough. MacAlman and his new assistant, White, had arrived at a Taiko Maru *class cargoman, with a listing of 2,958 gross tons. He held the opened manual above the lower hatch so Verne could take a glance. He nodded, but the masthead height of 95 feet that they had given orally was of immediate importance.*

Now with accurate periscope stadimeter ranges, Bill Burgan's plot and Richie's TDC had the same solution.

Captain Morton had ordered two tubes made ready forward and aft with torpedoes set to run at 6-foot depth, and when Verne called 80 starboard, Morton gave his assuring, "Any time, Verne."

Verne marked a constant bearing on her stack. "Set," came from Richie. The mainmast touched the wire, bringing an instant, "Fire!" Morton hit the plunger and the first torpedo left with a whine to hit under the freighter's mainmast. Marked on her bow, the second fish went to her foremast. Burgan was counting, and at approximately half the speed of a Mark-14, the run seemed endless. But accuracy, not speed, is the name of the torpedo game, and two violent detonations exactly as aimed obliterated the freighter. The time was 1715, still Saturday, the twenty-fifth.

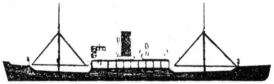

IKUTA MARU.   Gross tonnage: 2,968–2,984.
NAGATA MARU   Length: (w. l.) 307'.
TAIKO MARU.   Beam: 45'.
Draft: (loaded) 21½' (light) 7½'.

Speeds:
   Normal cruising—10 knots.
   Maximum—12½ knots.

4

Wahoo *continued on submerged, slowly circling the position of the sinking. As expected after such a violent explosion, only flotsam marked the area. Inhabitants of O Shima must have heard or seen the explosion, so it would be only a matter of time before some antisubmarine ship or plane would arrive, and the captain ordered the course for Tonjoson Wan. It lay across the Sea of Japan; Verne read the course, and steersman Wach steadied on 255. This was Morton's hit-and-run tactic, which left the enemy far behind, but there could be more.*

The crossing required 5 days, for north-south shipping sent the crew to battle stations day and night. Unfortunately for Wahoo, *the ships were Russian, and fortunately for them, their identification flags and lights were in order. Unknowingly, the Russians provided a target service heretofore omitted—that of a ship on a straight course. This at first had nearly stumped the new fire control party, who were sure they had missed a zig.*

When Wahoo *approached Tonjoson Wan, winds from the southeast brought rain and accompanying reduced visibility. So it was Carter and Lindeman under instruction on the SJ who made the first enemy contact. With dusk coming on, it was too late for a periscope attack, but not for a submerged observation from her quarter. With their ONI-208J opened on the chart desk, MacAlman and White made their own observations, arriving at* Masaki Maru *class cargoman listed at 1,238 tons.*

An end-around would not be required; opening the range until dark and then moving up to a bow position would assure a TBT surface attack.

A routine surfacing and maneuvers to a bow position were simple, almost too simple. The bells called hands to stations; Morton ordered three forward tubes readied, all torpedoes set to run at 6 feet, and conned Wahoo *to the normal course (perpendicular to the enemy's track). Verne, manning the forward TBT, had the cargoman's indistinct shape in sight and commenced calling bearings. The freighter's lookouts, peering into the blowing rain, had no chance of spotting a submarine's small silhouette blending into the dark sea. The range counter on the TDC read 800 yards; the angle on the target dial read 75. Captain Morton advised, "Any time, Verne," and a constant bearing directed a single torpedo to the freighter's midships.*

As prearranged, if this torpedo failed, a spread of two would follow. Bill had figured the divider for the Mark-18, 15 yards per second, and his count of 52 was smothered by the crack, whack, and rumble of the detonation. Verne reported the freighter broken in two and sunk; the torpedo hit 1 second early, added Bill. It was just past 1700 on October 2; the first sitting was starting chow, and a continuous movie would commence forward. This was like "days of yore"—a rubber of cribbage followed the evening meal, and then the captain went aft to seek out and thank every crewman.

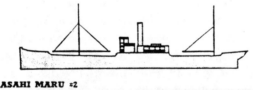

ASAHI MARU #2
BANEI MARU #7, HATTENZAN MARU, HIRANO MARU, MAOKA MARU, MASAKI MARU, MASAKI MARU #2, NOTORO MARU, ONO MARU #14, SAKISIMA MARU, SINSEI MARU #3, SINTO MARU, SINYO MARU #1, SYOHO MARU, TAKI MARU, TYOSAN MARU, YUMIHARI MARU #2
Similar: ITOSAKI MARU, NISSIN MARU, NISSYO MARU #8

Tonnages:			Constructed:	
Gross: 1,159–	D. W.: 2,118		1919	Japan
1,323				
Length:			Propulsion:	
W. L. (B. P.):	O. A.:		Machinery:	Reciprocating
220'			Screws: 1	N. H. P.: 117
Beam: 35'			R. P. M.:	@ Knots:
Drafts:			Fuel: Coal	Capacity: 240
Loaded: 16' 1"	Light: 4' 10"			tons
Speed:			Radius: 2,900 miles at 8 knots.	
Normal cruis-	Max.: 9			
ing: 8				
Potential naval value: AK.				
Remarks:				

Sawfish *had cleared the strait at 0230 on September 23, and turned right to search along the Sakhalin coast and to investigate the coaling station at Esutoru. En route early the next day she had attacked a small* freighter. The first Mark-18 torpedo hit *Sawfish*'s bow and didn't run; the second ran astern of the enemy. The coaling station was inactive, and *Sawfish* next patrolled south of Rebun Suido, the passage between the island and Hokkaido.

Though hugging the coast and covering the passes, *Sawfish*'s next opportunity did not come until September 28, with distant smoke and then two freighters passing Motsuta Misaki light. Able to close only one, Sands sent a spread of three Mark-18s. Again, the first hit *Sawfish*'s bow, and sound tracked the others beyond the target.

Three days later, while operating on the surface, *Sawfish* sighted smoke, raced ahead, and dived to attack a medium-sized passenger freighter. One of the first two Mark-18s hit *Sawfish*'s bow and apparently sank; the other was followed by sound astern of the target. A third torpedo was fired and also ran astern.

With the enemy ship not altering course and apparently unalerted, *Sawfish* surfaced for a 6-hour end-around, and dived for a second attack, this time with Mark-14 steam torpedoes. Maneuvering to a position 750 yards on her beam, Sands fired a spread of three torpedoes from the stern tubes. The first fish broached halfway to the target and ran erratically to the right, alerting the enemy, who avoided the others and opened up with his deck gun at the periscope. In so doing the ship made a target of herself, and *Sawfish* sent a fourth torpedo, which the enemy avoided.

Explosions had continued, and 100-foot depth seemed advisable. Torpedo reloads were completed, and at 1900, *Sawfish* surfaced to return to the position she previously had been patrolling.

5

On Wahoo's *fourth patrol, Morton had told us of his prewar excursion through Japan's Inland Sea. After stopping at Shimonoseki, they had sailed across the southern part of the Sea of Japan to Pusan, Korea. This latter passage had touched the northern end of the Tsushima Strait, the scene of the great Japanese victory over the Russian fleet. He had spoken of the heavy traffic along that last shipping lane, which had included everything from freighters to railroad train ferries.*

With torpedoes that would run true and detonate, and a lengthening dark of the moon to enable night surface attacks and evasion, the best time to attack there would come in about 4 days. Morton called for the conning tower chart, which Quartermaster Kemp spread out on the wardroom table, with dividers and parallel rules for plotting. The captain invited Kemp to sit down; he did so after retrieving the pertinent volume of Sailing Directions. *Neither the captain and navigator, nor the officers present and Kemp, could find any obstacles that could prevent* Wahoo *from penetrating to the position Captain Morton had circled on the chart. Rather, looking ahead, the constant northerly current of 2 knots would assist in evasion and withdrawal, for the position was at the "T" formed by the Tsushima Strait crossed by the Shimonoseki-Pusan shipping lane. Though none present had voiced it, there was one required element—a skipper with guts, and this* Wahoo *had in Morton's cautious, deliberate courage.*

Perchance, the course south lay atop the 130 east longitude line, but that would serve only as a base course for the greater part of the 360 miles. From it, Wahoo *would conduct her own reconnaissance. Any large ship would be attacked, but "spit-kits" would be avoided, and all daylight patrolling would be submerged to insure surprise.*

316

Back on the line and with a full battery charge, Wahoo *moved in on October 3. Verne and Kemp had good stars, and allowing for the current,* Wahoo *reached the selected position by 2200. Tracking had been manned in anticipation, and even those not going on the midwatch were up and about. They did not have long to wait, for the SJ was hot and soon had ships. One after another, their silhouettes showed that they were no larger than those already sunk, and at 0230 Morton ordered a retreat with the current to try again on the following night.*

A day submerged afforded those who had stayed up most of the night a welcome opportunity for shut-eye. By midafternoon, however, all hands seemed to be up and about and ready for another night. The lookouts' accounts of darkened ships turning on their running lights to avoid collision, others running with lights burning, and a lesser number continuing darkened had stirred the imagination. The number had probably become exaggerated, since the stories came from lookouts and their reliefs for the watches. After an early evening meal, with sacks ready to go up and over, Wahoo *surfaced into another black night. Two engines went on propulsion, the rest on charge, and in 2 hours she would be back on station.*

To clear the shipping lane for a better visual aspect after radar contact, and to still retain the three-way coverage, Captain Morton conned his submarine to a position between Tsushima Island and the coast of Kyushu and northeast of Ike Shima, and mentally noted, if hard pressed, this provided the shorter evasion route out into the East China Sea.

Again only small ships passed, and the captain had to conclude that the major steamers were now making southern Pacific runs. Still, the Tsushima Strait remained a major passage, so the patrol there would continue around the clock. At Verne's suggestion, Richie had been organizing section tracking parties. Primarily, this involved TDC instruction; the rest they knew anyway, so the regular watch would be responsible until battle stations. Duty Chief McGill was ordered to run the enlisted watch accordingly.

The low silhouettes of two patrols were immediately reported to the captain and exec, as are all ships. This was a change that could have significance. Verne came to the bridge to see them turn north; he then conned Wahoo *over to the approximate path they had followed, before going below to tell the captain. The time was 0200, halfway through the midwatch, and except for two more small merchantmen, the night passed quietly, while the boat maintained her position against the current.*

After stars on the first horizon, two blasts took her down. An air of excitement accompanied breakfast, for though Captain Morton had taken his submarine into taut places, heretofore he had promptly brought her out. Control's report of two patrols did not help, but the Bells of St. Mary's brought a cheer, as if they were the whistle for a kickoff.

The patrols had returned and were stationed about a thousand yards on either bow of a large ship presenting a sharp angle. There was no question about gaining an attack position, only that of sneaking past the near echo-ranging escort. That had not fazed the captain, who was already conning Wahoo towards the escort's stern, and maneuvering to present a small angle to the echo ranging.

Verne's angles, and stadimeter ranges from the estimated 130-foot height, flowed to Richie. And then came the first identification—a large transport. There was no need to identify her as enemy; the fact that she was zigging and escorted qualified her for torpedoes. Her speed of 15 knots, corresponding to Buckley's turn count, was close to plot and TDC's. Never before had Morton enjoyed a finer solution on a more valuable ship.

Four torpedo tubes had been readied forward and aft. The after room lost again as the captain ordered the outer doors opened forward and the torpedo depth setting increased to 10 feet. Verne's angles were receiving Richie's, "Checks," and Morton made a final comparison between plot and TDC, the latter's dial showing an angle of 80 port.

"Any time, Verne," he announced in a reassuring voice, and then stepped over to the firing panel. There would be a small change in the points of aim to secure maximum torpedo divergence: Verne's constant bearings and Morton's plunger sent torpedoes to hit the transport aft, then under the after end of her long superstructure, followed by the third under her bridge, and the fourth to hit forward.

The momentary shudder, the zing, and the poppet pressure were all normal as the whine of four Mark-18s through the hull quickly faded, but not from Buckley and Carter on sound, who simultaneously called, "All straight and normal." The time for the 950-yard torpedo run should be 63 seconds, and Bill picked up the count at 30 to go. On Morton's nod, Verne made a cautious sweep to report the enemy proceeding on course. With 5 seconds to go he was raising the scope again when the crack and whack of the first warhead detonation hit Wahoo. *The second, he described with a single word, and then passed the scope to the captain for the final two. The devastation was awesome. The captain reported the ship capsizing and then sunk. Bill's recorded time from the first detonation was just under 1 minute.*

Sporadic depth charges rained, but a cautious look by Verne had shown the escorts milling around beyond the sinking. It was time to make tracks during the confusion, and Wahoo *headed northeast to clear the small island of Okino Shima and then north into the Sea of Japan.*

In the wardroom, Verne and the captain were relaxing over a cribbage game, now that the tops of the escorts had dropped below the periscope's horizon. After a game, they turned to the copy of ONI-208J, which MacAlman had brought to the wardroom. The long superstructure marked the ship as a transport, but the book showed none with her type of low stack and cruiser stern. She was probably too new to have been included in the manual, so the Doc proceeded to the conning tower to record one transport of about 9,000 tons. Heading south, she had to have been carrying troops. It was a sobering thought, but eased by the knowledge that a like number of our soldiers might thus have been saved. This time starting forward, Morton commenced his turn through the boat to seek out, thank, and congratulate each member of his crew.

Note from the Author

Tokyo's Domei news reported that on 5 October, a steamer was sunk by an American submarine off the west coast of Honshu, near the Tsushima Strait. The ship sank after several seconds, with 544 people losing their lives. (It had to have been *Wahoo*'s.)

Time magazine reported this on 18 October, and compared the achievement to German Gunther Prien's entry into Scapa Flow. (Had *Time* known that Morton had actually penetrated to the East China Sea, the feat would have been incomparable.)

---

6 _____

The muffled sounds from distant depth charges had faded, for Wahoo's *turns for 6 knots and 2 more from the current had cleared the area. By noon, they had disappeared altogether. Tonjoson Wan was beckoning, and three blasts with engine bells initiated a high-speed surface run on course 355. If not driven down by a plane,* Wahoo, *at four-engine speed, should reach the last broad promontory before the great bay by dark, and she would be back in business.*

It was probably unnecessary to warn the lookouts, for all had seen the small chart now on display atop the gyro, but a good look at their submarine's somewhat precarious position would do no harm. The total run to Imun Mal, which Kemp had marked on the chart, stepped off at 120 miles, and by the first dogwatch, 1600, the latest position showed Wahoo *more than halfway there.*

The exhilaration from the last attack, in fact the whole patrol, had not subsided. Three ships down with the first seven torpedoes must have been some sort of a record, and this was not the halfway point for the time in the Sea of Japan. A few of the older hands, with many patrols, were not so vocal—they had gone to sea because they loved ships, but each one was a necessary step in bringing this war to a close, and for that they could cheer with their younger shipmates. There was not much time to consider these things, for on the very next midwatch Fire Control-man Logue raised a pip on the SJ where no island could be.

Hiram Greene and Don Brown assisted by Simonetti assumed section tracking, while Verne, spelling the captain, took the conn until the contact was investigated. The ship was heading south towards Imun Mal, which Wahoo *had passed at dusk. The broad point lay shoreward, but had a shoal area extending some miles to sea, and so would a passing ship.*

Through 7 × 50s, Verne was able to make out the ship as a cargoman of about the same size as the Masaki Maru, *the freighter* Wahoo *had sunk to the north on October 1. Though there would be no advantage of wind and rain, Verne believed that a similar attack could be made, or there was plenty of time to be waiting for her off the point at dawn.*

Hiram came up to take the conn, and Verne went below to advise his skipper of the two possibilities. Morton chose a precise submerged attack, but came topside before making the final judgment. It was, after all, a captain's decision. He conned his ship 5 miles to seaward prior to heading her south and turning the conn back to Hiram.

For insurance and to provide time for a cautious approach to Imun Mal, Verne added a third engine and informed the captain. Abreast the point before the morning twilight, Wahoo *stopped to confirm her DR with Buckley's soundings as she moved cautiously westward towards the abrupt, 100-fathom curve. A sudden, though expected, 26 fathoms fixed her position and Verne conned* Wahoo *a mile to the east for diving at dawn.*

Morning twilight's first horizon gave the navigator and Kemp a fine opportunity for star sights, which further fixed their location. Arriving on the bridge, Morton conned his boat closer to the 100-fathom curve, and pulled the plug when the enemy's tops, in line, came over the horizon. Confidently, the crew had manned their battle stations on diving, so the Bells of St. Mary's again were only a confirming formality.

The freighter's speed had been determined by the miles steamed since first sighted, allowing for the current, and was again confirmed when her hull came over the horizon—both 8 knots. Her course had been restricted by the shoals close to the 100-fathom curve, and measured 150 on the conning tower chart. Captain Morton was conning Wahoo *to reach a position 800 yards from her restricted track when she would pass astern.*

Only one maneuver could have saved the freighter—an abrupt, dawn change of course to seaward—but the captain had already countered that by having three tubes made ready forward as well as aft. Verne's angles and bearings kept pace with the TDC. There was no need for further consideration of the current; both submarine and freighter were being affected similarly, and so it would be with a torpedo and the target. The outer doors were opened aft; Morton gave his, "Any time, Verne," and instantly the exec had marked a constant bearing. The first torpedo was on its way to hit below the freighter's mainmast, and was followed by another to detonate under the foremast.

All signs were normal, and the captain called Chief Carr to the conning tower to man the search scope at 15 seconds to go, advising him and Verne to remember details of the ship. The duration of the 1,300-yard torpedo run would be 87 seconds, and even Bill seemed to be counting slowly. Kemp raised the scopes, and instantly came the first crack, whack, and shaking explosion. Seven seconds later came a repeat. They were early, but only because of a range error which did not affect the lead angle or the accuracy. Chief Carr and Verne had identical reports: by the time the steam and smoke had blown clear, the freighter had completely disappeared.

Wahoo continued eastward, and while their memories were fresh from the fleeting glimpses, Carr and the exec pored over ONI-208J. The only ship with the same configuration was about twice the target's size, so they recorded her as Kanko Maru No. 2 of 1,288 gross tons.

Surfacing 30 minutes after the attack, Wahoo *steadied on course 080 which would take her close to Ullung Do. This volcanic island, no more than 10 miles in diameter, had a 3,221-foot peak that might well serve as a beacon for larger north-south ships. Since it lay not far off the route, Morton wanted to give it at least a passing glance. The two engines on propulsion would have* Wahoo *there by noon. At the moment, breakfast was being served, and in the wardroom it would be difficult to describe a happier mess. If the sounds of comradeship drifting into the control room from the crew's mess were a true indication, then the same mood was present there.*

Ullung Do's peak came in sight at midmorning and continued to rise with every mile, the sight encouraging the lookouts and the search scope to find a mast ahead. As a check on the SJ and a practical demonstration, Verne and Kemp recorded the bearing of the peak when it was broad on the bow and the simultaneous reading of the mileage counter of the DRI. A similar recording when the peak was abeam showed the distance run matching the radar range, for they were two legs of an isosceles triangle. It would, of course, fix Wahoo's *position without the radar, and might stir a seaman's interest in striking for quartermaster or signalman; already, Kemp was showing that it worked on beam and quarter too.*

On passing the island, Verne changed course to 060 as had been laid down on the chart, the duty chief's messenger informing the captain. At the end of the fine pencil line lay Oga Hanto, a short, abrupt peninsula about 40 miles south of Tsugaru Strait and 350 miles dead ahead. Coming to the conning tower and noting the distance, Morton ordered a third engine on propulsion so Wahoo *could approach Oga Hanto during the second night, October 7.*

Sawfish had made no further contacts in the area she had been patrolling, so just after midnight on October 3, she set course for Oga Hanto, about 2 days' run to the south, making the transit in rain and through heavy seas. Smoke from three ships before breakfast on October 5 proved too distant to close, but during the first dogwatch, smoke developed into two other ships, which offered promise for an end-around. From her position 23 miles southwest of Oga Hanto, Captain Sands conned his submarine to a favorable approach position. Diving at 2215 to 40-foot keel depth, he conducted the approach by SJ radar and sound. With the TDC checking with both inputs, he ordered the normal 64 feet and fired a spread of three steam torpedoes by TDC from a range of 1,300 yards. Sound reported the dull thud from two of them on time, but again there were no detonations.

At 1600 on October 6, from a point 6 miles west of Oga Hanto, *Sawfish* made her next contact on telltale smoke. It developed into a small, loaded freighter. Firing a spread of three Mark-18s at 8-second intervals, at least two missed astern as followed by sound. Thirty seconds after the first firing, a resounding thud was heard throughout the boat. (The second torpedo might very well have gone into a circular run and hit *Sawfish* seconds before arming.)

Sawfish's Mark-14 steam torpedo exploder performance had been comparable to *Wahoo*'s, and with this last Mark-18 performance, confirming that they were all running slower than designed, Captain Sands had decided to return to Base with the remaining Mark-18s. There, the experts might have the answer, whether it involved heaters, raising the specific gravity of the batteries, or modifying the TDC. In the Sea of Japan, 3,450 miles away was no place for experimenting, and *Sawfish* headed for La Perouse Strait.

In his endorsement to *Sawfish*'s patrol report, the division commander wrote: "The performance of the Mark-18 electric torpedo is disappointing. Obviously, much work and test firings will have to be done before this torpedo is suitable for issue to our submarines."

Sawfish's Mark-14 steam torpedoes, like *Wahoo*'s on her sixth patrol, were duds.

A falling barometer gave a few hours' warning of increasing seas and rain. They combined to make a daytime approach to the promontory more promising, and the third engine was taken off propulsion. At midaf-

ternoon, October 8, Wahoo *closed the coast submerged. Through the periscope, the headland of Oga Hanto reached high above the waves and surf; it would have been unnerving to a surface ship. On the chart, the 20-fathom line was shown within 10 miles of the promontory's hook-like tip. On either side of the short peninsula were soundings of 10 fathoms. Unaffected by the surface wind,* Wahoo *was able to reconnoiter the point and make tentative plans for attacking ships passing the point in either direction.*

Satisfied, Morton conned his submarine to the west when visibility through the scopes faded, and she surfaced into the rain and diminishing seas. The duty chiefs rotated the watch regularly, from wheel to radar to sound and then lookout. It rested the eyes between billets and brought the lookout in his wet rain clothes to the warmth below. Lucky indeed were hands with the laundry detail, which had become a popular watch.

Fishermen had apparently sought cover, and perhaps larger ships were waiting in the shelter of the Tsugaru Strait, mindful of the extra fuel the wind and remaining seas would consume. For these reasons, or just by chance, no ships rounded Oga Hanto on the evening watch, for the SJ would have spotted them. Hiram and Don assumed the mid-watch, taking turns topside, and when in the conning tower keeping Wahoo *in position with minor changes of course and propeller turns.*

The musical chairs of rotating the watch had taken the usual 10 minutes or so, when Yeoman White, as if it were routine, reported an SJ pip to the north. The clock read 0214 on this October 9 when the Bells of St. Mary's bonged throughout the submarine.

Don cranked the initial range of 13,000 yards and the bearing into the TDC, setting the target dial for a zero angle before turning on the machine. Richie's school was paying off, for a new range and bearing, after battle stations had been manned, gave an initial solution. Bill had plotted both setups on the navigational chart and picked off a similar course and speed—a course of almost due south and the initial 8 knots that had been intentionally left set in the TDC. Bill's plot was more meaningful to the captain, however, for he could see that the enemy would pass well off Oga Hanto.

Morton kept Wahoo *on the enemy's projected track, and ordered three tubes made ready forward and aft. It was not until the range had closed to 5,000 yards that Verne could make her out in the blowing*

*rain, and he had the wind to his back. At 4,000 yards the captain
followed his plan by keeping the stern to the enemy, firing to seaward
as required by the op-order, already being on an evasion course, while
keeping her lookouts peering into the southwest wind and spume.*

*Verne called bearings only, for even as the angle opened, TDC's
target dial would be better. He could see enough, however, to identify
the enemy as another freighter, similar to the* Kanko Maru, *but about
twice her size. His wire was drawing close to astern when the captain
gave his, "Any time, Verne."*

*Verne's rapid constant bearings sent stern torpedoes to the mainmast,
midships, and left to the foremast. The shudder, zing, poppet pressure,
and whine for each torpedo seemed normal.*

*"All back emergency! Wild torpedo to starboard!" blared from the
conning tower speaker. Instantly, Simonetti twisted the maneuvering
telegraphs and Morton bounded up the hatch, swinging the collision
alarm on the way. The sirens would be wailing in each compartment.
All doors dogged shut, and the ventilation clapper valves would seal
each room, giving it the strength of the pressure hull. Within seconds,
talkers reported, "Secured for collision." Morton could see the circling,
porpoising torpedo abeam and curving towards* Wahoo. *Only the 5 million watts pulling the boat astern could save her. A final right rudder
to throw the bow clear of the onrushing torpedo offered the only chance,
and the captain called, "Blow safety! Blow negative! Brace yourselves!"*

A violent, deep detonation shook Wahoo, *raising her as would the
sea of a typhoon, and then plunged her foredeck deep into the seas.*

*Two sharp detonations marked the end of the freighter after a 1-
minute torpedo run, but it brought little cheer. By their sound-powered
phones, the talkers checked in from aft forward. Remarkably, few serious
injuries had been sustained, probably due to Morton's last instruction.*

*As expected, from the forward torpedo room there could be no reply,
but other doors and clapper valves were opened and the crew went
about resetting circuit breakers and getting their ship in order.*

*The captain had blown bow buoyancy, raising the foredeck a little,
and slowed to regain rudder control. Simonetti could now keep the
boat's stern on due west as she sought the relative sanctuary beyond
the coastal shipping and patrols. Knowing that* Wahoo *could not dive
and surface again in her present condition, Morton sought a secure
route for a dash through La Perouse Strait. This would depend on success*

in raising the bow. The alternatives of scuttling, not in Wahoo's *makeup, or seeking asylum with internment at Vladivostok would not be considered while there existed any chance of returning the Mark-18s to prevent another such accident. Verne, completing a turn aft, fully agreed, and had figures to show that if the bow could be raised,* Wahoo *could dive, and surface stern first if on soundings of less than 20 fathoms.*

John Campbell and Chief McGill, the best in the boat, set about the problem of expelling the seas from the forward torpedo room, which could have become a great ballast tank. There would be insufficient air from the banks, but couldn't the detonation have ruptured one of the torpedo room's inside ballast tanks, whose outer wall, like a letter b *or* d, *is a part of the pressure hull? The test would be easy—just start the turbos. The captain was more than ready, for though it may have been the better view in daylight, more of the forward deck seemed undersea, as when flooding the forward group to launch a rubber boat from on deck.*

The screeching hyenas came up to speed, and McGill, by chance at his battle station, opened the gate stop valve. One after another, bubbles reached the surface above and forward of the flood openings, except to starboard forward. That ballast tank had indeed been ruptured into the torpedo room; the great volume of low-pressure air must be rising in the torpedo room and forcing the sea out of the rupture.

A half-hour blow brought the bullnose above the sea, and there it would remain until the auxiliarymen could install a sheet-metal dutchman to stop the air to the after ballast tanks so as to gain full 12-pounds pressure forward. The bow was high enough, however, for Morton to order, "All ahead two-thirds, reverse course," to continue seaward. The rain cooperated, providing security; the turbos raised her bow steadily, and then two more engines went on the line. So Wahoo *could reach La Perouse Strait within 2 days, for a foul-weather passage, or at night if clear.*

To the north, 2 days before, on October 7, *Sawfish* had dived on sighting a floatplane and received one bomb, not close. In succession, the plane was relieved by two light bombers, who kept *Sawfish* down till dark. Entering La Perouse Strait at 0030 on October 9, she outran the first patrol and avoided two others, the silhouette of the larger resembling a destroyer.

Verne ordered the tank compass moved from control to the conning tower and then plotted the route to pass well south of O Shima, site of the first sinking, and from there due north, on past Rebun Jima until Wahoo *could head for La Perouse Strait from the west. Within the strait, the track had been laid down well north of Cape Soya, close to the 20-fathom line. Early sighting by the continuous watch manning both periscopes had permitted maneuvers to avoid the few masts sighted. At night the lookouts' 7 × 50s did the same. But on nearing the strait, thin masts disclosed patrols astern, forcing Morton to accept the more dangerous daytime passage. So early in the morning watch of October 11, 10 days ahead of her schedule,* Wahoo *was passing the 20-mile-wide Cape Soya Strait. Morning twilight had shown her cruising under an overcast, too low and heavy for planes, but permitting the navigator to check the position with sextant angles between landmarks shown on the chart, and use of the three-arm protractor.*

By the forenoon watch, the overcast had become lighter, and lookouts then searched their sectors continuously from the horizon to sky. The violent, shaking clap from an artillery shell close overhead, and the whack, then swish-swish-swish from its splash and ricochet shocked the lookouts, but not the OOD, who cleared the bridge, nor Morton, engaged in conning his submarine away from the giant smoke ring rolling out to seaward from the nearest promontory, Soya Misaki. Before another salvo, Wahoo *would be presenting a minimum target to the enemy. The advantage was brief, for the next salvo came even closer. Staying on the surface was wasting critical time, for the enemy would already have requested antisubmarine forces, and* Wahoo *should be moving as far away as possible from the attack area. Confidently, Morton ordered, "Take her down."* Wahoo *dived with an up angle, leveling off on the bottom, and proceeded eastward to clear the area of the artillery attack and La Perouse Strait.*

The coast artillery battery had been installed during September of 1941, mounting type 96, 4m by 15cm guns, the equivalent of our 6-inch, 26-caliber guns. The battery commander had asked for a plane from the Ominato Air Fleet, flying out of Wakkani, northern Hokkaido. For clarity, the report is arranged chronologically, showing the time of drops or arrival.

0920   Floatplane #19, having arrived in about an hour, found an oil slick some 5 meters wide and 10 meters long (apparently from

Wahoo's No. 1 fuel tank abreast the wardroom and next to the Mark-18 detonation). Circling, the pilot could identify a black

0945   conning tower and, after summoning more aircraft, dropped one bomb on what he described as a black hull with a white wake, and a second bomb, which brought up bubbles and oil.

Aircraft #2 arrived and dropped four small-type bombs, which brought up oil.

1025   Floatplane #19 investigated the spot and dropped another bomb, but saw no oil.

Just-arrived Aircraft #20 investigated the same location, drop-

1034   ping another bomb without raising any oil.

1135   Floatplane #19 guided Submarine Chaser #15 to the area of the attack. This ship, in the Fifth Fleet, closed the area on receipt

1203   of an aircraft report, and dropped nine depth charges. Four min-

1207   utes later, 200 meters to the northwest, she dropped seven more charges. In the great column of sea and spume above the detonations, a large piece of bright metal was seen and identified as part of a propeller blade.

1218   Submarine Chaser #15 dropped one more depth charge.

1221   Submarine Chaser #43 dropped six depth charges.

1321   Aircraft #6 arrived and dropped two bombs.

1330   Auxiliary Minesweeper #18 arrived.

1350   Searching aircraft reported that neither the submarine nor her wake was visible.

If *Wahoo* had had both screws after these recorded attacks, she might have surfaced after dark. An axiom of antisubmarine warfare, however, is to stay with the enemy, for one never knows the extent of troubles that may exist below. The Japanese had gone further, enlisting assistance from all available forces in an overwhelming attack. A total of sixty-three depth charges or large bombs and forty smaller bombs had been dropped. The expanding oil slick, which continued moving eastward, had steadied by nightfall. It was then about 60 meters wide and 3 nautical miles long, with air bubbles breaking its surface. An early sample showed the slick to be of high-grade diesel fuel.

Sadly, there could be no doubt. Our beloved *Wahoo* had indeed gone on down to Davy Jones's locker, where the angels must have wept as they received her brave crew and their most courageous captain, who had done so much for their country and had come so close to success in *Wahoo*'s greatest mission, to save our submarines from Mark-18 disasters. Had *Wahoo* not been sighted, Morton would undoubtedly have succeeded in his valiant mission to bring her home, so other boats would be spared a like fate.

EPILOGUE

As noted before, *Time* magazine of October 18, 1943, reported a Tokyo broadcast that a steamer had been torpedoed in the Tsushima Strait, sinking in seconds with the loss of 544 nationals. It was *Wahoo*'s transport, *Konron Maru,* of 9,000 tons, loaded with troops and heading for the battle zones. In order, the others were: *Taiko, Masaki,* and *Kanko Maru,* 1,288 tons; and *Kanko Maru,* 2,962 tons, as shown in ONI-208J below.

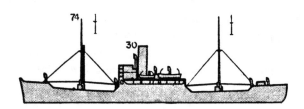

**IMIZU MARU, KANKO MARU, KEIKO MARU, RAKUTO MARU,
RYUKO MARU, ZUIKO MARU**

Tonnages:
  Gross: 2,578-2,962 D. W.:
                       3,787-4,094

Length:
  W. L. (B. P.): O. A.:
    298-305'
Beam: 45'
Drafts:
  Loaded: 20½' Light: 7½'
Speed:
  Normal cruising: Max.: 14
    11½

Constructed:
  1935-38   Japan

Propulsion:
  Machinery: Reciprocating
  Screws: 1   H. P.:
  R. P. M.:   @ Knots:
  Fuel: Coal   Capacity: 318 tons
  Radius: 5,500 miles at 11½ knots

Potential naval value: AM, AP, AH, patrol vessel.
Remarks: RYUKO MARU operating as AH-7.

Cutouts from archives' duplicates formed the following proposed citation, apparently little if at all known within the Submarine Force.

MORTON, Dudley W.   Comdr. USN

U.S.S. WAHOO   Pacific

Recommended for MEDAL OF HONOR by Sub.Bd. of Awds Ltr FB-5-102/P15 Serial 0085 SECRET ltr dated 2 Dec. 1943. Rec'd. Bd. D&M 3-27-44

Awarded: NAVY CROSS—5 April 1944 Bd.Awds.Mtg.

"For extraordinary heroism above and beyond the call of duty and conspicuous intrepidity as commanding officer of a submarine in action against enemy vessels in patrolled enemy waters. With great courage, aggressiveness and submarine warfare efficiency, he entered dangerous, confined and shallow waters where he sank at least one important enemy vessel. This feat alone ranks with the most daring operations of any submarine exploit of World Navies to date. Other successes in this area are unknown since his submarine failed to return from this patrol and it is presumed that he gave his life and his ship to the service of his country. His courage, initiative, resourcefulness, and inspiring leadership combined with excellent judgment and skill during this and three previous patrols have served as an inspiration to all submarine personnel. His conduct on this, as well as on all his previous patrols, is in keeping with the highest traditions of the Naval Service."

The proposed citation was both weak and premature. Had it been submitted a year later, the Secretary of the Navy would have returned it, directing that it be resubmitted after the close of hostilities, when more specific information might be available. This is the action taken in my own case. Only now, with the Japanese report of the final encounter just received during this writing, does Morton's valiant action become irrefutable. I therefore will continue pressing for the elevation of this Navy Cross (the award for sinking three ships) to the Medal of Honor, with an authority who will follow the awards policy existing at that time, and which appears early in this book. From the same authority, I will seek a Second Presidential Unit Citation for *Wahoo*'s fourth patrol. The nine ships made this the second highest patrol in the 1,560 U.S.

total, and the second citation was not recommended at the time since action was still in progress on her first such award. She was also uncited for her fourth through seventh patrols, in which she sank seventeen ships, more than any other submarine receiving the PUC for multiple patrols and twice the number of sinkings of several boats that were so awarded, including one for her second such award. No one deliberately set aside just awards; further information had come slowly, *Wahoo* had been lost, and until now, time had just passed her by.

Starting with 39 fleet submarines and 12 S-boats for the whole Pacific, 207 more had been commissioned during the war. Nearly all made anti-shipping patrols or carried out one or more very taut special missions. Though exploders and torpedoes gave trouble during periods, we were not alone with torpedo problems, and other nations had solved theirs. Our submarines, however, were the best in the world, with a single-salvo firepower for conventional weapons that has not been equaled by submarines since.

Our submarines sank over 1,300 merchantmen, half again the number sunk by all other forces combined. Over 200 warships were sunk, which exceeded even the number sunk by U.S. Naval Air; and, in addition, there were 300 special missions. All of this was accomplished by a force manned by only 2% of the United States Navy's personnel. After the war, Japanese admirals and generals alike placed U.S. submarine operations first in the factors leading to the fall of the Empire.

These results were not achieved without the most severe penalties: *Sealion,* bombed at Cavite in the Philippines with all but four surviving, was our first loss. Three hands were saved from *S-26,* lost en route to patrol. *R-12,* lost in training, had twenty-four survivors. Eight crewmen from *Flier* eventually reached shore. From four groundings on patrol, all hands were miraculously saved. *Tang* and *Tullibee,* sunk by their own Mark-18 torpedoes, had nine and one survive, respectively, who were repatriated with 158 prisoners from seven other boats. Sadly, from thirty-seven other submarines, bringing the total to fifty-two, there were no survivors, and their brave stories, except for *Wahoo*'s, we shall never know.

With 3,505 shipmates still on patrol, our submariners had the highest casualty rate in the armed forces, six times that in surface ships, for boats engaged the enemy continuously throughout the war, except for about 3 weeks between the 2-month patrols. And yet, they were all volunteers, many of whom volunteered again for billets in leading boats.

Sadly, the following *Wahoo* shipmates were lost in their subsequent submarines:

Jesse L. Appel	Stephen Kohut
John W. Clary	Fertig B. Krause, Jr.
Jack E. Clough	John A. Moore
William E. Coultas	Cecil C. Robertson
Helmit O. Dietrich	Earl C. Schrier
Oakley R. Frash	Charles A. Zimmerman

Commander Kennedy did receive the Silver Star medal, and then another in his subsequent destroyer command. Commander MacMillan sank eleven ships with *Thresher,* receiving two Navy Crosses and the Legion of Merit. Commander Moore in *Grayback* sank ten ships, receiving two Navy Crosses. And so, a bit of Morton and *Wahoo* had accompanied each of them, including George Grider's seven ships and two Navy Crosses when commanding *Flasher*.

Though her life was short, her sinkings placed *Wahoo* within the first four boats, and Morton tied for second place among the skippers. For best patrol, he was again in second place in the 1,560 U.S. total. But these are just numbers, and submariners will remember the captain who shook off the shackles and set the pace, Mush Morton.

THE SECRETARY OF THE NAVY

WASHINGTON

The President of the United States takes pleasure in presenting the PRESIDENTIAL UNIT CITATION to the

UNITED STATES SHIP WAHOO

for service as set forth in the following

CITATION:

"For distinctive performance in combat in the New Guinea Area, January 16 to February 7, 1943. In bold defiance of an enemy destroyer attempting to run her down in a confined harbor, the WAHOO remained at periscope depth to counter with a daring attack, sinking the Japanese vessel by her torpedo fire. Pursuing similar tactics while under sustained fire, she fought a fourteen hour battle, attacking an unescorted armed enemy convoy and destroying the entire force, two freighters, one tanker and one transport and their personnel. The high combat efficiency of the WAHOO, her officers and men, is exemplified in the destruction of 31,890 tons of enemy shipping during a War Patrol from which she escaped intact."

For the President,

Frank Knox

Secretary of the Navy.

GLOSSARY _____

After trim. Variable ballast tank to adjust submarine's tilting moment and weight.

Air banks. Group of 11-cubic-foot air bottles in midships ballast tanks for storing high-pressure air to charge torpedoes; blow tanks; and, reduced from 3,000 to 200 pounds per square inch, for other uses.

Angle on the bow. The angle formed by the longitudinal axis of a ship and the line of sight from the submarine intersecting her.

A-scope. A radar screen giving a horizontal presentation.

Auxiliary tanks. Three variable midships ballast tanks, one generally reserved for fresh water.

Ballast tanks. Spaces between the pressure hull and outer hull not reserved for fuel, and located inside the pressure hull in the torpedo rooms. They are blown dry when surfaced and completely flooded when submerged.

Bathythermograph. An instrument to record sea temperature at the submarine's depth and to show any abrupt change or gradient which will reflect enemy echo ranging.

Bendix log. An underwater manometer for measuring speed.

Betty. Japanese patrol torpedo plane or bomber.

Bow buoyancy. A ballast tank to give extra buoyancy forward when surfacing in heavy weather or in an emergency.

Bow planes. A pair of large horizontal rudders, rigged out on diving to help give the initial down angle and then in conjunction with the stern planes, to control depth.

Can. Storage batteries.

Cavitation. The formation of pockets of vacuum by rotating propeller blades. The collapsing vacuum creates propeller noise.

CinCPac. Commander-in-Chief Pacific Fleet.

Clamp down. Going over decks in living spaces with a damp swab.

ComSubDiv. Submarine Division Commander.

ComSubPac. Commander Submarine Force Pacific Fleet.

ComSubSoWesPac. Commander Submarine Forces Southwest Pacific Fleet.

Conn. The authority directing the steersman or the individual act directing and thus maneuvering a ship.

Conning tower. A small horizontal full between the bridge and the control room. It contains all the ship and torpedo control devices: steering stand, chart desk, sonar gear, torpedo data computer and its angle solver, the SJ surface search radar, torpedo firing panel, Pit log, dead-reckoning indicator, bathythermograph, and two periscopes.

Control room. The midships compartment containing all diving controls: the ship's gyrocompass (and its auxiliary when available), an auxiliary steering stand, the AC switchboard, and the radio room.

CPO. Chief Petty Officer.

DE. A destroyer escort.

DivCom. Division Commander.

Dogs. The pawls securing a watertight hatch or door.

Dogwatch. Normally the 1600 to 1800 or the 1800 to 2000 watches, which are dogged or halved for the crew.

DR. Dead-reckoning position obtained from ship's course or speed.

Drain pump. A two-piston, high-pressure pump for pumping to sea.

DRI. Dead-reckoning indicator with inputs from Pit or Bendix log and gyrocompass. Dials show latitude and longitude.

End-around. Surface and submerged maneuver to pass a ship and gain a position ahead.

Engine-air induction. Large mushroom valve and piping to provide air for the diesels.

Fire control. The mechanics of directing gunfire or torpedoes.

Fire by five. Loud and clear radio signal or voice.

Fix. An accurate position by star sights or bearings of land positions.

Forward trim. Variable ballast tank used to adjust boat's tilting moment and weight.

Fox. Radio broadcast schedule for messages for submarines.

Gradient. A layer where the temperature of seawater and to a lesser degree its density changes quickly and will bend sound waves of echo ranging clear of a submarine below the layer.

Gyro angle. The angle set into each torpedo's gyro by the TDC so its steering mechanism will keep the torpedo on course to hit the point of aim.

Hull-down. A ship beyond the horizon with only masts showing.

IC switchboard. Interior communications switchboard. Handles AC electricity for gyrocompass, torpedo data computer, radios, sound.

ISWAS. A hand-held circular slide rule with azimuth scales and pointer on the back to figure distance to the track and tactical courses.

JK. Supersonic listening sound head.

JP. An amplified sonic receiver.

Limber holes. The scalloped openings in the superstructure where it meets the ballast tanks or pressure hull.

Losing bearing. Dropping behind when trying to overtake and pass a ship.

Mark-18. A new electric powered, wakeless torpedo with a speed of 27 knots and a range of about 4000 yards.

Mark-14. A steam torpedo (alcohol and compressed air) with a range of 5000 yards at 47 knots and 9000 yards at 31 knots.

Maru. A suffix to the names of Japanese merchant ships: hence, in submarine language, any Japanese ship except a warship.

Momsen lung. A breathing apparatus for escape and as a life preserver when reaching the surface.

Negative tank. A tank holding 14,000 pounds of ballast to accelerate diving.

Normal approach course. An approach course perpendicular to the bearing of the enemy. It will reach the enemy if possible.

Normal course. An approach course perpendicular to the track of the enemy.

One bell. A single order to maneuvering.

1MC. The submarine announcing system which includes the diving alarm, collision alarm, and general alarm (battle stations) in a somewhat melodious note, frequently call the Bells of St. Mary's.

ONI-208J. Identification manual of Japanese merchant ships, used by submarines to help in identifying ships.

PBM. A U.S. Martin Catalina patrol bomber.

PC. A patrol craft about half the length of a destroyer.

PCO. Prospective commanding officer, normally reporting from another related assignment or from a smaller submarine, making a refresher and updating patrol before taking his own fleet boat command.

Pit log. A common name for all logs, from the original Pitometer log.

Point. A point of the compass, accurately 11¼ degrees; the best way for lookouts to report direction with each sector divided into eight points (one point abaft the starboard beam).

Poppet valve. Valve to vent residual impulse air into the boat after a torpedo firing, rather than having it form a great bubble, which would mark the submarine's position.

Pressure hull. The submarine's inner hull and conning tower; built to withstand sea pressure at the stipulated test depth plus a large safety factor.

QC. The echo-ranging half of a sound head.

Relative bearing. The direction or bearing in degrees measured clockwise from own ship's bow.

Safety. A special ballast tank with the strength of the pressure hull, which can be blown and the flood valve closed to compensate for some flooding in the boat.

S-boat. A numbered class of post-world War I submarines still operating in World War II.

SD. Nondirectional air-search radar.

Stadimeter. Periscope rangefinder requiring target's height or length to determine range and angle on the bow, respectively.

Stern planes. A pair of horizontal rudders that control the angle on the boat and, working with the bow planes, the depth.

TBT. Torpedo bearing transmitters, one forward and aft, receive hinge pin of 7 x 50 binoculars fitted with vertical hair to transmit relative bearings to conning tower.

TDC. Torpedo data computer. Keeps the target range current and displays the relative aspects of own ship and target continuously. The angle-solver section computes the hitting gyro angle continuously and keeps it set on the gyros in the torpedoes.

Torpedo gyro. The internal gyro that is spun on firing and guides the torpedo course set at the instant of firing.

Torpex. An explosive in torpedo warheads composed of TNT and metal flakes.

Trim pump. A rotary pump for shifting ballast and pumping to sea.

True bearing. The bearing in degrees measured clockwise from the earth's true north. In practice, this is duplicated by the submarine's gyrocompass.

Ultra. A priority, classified message containing information derived from broken Japanese codes.

Very star. Various signal flares fired from a large-barrel pistol.

Zeke. A Japanese Zero fighter or bomber.

INDEX

Anders, Floyd, 169
Appel, Jesse L., 43, 101
Argonaut, 1, 2, 17, 116, 117
Ater, Richard W., 104
Awards, 274–75

Bair, Arthur L., 188
Barchet, Steven, 2
Bass, Raymond, 259
Bougainville, 77
Brisbane, 109
Brown, Donald R., 303, 309, 311,
    325
Buckley, James P., 135–40, 149,
    210, 263, 299, 311, 321
Burgan, Willian W., 303, 309, 311,
    325

Campbell, John S., 117, 163, 216,
    289, 327
Caroline Islands, 34
Carr, William J., 129, 130, 226, 228,
    286, 287
Carter, James E., 60, 135, 140, 141,
    149, 313, 318
Chester, 1
Chisholm, Fred B., 156–57, 224
Chiyoda, 55
Cribbage, 201, 211

Deaton, Lynwood N., 52, 92, 295
Dooley, David E., 21, 102
Dye, Ira, 28, 48

East China Sea, 189
English, Robert E., 27, 73

Fiedler, Eugene, 291
Fife, James, 111
Flying Fish, 27, 43, 56
Frash, Oakley, 28

Gerlacher, Wesley L., 216
Glinski, Henry P., 156
Greene, Hiram M., 303, 309, 320,
    321, 325
Grider, George W., 7, 12–14, 16,
    17, 21, 49, 101, 125, 134, 157,
    161
Griggs, John B., 67, 284
Grouper, 102, 117

Hall, James C., 81
Hartman, Leon M., 47
Henderson, Richie N., 28, 40, 130,
    187, 203, 210, 222, 260, 317
Honshu, 254
Hunter, Deville G., 12, 13, 14, 20,
    40, 89, 145, 147, 148, 219

Jackson, Chandler, C., 6, 10, 17, 18, 19, 22, 135–40, 145, 157, 163, 210, 284, 287
Jayson, Jaun O., 117, 124
Johnson, Kindred B., 10, 13, 51, 288, 295

Keeter, Dalton C., 125, 133, 157, 222, 283
Kemp, Wendell W., 258, 260, 289, 292, 309, 316, 323
Kennedy, Marvin G., 11, 12, 13, 14, 111
Kilty, 16, 17, 18
Kohl, Jerome T., 203, 210
Krause, Fertig B. Jr., 16, 17, 19, 20–22, 32, 39, 50, 89, 148, 210, 225
Kurils, 254

Lane, James E., 287
Lapon, 289
Lassing, Lt. (jg), 14
Lemert, Richard H., 186, 222, 289
Lenox, Andy, 1, 125, 128, 131, 157, 283, 284
Lindemann, Clarence A., 313
Lindhe, Leslie J., 156
Litchfield, 22, 23, 287
Lockwood, Charles, 180
Logue, Robert B., 320

MacAlman, Stuart E., 258–59, 263, 287
MacMillan, Duncan C., 10, 78, 199, 211, 222, 225, 313
Manalesay, Jesus C., 117, 124, 259
Mare Island, 2, 3, 10, 12–13, 15, 277–78
Mayberry, Clyde C., 194, 197
McCandles, Commodore, 13

McGill, Thomas J., 39, 42, 52, 53, 89, 125, 219, 224, 253, 317, 327
McSpadden, Donald J., 52, 92, 288, 295
Midway Atoll, 2, 11, 183, 241, 289, 300, 306
Misch, George, 67, 74, 151, 157, 311
Moore, Johnny, 249, 257, 262
Morton, Dudley W., 71, 102, 112, 114, 127, 134, 153–54, 157, 164–65, 181–82, 191, 194, 201, 204, 207, 215, 221, 226–27, 235, 250, 258, 262, 271, 278, 287, 289, 292, 296, 299, 303, 312, 314, 316, 318–19, 326–27, 328

Narwhal, 11

O'Brien, Forest L., 47
O'Kane, Richard H., early naval career, 1–3

P-28, 73, 74
Paine, Roger W. Jr., 7, 13, 17, 31, 46, 148, 161, 187, 286, 287
Patterson, 120–23
PC-570, 14
Pearl Harbor, 2, 23, 61, 171, 274, 287, 300
Permit, 289
Phillips, Paul D., 13, 14, 17, 150, 293
Plunger, 289
Pompano, 7
Pruitt, 1, 18, 101, 152, 222

Rau, Russel H. (Pappy), 7, 11, 17, 18, 21, 27, 46, 135
Redford, Burnell A., 186
Rennels, Juano L., 287, 293
Roosevelt, Franklin D., 2

Rowls, John C., 13, 150, 153
Ryujo, 57–58

Sands, Eugene, 304, 315, 324
Sawfish, 302, 307, 314, 315, 324, 327
Sea of Japan, 290, 310
Simonetti, Alfred, 18, 57, 129, 135–40, 169, 210, 320, 326
Sinkings (listed chronologically), **Patrol One,** *Keiyo Maru,* 49–51; **Patrol Two,** *Syoei Maru,* 89–91, *I-15,* 97; **Patrol Three,** *Asashio,* 137–40, *Dakar Maru,* 147, *Seiwa Maru,* 150–51, *Manzyu Maru,* 158–59, *Arizona Maru,* 161; **Patrol Four,** *Nanka Maru,* 203, *Tottori Maru,* 206, *Seiwa Maru,* 210–11, *Nitu Maru,* 211–13, *Katyosan Maru,* 216–18, *Syoyo Maru,* 222–23, *Sinsei Maru,* 226–29, *Hadachi Maru,* 227–28, trawler (wrecked), 230–31, *Kimisima Maru,* 234–36; **Patrol Five,** *Yuki Maru,* 261, *Huzisan Maru,* 267, *Hawaii Maru,* 267; **Patrol Seven,** *Taiko Maru,* 311–12, *Masaki Maru,* 313–14, *Konron Maru,* 318–19, *Kanko Maru,* 321–22, *Kanko Maru* no. 2, 325–26

Skipjack, 7
Skjonsby, Verne L., 287, 294, 311, 314, 317, 319, 322, 326, 327
Smith, C. J., 27
Smith, Donald O., 46, 226
Solomons, The, 79
Sterling, Forest, 70, 87, 96, 117, 282, 286, 306, 309
Swinburn, E. R., 13

Telescopic periscope well, 219
Terrell, William C., 311
Truk, 34
Tunney, Gene, 304, 305
Tyler, Ralph O., 156, 238

Vitiaz Strait, 132

Wach, Ludwig J., 44, 160, 226
Wahoo's Commandos, 230–31
Ware, Norman C., 10, 18, 47
Watkins, Frank, 27
Wewak, 135–40
Whipp, Kenneth C., 157
White, William T., 306, 311, 325

Yellow Sea, 198